PROVEN
STRATEGIES IN
COMPETITIVE
INTELLIGENCE

PROVEN
STRATEGIES IN
COMPETITIVE
INTELLIGENCE

LESSONS FROM THE TRENCHES

EDITED BY JOHN E. PRESCOTT AND STEPHEN H. MILLER
SOCIETY OF COMPETITIVE INTELLIGENCE PROFESSIONALS

JOHN WILEY & SONS, INC.

New York • Chichester • Weinheim • Brisbane • Singapore • Toronto

Published by John Wiley & Sons, Inc.
Published simultaneously in Canada.

ISBN 0-471-40178-1

Printed in the United States of America.
10 9 8 7 6 5 4 3 2 1

This book is dedicated to
CI practitioners throughout the world.

CONTENTS

PART 1
COMPETITIVE BUSINESS INTELLIGENCE: CORPORATE CASE STUDIES

PART 2
Competitive Technical Intelligence

PREFACE
Corporations Get Smart

Increasingly, management strategists are relying on a frequently misunderstood practice known as competitive intelligence (CI). From out of the shadows of corporate "spy vs. spy" stereotypes, today's CI professionals are legally and ethically collecting, analyzing, and applying information about the capabilities, vulnerabilities, and intentions of their competitors, and monitoring developments within the overall competitive environment (such as previously unseen rivals over the horizon, or new technologies that could change everything). The goal: actionable intelligence that will provide a competitive edge. Or, in the words of strategy guru Liam Fahey, "to help the firm outwit, outmaneuver, and outperform current, emerging, and potential competitors. . . .We look at competitors as a way of analyzing ourselves and asking, *How good are we?*"★

According to former NutraSweet CEO and Chairman Robert E. Flynn: "*CI is worth up to $50 million per year to our company. That is a combination of revenues gained and revenues 'not lost' to competitive activity. I believe in CI, our senior managers believe in it, and together we have created a corporate culture that supports it.*"

Similarly, former Kellogg USA President Gary Costly warns, "*The big payoff for competitive intelligence is that it will point out weakness that you have internally because of the strengths of your competitors. Companies that don't do this will fail.*"

Realizing their need to hone competitive strategy, a growing number of the biggest global companies have established world-class CI functions within their firms. A full 82 percent of the largest U.S.-based multinational

★ See Liam Fahey, *Competitors: Outwitting, Outmaneuvering, and Outperforming* (New York: John Wiley & Sons, 1998).

companies with annual revenues of more than $10 billion now have an organized intelligence unit, according to a 1998 survey by The Futures Group. Among all U.S.-based companies with revenues above $1 billion, 60 percent claim to have an organized competitive intelligence system. Still, most midsize-to-large companies—and an even larger percentage of small-to-midsize firms—lack dedicated CI operations, despite the fact that most business leaders recognize that their success depends on looking forward and moving more quickly than the competition.

Admittedly, most companies, large and small, have always made efforts to keep tabs on their rivals in some fashion without knowing that the activity is called *competitive intelligence*. But they could be doing a far better job of it, which is the impetus behind SCIP, the Society of Competitive Intelligence Professionals (www.scip.org). Established in 1986, SCIP is a global not-for-profit association. Its members conduct competitive research and analysis for their companies, and help management to plan competitive strategy.

Economic espionage, SCIP emphasizes, represents a *failure* of CI, which uses open sources and other forms of ethical inquiry. Promoting CI as a discipline bound by a strict Code of Ethics and practiced by trained professionals is the Society's paramount goal.

CHALLENGING CORPORATE INSULARITY

SCIP members have professionalized CI's methods. These include not only the basics—identifying information sources, gathering data, and analyzing the collected information—but applying cutting-edge tools and techniques such as (among others) wargame exercises with alternate competitive scenarios to test the "what ifs" that lie ahead; data mining information already in operational files so it can be applied to analytical tasks; technology scouting via patent tracking and other tools that reveal areas in which competitors are likely to make breakthroughs; and so on.

Trying to remain cognizant of competitors' intentions and of unanticipated marketplace developments by scanning open-source public records; carefully monitoring the Internet and mass media; talking with customers, suppliers, partners, employees, industry experts, and other knowledgeable parties; creating psychological profiles of top decision makers; and attending trade shows and conferences smartly—with the aim of gathering data on what rivals are up to and incorporating that awareness into business planning—all of these are competitive intelligence activities. And so is taking that information, boiling it down, shaping an analysis of a competitor's situation in order to yield insights into its present status and future objectives, and determining how all of this compares with one's own strategy—while raising red flags about fresh competition from unexpected quarters.

Great attention has been paid of late to "knowledge management," and much less has been given to CI. True, CI has benefited from advances in information technology infrastructure and the elevation of knowledge management into a dominant corporate function. Moreover, the integration of knowledge management throughout organizational structures is helping to raise awareness of CI's value. Knowledge, after all, must be produced and analyzed before it can be communicated and "managed." This applies both to internally generated data and to intelligence from outside the corporate walls, which can challenge the insularity that often hobbles corporate decision makers.

Yet, too many businesses still have not incorporated CI into their organizational structure and corporate culture, much less into their IT framework (i.e., establishing an interactive CI area within their corporate intranet and making it accessible throughout the organization, from the CEO to the sales reps). That puts them at a disadvantage when other companies have implemented companywide efforts for collecting, analyzing, and disseminating competitive intelligence.

COMPETITIVE INTELLIGENCE REVIEW: LEARNING FROM THE BEST

In 1990, SCIP launched its peer-reviewed journal, *Competitive Intelligence Review.* Over the years, it has become the premier forum for "practical scholarship" pertaining to all aspects of the CI field. In particular, it has been recognized for its outstanding corporate case studies. These have included in-depth examinations of competitive intelligence (and competitive *technical* intelligence) at IBM, Xerox, Daimler-Benz, Chevron, and NutraSweet, to name just some of the research-intensive corporations whose CI operations have been detailed in our pages and are now collected in this volume.

Often, these studies were written by the directors of CI at the subject companies, but occasionally we've gone straight to the top and heard from CI-savvy CEOs, such as Robert Galvin of Motorola, John Pepper of Procter & Gamble, and Hans Gieskes of Lexis–Nexis. These business leaders provide insight into how their corporations structure and run CI operations (and foster CI-supportive cultures).

Other articles, including benchmarking studies conducted by leading academics and CI consultants, provide outsiders' analyses of the best corporate CI practices.

As readers will soon discover, not everyone agrees on the specifics of how a CI function should be organized (i.e., the great "centralization" vs. "decentralization" debate). Moreover, it goes without saying that the CI operations discussed within these pages operated—and succeeded—within highly specific organizational contexts. Nevertheless, as practice models, they provide insights that transcend those specifications, and we trust that examining and comparing these different approaches will provide even old CI hands with fresh perspectives.

SNAPSHOTS IN TIME

These articles are reprinted from *Competitive Intelligence Review* as they originally appeared, with only minor editorial changes. They are "snapshots in time" of the CI operations under discussion when the authors wrote about them. (Authors' positions and affiliations also date, for the most part, to when the articles were originally published.)

The editors felt that any attempt to "update" these studies would only result in confusion between time periods, or would necessitate a completely new and different work. No corporate model is stagnant, and any description of corporate operations, by necessity, describes what *was*. This in no way diminishes the valuable lessons to be learned by studying highly effective CI models at a given point in time.

No one can deliver an "out-of-the-box" turnkey solution to competitive intelligence, but these examples of how best-practice companies monitor the competitive landscape and factor that information into competitive strategy will, we hope, inspire others to give CI the high priority it must have if businesses are to thrive in today's new economy.

While this volume focuses on corporate models and systems, we hope in the near future to publish a companion volume that explicates CI tools, techniques, and analytical methodologies, also from the pages of *Competitive Intelligence Review*.

PURSUING COMPETITIVE ADVANTAGE

Augmenting innovation, honing marketing, going global, and improving the use of electronic data are just some of the competitive intelligence topics we are pleased to present herein, helping readers to take CI to new levels for their companies and clients.

In a global market saturated in data traversing the earth in nanoseconds, the need to turn competitor information into actionable intelligence has never been greater. CI professionals are pledged to providing their companies with the tools needed to stay fast, focused, and flexible in the pursuit and maintenance of competitive advantage.

STEPHEN H. MILLER
Society of Competitive Intelligence Professionals

INTRODUCTION

Competitive Intelligence—Lessons from the Trenches

John E. Prescott, Ph.D.
JOSEPH M. KATZ GRADUATE SCHOOL OF BUSINESS, UNIVERSITY OF PITTSBURGH

Competitive intelligence (CI) is embedded in the fiber of businesses throughout the world. Only a few years ago, this statement would have been questioned. Today, the institutionalization of CI practices is the result of the confluence of several forces, including practitioners demonstrating its value to managers, an evolving set of increasingly sophisticated frameworks and analytical tools, and a well-connected network of CI professionals dispersed throughout the world.

Noticeably absent in this set of forces are traditional explanations such as the globalization of business and the advent of information technology. Both of these forces are enablers to the institutionalization of CI, but the main impetus has been the hard work of dedicated CI professionals, which has resulted in a growing discipline that mandates its incorporation into decision-making processes. Managers have little excuse for being blindsided by competitors' initiatives, overzealous regulators, and disruptive technology. As the cases in this book demonstrate, well-organized CI processes lead to sustainable and profitable growth. This introductory chapter illustrates four key lessons that can be gleaned from the articles that comprise this book. Armed with these lessons, CI professionals and their management can direct the profession to new heights.

John E. Prescott, Ph.D., can be contacted at the Joseph M. Katz Graduate School of Business, University of Pittsburgh, 246 Mervis Hall, Pittsburgh, PA 15260, USA; Tel: 1-412-648-1573; Fax: 1-412-648-1693; E-mail: *prescott@katz.pitt.edu*.

INTRODUCTION

EMERGING FROM THE SHADOWS

Competitive intelligence in business organizations has benefited greatly from military and government intelligence practices and knowledge. Many of the pioneers in the business intelligence community migrated from a variety of governmental organizations. They brought a set of concepts and insights that had been refined over centuries. Most notably, Sun Tzu's (Griffith, 1971) classic work on military intelligence is widely read, and he is credited with being the father of intelligence. More recently, the James Bond series of movies and John LeCarré's (1963) set of novels, based on his experience in the British secret service and written in his captivating style, captured the imagination of the general public. In the United States, two recent publications: *Intelligence Essentials for Everyone* (Krizan, 1999) and *A Compendium of Analytic Tradecraft Notes* (Directorate of Intelligence, 1997) summarize key aspects of the intelligence production process. All of these works have sensitized the business community to the value of intelligence. Equally important, they have framed public opinion to think of intelligence in terms such as clandestine, stealthy, secret agents, and espionage.

Amid this atmosphere, the business community has begun to develop a set of intelligence concepts and analytical frameworks appropriate for their context and acceptable to scrutinizing stakeholders. Led by SCIP—the Society of Competitive Intelligence Professionals (www.scip.org)—and a few academics, the field of competitive intelligence emerged. National security intelligence taught businesses the value of the intelligence cycle. However, a profit motivation that underlies most businesses requires significant modifications to lessons learned from national security intelligence.

Most of the cases in this book represent leading-edge firms that are experimenting with the development of competitive intelligence systems, tools, and practices that contribute to sustainable and profitable growth. Some firms, such as IBM, Xerox, Motorola, Nutrasweet, Avnet, Merck, Procter & Gamble, Intel, and Microsoft, have developed CI into a core capability.

Many of the articles in this book have lists of do's and don'ts. It has become increasingly common for CI practitioners and academics to develop lists as a way to assist others in avoiding potential pitfalls, and to allow practitioners to more quickly move down the learning curve. These lists have been very helpful, but they focus on "What?"—that is, do's don'ts. An alternative—and, I would argue, a more sophisticated way to proceed—is to focus on "How?" An emphasis on "How?" centers on the processes that underlie a set of activities.

Process maps are one approach to exploring "How?" One advantage of process maps is that they allow us to more fully understand how to manage a particular set of activities. As an illustration of how the two approaches can be contrasted, I will focus on do and don't lists for two of the lessons and process maps for the other two lessons.

FOUR OVERARCHING LESSONS FROM THE TRENCHES

Four overarching lessons that emerged from the cases in this book can benefit firms as they implement their CI efforts. The four overarching lessons are each described below.

Lesson 1

CI programs require a clearly articulated role that emerges through a process of (re)learning the intelligence needs of organizational members.

One of the most perplexing and frustrating questions for a CI program is how to determine its role or focus. Without a clearly articulated role, a CI program will flounder or, worse, become a center for ad hoc requests. One of the most vocal aspects of the debate runs as follows: "If you do not report to the CEO, you cannot be a successful CI program." Those who espouse this position are either overly pessimistic or naive. There is no empirical evidence that CI programs that report to CEOs are more successful, or last longer, than those that do not report to CEOs. All of us would embrace the opportunity to closely interact with top management. A recent study that I conducted with the American Productivity and Quality Center (APQC, 1999) reveals that top-management support is critical to the launching of a CI effort. However, the location and ultimate role of a CI program are determined by other forces, such as underperforming assets, competitor initiatives, the impact of nonmarket forces such as regulation, and the support of champions located virtually anywhere in the company.

Several of the articles in this book illustrate the issues involved with determining the role of a CI effort. The articles describing CI practices at IBM and Xerox show how those corporations addressed this critical issue. The articles by Lackman and colleagues (p. 195), which benchmarked CI functions; by Marceau and Sawka (p. 148), on developing CI programs in telecoms; and the roundtable discussion (see Bryant et al., p. 308), all provide useful tips for determining the role of a CI program. From these articles we can draw a few conclusions:

- *CI programs are primarily located in marketing, planning, and R&D functions in organizations.* Most CI professionals spend less than 50 percent of their time directly on intelligence activities. Independent CI departments that directly report to the CEO are rare. There has been an increase in the number of CI programs that report to the finance department. Procter & Gamble is an example.

- *The role of a CI program is driven by business needs that are often rooted in underperforming assets.* Few CI operations are started because management is acting proactively. A business issue is the catalyst for launching a CI effort. Intelligence professionals must make the most of the opportunity presented by the catalyst.

- *A defined role is important, but an entire administrative structure needs to be developed to successfully implement the chosen focus.* Core work processes, such as request-handling and analytical frameworks, need to be documented.

These conclusions are important, but they do not adequately address the heart of the question: How is the role of a CI effort determined? In this regard, the article—by Jan P. Herring (p. 240)—describes a process for determining key intelligence topics (KITs). Herring modified the national security approach for determining essential elements of intelligence to the business sector. The process he developed and the empirical results from his consulting confirm that the roles of CI efforts fall into three categories:

- Strategic decisions and actions (tactics).
- Early-warning topics.
- Knowledge of, and learning from, key players.

Regardless of the location of a CI effort, its role is some combination of these three categories.

The KIT process provides a practical mechanism for determining the intelligence needs of managers. However, Lesson 1 suggests that the process is one of (re)learning, and one approach for (re)learning is to conduct intelligence audits periodically. The need for (re)learning intelligence is based on two facts: (1) in most industries, the competitive landscape changes over time (D'Aveni, 1994), and (2) managerial turnover results in new and different intelligence needs.

The issue is more complicated than simply conducting KIT assessments periodically. The intelligence needs for senior-level managers who deal with strategic issues are fundamentally different from the intelligence needs at the tactical level of the organization. For example, senior managers need to understand the evolving dynamics of their industry and its future profit potential; the sales force needs to close deals. The Miree and Prescott article, with APQC (p. 216) addressed the question of how organizations coordinate their strategic and tactical intelligence. The results of the study identified a set of mechanisms that best-practice companies use to TAP-IN™ to strategic and tactical intelligence needs. The components of TAP-IN are:

- Teams, IT, and training.
- Allocation of personnel to strategic and tactical intelligence.
- Planning—How is CI integrated into planning?
- Interaction with CI clients through dialogue.
- Network positions of the CI group.

We argue and demonstrate that CI functions that apply the TAP-INs in specific ways are able to coordinate strategic and tactical intelligence and thus (re)learn the intelligence needs throughout the organization. In this way, the role of a CI effort is clearly articulated through a close coordination of strategic and tactical intelligence needs.

Here is a summary of what we have learned regarding this lesson:

- The role(s) of a CI program should be tied to business issues that have important performance consequences.
- The KIT process is a very practical approach for initially cataloging the potential role(s) of a CI program.

- As a CI program matures, applying the TAP-IN process ensures the coordination of strategic and tactical intelligence and thus facilitates the (re)learning process.

A related issue that has spawned considerable debate is whether CI operations should be decentralized or centralized. The TAP-IN process demonstrates that, regardless of the degree of centralization, strategic and tactical intelligence must be coordinated. When organizations have multiple CI units spread across a variety of businesses, the coordination of intelligence takes on another dimension.

> In a diversified company, businesses that have similar customers/ competitors and share resources should centralize their CI efforts. But if there are few commonalities across businesses, CI units should share best practices but not centralize their efforts.

There is a simple heuristic for determining the degree of centralization of CI efforts in a diversified company: Businesses that have similar customers/competitors and share resources (e.g., manufacturing, marketing, R&D) should centralize their CI efforts. In diversified companies that have few commonalities across businesses, CI units should share best practices but not centralize their efforts.

Lesson 2

The set of outputs from a CI program must be disseminated on a timely basis, provide actionable implications, and be perceived as credible and trustworthy.

One of the most important objectives for CI professionals is to reduce the time they spend in providing answers to ad hoc requests, and increase their level of participation on decision-making teams. This is not to imply that ad hoc requests are unimportant. Quite to the contrary, answers to ad hoc requests provide valuable intelligence. However, an intelligence unit that focuses most of its time and resources on ad hoc requests will not be perceived as an integral part of key decision-making teams. In other words, CI professionals will not be sitting at the table and, without a seat at the table, it is difficult to sell the implications of an analysis. The critical question that needs to be answered is: How does a CI function develop a set of products and services that gains the credibility and trust of intelligence users?

1. *An intelligence question should be framed with an analytical tool.* Scores of analytical tools and frameworks are available to the CI professional [Gilad & Herring, 1996, Parts A and B; Prescott & Grant, 1988]. CI practitioners recognize that blending hard numbers with interviews and unobtrusive measures provides a richer understanding of an intelligence question. Another benefit of applying analytical tools and frameworks is that they are perceived as being "objective." In most cases, references and examples from other applications of the tool can be provided to skeptical intelligence users. Credibility is enhanced when one is able to document that a tool has been used by others and deemed appropriate for the question at hand.

2. *Effective communication dominates analysis.* Unless the message from the analysis is communicated effectively, trust and credibility with intelligence users will not be enhanced. There are a few simple heuristics for effectively communicating your intelligence. Ensuring that intelligence is context-based is critical; that is, in what context are your conclusions appropriate?

Formatting your conclusions and implications in a way that appeals to your intelligence users is a second heuristic. A third heuristic that is practiced extremely well by Sequent Computer Company is to develop redundancies in products. The article by Hans Gieskes (p. 69), describing CI at Lexis-Nexis, is another good example. Redundancy in products means that the same intelligence is packaged in multiple ways. For example, at Sequent Computer, the same intelligence can be found in an electronic form, a paper version, verbally relayed, and, in some cases, on a CD. Having such redundancies recognizes that intelligence users have different preferences for how they want to receive intelligence.

3. *Ethical mishaps will destroy credibility and trust.* Ethical issues of CI have received more attention than any other topic in the field. Given the intellectual property concerns of businesses, a focus on ethics is critical. SCIP has developed a Code of Ethics (www.scip.org/ci/ethics.html) that has become the standard in our industry.

However, it is naive for us to assume that even SCIP's code will address all ethical situations around the globe. It is imperative that CI professionals understand the laws, customs, and ethical standards of the countries in which they are conducting CI. For example, many of the CI programs mentioned in this book operate across multiple countries. Few CI professionals have the capability to appreciate the ethical issues in all of these countries. I strongly encourage CI professionals to develop a positive working relationship with their legal counsels in the countries in which they compete. More to the point, Open Source Solution (OSS)—a nonprofit organization started by an ex-marine intelligence officer, Robert Steel— has repeatedly demonstrated that publicly available information, when properly analyzed, provides significant intelligence. Having noted this finding, countries differ in what is considered open-source information and the implications for intelligence analysis.

The above conclusions are important, but they do not fully address "how" a CI professional develops trust and credibility (Leana & Rousseau, 2000) with intelligence users as they evolve their product portfolio. Part of my recent study with APQC (1999) addressed this important "how" question.

A PROCESS MODEL FOR BUILDING TRUST AND CREDIBILITY WITH INTELLIGENCE USERS

Rick Heibel, manager of competitive intelligence at Caterpillar, knew he was developing a positive working relationship with his chief financial officer (CFO). The CFO had been a champion of CI and regularly discussed intelligence topics at top management's strategic review council. Rick knew he could not rest on past success. He needed to develop a plan that would build trust and credibility with intelligence users throughout the organization.

Figure 1 shows a process for developing trust and credibility with intelligence users. It was developed through my research with scores of companies and the four CI benchmarking studies at APQC. I will demonstrate how the process works by continuing my discussion of Caterpillar's best-practice CI function.

Under Rick's direction, the CI function was located in a service group at the corporate headquarters. Being located in a service, as opposed to a product group, resulted in what Rick termed "enterprise neutrality." The neutrality existed because CI was not located in any of the product and market groups that had profit-and-loss responsibility. In other words, CI was politically neutral. With this background, we can now illustrate how Rick and his team managed the process of developing a portfolio of products that were timely, actionable, and perceived as highly credible. The discussion will follow the process flow depicted in Figure 1.

As was demonstrated with Lesson 1, intelligence users are the primary drivers of a CI effort. For Caterpillar, the primary KITs were to provide early warning of the emergence of new competitors, and profiles for a set of the current competitors. At the time of the case, the Asian Crisis was a key market event of interest because many of Caterpillar's strongest competitors

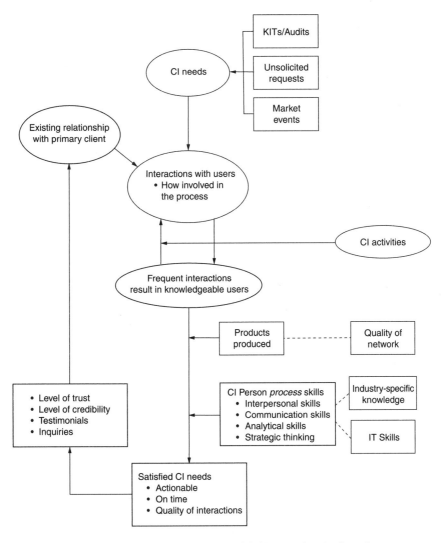

Figure 1 Building trust and credibility in the CI function.

were Asian-based. CI outputs were shared with the product and market groups throughout Caterpillar, using a variety of methods including briefings, reports, and the corporate intranet.

The next phase in the process of developing trust and credibility is to determine how involved managers will be in the intelligence process. A useful way to frame this phase is to use the components of the intelligence cycle: agreement on intelligence needs; collection of information; analysis to develop conclusions and implications; dissemination of intelligence; and feedback. At Caterpillar, managers prioritized intelligence needs and provided feedback throughout the life of a project. Implementation of recommendations resulting from the intelligence was the responsibility of product and market managers.

Having reached an understanding of the managerial and CI roles in the intelligence cycle, the CI group turned its attention to the collection and analysis of information to develop and update baseline profiles for competitors. During the collection and analysis steps, Rick and his team had frequent face-to-face interactions with managers. These frequent interactions resulted in knowledgeable users who facilitated midcourse adjustments to collection and analysis priorities.

The degree to which intelligence users are satisfied with the outputs of a CI group is influenced by two important factors:

1. The quality of CI products.
2. The process skills of CI personnel.

At Caterpillar, Rick had this philosophy: no assignment was too small to warrant attention; information and resulting intelligence would not be filtered (i.e., sanitized); all individuals providing intelligence would be acknowledged; and feedback was requested on all products. Rick's group also answered ad hoc requests and participated in competitor response modeling and new product development teams. The CFO noted that one of the strengths of the CI group was its process skills.

Rick's team was perceived as adding value because of its focus on how competitive initiatives affected price realization, market share, and profits. This bottom-line orientation resulted in actionable intelligence not only for product and market managers, but also for the strategic review council.

The outputs of the process described above and depicted in Figure 1 resulted in increased levels of trust, credibility, testimonials, and inquiries. Some of the indicators that demonstrate the positive outcomes of Rick's group include: increases to the CI budget, executives' mention of CI in speeches, increased levels of CI training for current and new employees, and CI group participation in the strategy review conference. Based on additional feedback, Rick and his team are creating new CI products. Their positive relationships with intelligence users and their new initiatives are stretching their resources. Having established a high level of trust and credibility, Rick now ponders how to maintain the momentum.

The objective of every CI professional is to "sit at the table" and positively impact the performance of the organization. In developing a CI product portfolio that focuses on actionable intelligence, timeliness and high-quality interactions with intelligence users build trust and credibility. It may take some time, but those who follow the conclusions drawn from the articles cited in this section, and the process described above, will soon be "sitting at the table."

Lesson 3

In organizations, an intelligence-driven culture is built one person at a time, through intelligence skill enhancement, human network development, and mechanisms that facilitate the flow of information.

The creation and use of intelligence is a social process. Unfortunately, the vast majority of articles and books focus on the technical aspects of creating intelligence. We identified nine articles that recognize, and incorporate suggestions for focusing on, the social aspects of intelligence. Robert Galvin of Motorola recognizes the value of the social processes underlying intelligence activities when he encourages CI professionals to adopt an anthropological perspective.

The overarching goal embedded in this lesson is for intelligence activities to be integrated into the daily tasks of everyone. I am not suggesting that an embedded intelligence culture reduces the need for a formal CI function. Quite to the contrary, an organization in which intelligence becomes second nature requires a well-coordinated intelligence function to nurture the culture. The firms participating in the APQC benchmarking study, "Leveraging Information for Action," as well as the Nutrasweet, Motorola, and Avnet case studies, illustrate the value of an organized CI system for developing an intelligence culture. Drawing on these articles, four conclusions have been developed to inform us regarding our third lesson.

1. *Develop a promotional plan for your CI function.* Perhaps Max Downham, former vice president of mission and strategy at NutraSweet, summarizes this conclusion best when he notes that intelligence concepts have not traditionally been considered to be an essential corporate function. Often, managers have not been exposed to the concepts of intelligence in a way that is directly linked to the bottom line. Everyone acknowledges that intelligence contributes to sales, manufacturing, marketing, and R&D, but it is sometimes difficult to neatly fit intelligence into daily corporate activities. A promotional plan is a structured approach to raising the level of awareness for CI capabilities. At the same time, it allows you to address how intelligence contributes to the bottom line.

A variety of ways can be used to launch a promotional effort. For example:

- Boehringer Ingleheim and Bell Atlantic conducted presentations on the basics of CI throughout their organizations.
- Telcordia and GlaxoWellcome had face-to-face meetings with potential CI users.
- Caterpillar developed promotional brochures and distributed them across the company.
- Fidelity's CI unit participated in in-house sales force conferences.

Many companies use demonstration projects to illustrate their CI capabilities. In the early stages of a promotional campaign, CI professionals will need to "push" their services out to potential users. It is no coincidence that newsletters are the most popular CI product of a new CI operation—even though evidence suggests that they are not particularly effective.

A promotional plan will initially create "top of the mind" awareness. It is imperative for the CI group to follow up on any requests for intelligence. Typically, there will be a large number of ad hoc requests. To keep from being swamped, develop a request-handling process; that is, develop an explicit set of steps for how an intelligence request will be answered. Priority setting and the development of a referral process permit you to gently say no to intelligence requests while still being helpful. As your set of products and services evolves over time, your promotional plan will need to keep pace. Employees at all levels of the organization come and go, so link your promotional plan to new employee orientation programs.

2. *Involve all employees in CI training.* One of the great debates is whether an intelligence analyst is born or can be developed. Like most debates of this type, the truth lies somewhere in the middle. My work with Texas Instruments developed a skill-based approach to training analysts that is generalizable across a wide set of professionals. However, our focus here is on any employee, not on training analysts. The task is much simpler but probably more important. Virtually all employees can be trained to provide information to the CI group. They are most likely to do so if they receive valuable information in return.

> Virtually all employees can be trained to provide information to the CI group. They are most likely to do so if they receive valuable information in return.

The most effective CI training occurs when it is linked to strategy and tactics. When CI training is linked to an employee's job responsibilities and shown to contribute to bottom-line performance, there will be immediate buy-in.

To me, the key skills developed in training of this type are observation skills. An example will demonstrate my point. An employee at a utility company had received basic CI training. She was driving to work one day when she noticed a train carrying many carloads of piping. When she arrived at work, she called the CI group and reported her sighting. After a little digging, the CI group discovered that a competing utility company was building a pipeline into a new residential development. As a result of her observation, the firm was able to initiate a competitive response that saved significant revenues.

3. *Develop human-intelligence networks that match your strategy.* Only recently have CI professionals recognized the important of developing a human-intelligence network. A well-developed human-intelligence network is the most effective mechanism for collecting high-quality information (Nolan, 1999). Companies such as Compaq, Shell Services International, and Telcordia have designed their CI function around networking concepts (Scott, 1992).

Recent research indicates that CI groups develop two types of networks, based on their strategic thrust (APQC, 1999). If a CI group focuses on complex projects and it is imperative that individuals in the network can be relied on to assist in transferring tacit knowledge, then a coordinated–tight network is most effective. Because tacit knowledge is valuable and difficult to transfer, individuals are often reluctant to share their knowledge with just anyone. Coordinated–tight networks focus on developing close relationships with a few individuals. These close relationships facilitate the transfer of tacit knowledge because a high level of trust between individuals has been established.

One limitation of this type of network is its rather narrow search capability. High levels of energy are devoted to nurturing a few high-quality relationships, and the trade-off is a lack of network breadth. The article by Amy Berger of Larscom Corporation (p. 168) is an example of developing a coordinated–tight network to support a sales force. Central to this support is the development of CI products that allow the network to flourish and the sales force to win bids. Over time, the high-quality, trust-based relationships built with the sales force allow the exchange of tacit knowledge.

In contrast, many CI groups need to be able to cast their nets widely to collect diverse information. This type of network is required where there are many intelligence users with varying intelligence needs. Decentralized-loose networks are designed to emphasize diversity. In this case, the CI professional is interested in establishing relationships with a wide variety of individuals.

Given the focus on diversity, developing deep and trusting relationships is more difficult. Thus, this type of network allows one to search broadly and quickly but trades off the ability to transfer tacit knowledge. The external watch process at Chevron, described by Derek L. Ransley (p. 286), represents a decentralized-loose network. Dr. Ransley describes how a well-defined network of diverse individuals and groups can be used to develop an early warning system for new technologies that have strategic implications for Chevron's businesses.

Human–intelligence networks need to be developed using principles based in sociology and organizational theory (Nohria & Eccles, 1992). Europeans and Asians, in particular, are more comfortable with sociological principles than North Americans are. Recent research conducted by Tom Tao and myself (2000) in China found that one of the significant differences between North American and Chinese CI efforts was the use of *Guanxi* (networks). We need to devote additional research effort to understanding networks and their impact on a CI program's effectiveness.

4. *Analyze how intelligence flows in your organization.* We have all heard the adage "Information is power." It is used to explain why

information does not flow effectively in organizations. There is some truth to this conventional wisdom, but the reasons why information flows are more complicated. Robert Mauch, president and CEO of AmeriGas Propane, Inc., underscored this point in the CEO roundtable when he stated:

> You need to create an environment where the competitive intelligence officer can share competitive information with different managers at varying levels of the organization in a way that causes the manager to use the information to solve a problem or to achieve an objective." (Symposium: *Understanding the Competition*)

Currently, the panacea for facilitating the flow of information is information technology (IT). IT has become a great enabler for facilitating the flow of information. Companies such as Dow use IT to manage CI projects around the world. Others, such as Procter & Gamble and Corning, have created knowledge warehouses where experts and past research studies can be easily located.

IT is a wonderful tool, but our understanding of information flows needs to be more broadly based. Mohinder Dugal, Patrick Gibbons, and I have been examining four mechanisms that act as barriers and facilitators of information flow. *Behavioral mechanisms* are those related to the personalities and traits of individuals. The adage "Information is power" would fit into this category. *Political mechanisms* involve differences in goals and aspirations among managers. *Organizational systems,* a third set of mechanisms, include decision-making processes, IT, reward structures, and other systems. The last set of mechanisms comprises the varying *mental models* used by managers to frame and interpret information.

> Contrary to popular folklore, behavioral and political mechanisms are not the primary barriers to the flow of information. Organizational systems and differing mental models are the primary barriers.

Interestingly, our diagnostic research is showing that, contrary to popular folklore, behavioral and political mechanisms are not the primary barriers to the flow of information. Organizational systems and differing mental models are the primary barriers. Additional research is needed, but CI groups now have a way to diagnose the reasons for the quality of information flows in their organization.

Lesson 4

The evolution of CI programs is a natural phenomenon driven by the needs of the corporation, feedback, and quality-enhancement techniques.

To survive, a CI program needs a plan to manage its evolution. Two articles focus on the evolution of CI. John E. Pepper, former chairman of Procter & Gamble describes the evolution of CI under his leadership (p. 23). His perspectives on how CI groups need to evolve coincide with a framework presented below. Dr. Wayne A. Rosenkrans of AstraZeneca Pharmaceuticals describes a model of CI that evolved from SCIP's board of directors (p. 297). In essence, the model represents the value chain for the CI industry. Both articles provide valuable points for CI professionals.

My own focus will center on "how" CI professionals can manage the evolution process. I draw on my research and interaction with CI professionals to develop an evolutionary framework.

Figure 2 depicts a process for a CI function's evolution over time. I will describe the framework using Compaq as an example. Compaq is in the fast-moving computer industry. Every day, two or three new products or modifications are introduced at Compaq. This is an amazing rate of change. Ensuring that Compaq managers, working in industries that have blurry and converging boundaries, are informed of the latest developments is a formidable task.

Currently, the evolutionary drivers of CI include the implications of increasing levels of out-of-the-box revenues, competitor Internet strategies, imminent alliance and merger activity, and early warning of new competitors. Given this background, the CI group, under the direction of Bill Mutell, reassessed its vision. Ideally, the group desired to "sit outside the CEO's door" and become indispensable to top management. This was the vision that they wanted to achieve, but visions need to be converted into reality through an accurate assessment of capabilities and a deployment of resources.

Having developed their vision, Bill's next step was to assess their current position and the challenges involved in achieving their vision. At the time of the analysis, the CI group was focusing its efforts on strategic intelligence for corporate managers, providing early warning, and demonstrating how CI contributes to financial success. The group had developed a hub-and-spoke CI process that linked corporate CI efforts to decentralized tactical intelligence.

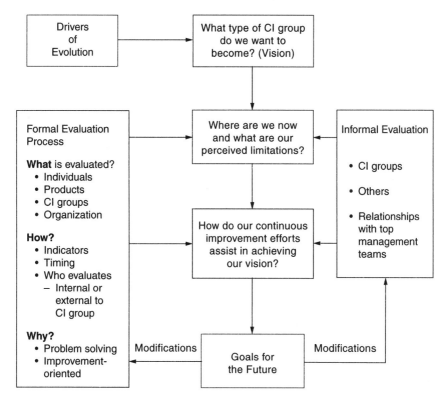

Figure 2   The evolution of CI programs.

Central to assessing the group's current position was the incorporation of both formal and informal evaluation processes. Informally, the CI group:

- Catalogued all feedback received from the 200+ strategic reports during the past year.
- Tagged e-mail.
- Noted verbiage from CI reports that executives used in speeches.
- Developed close relationships with the strategic planning department.

There were formal evaluations of the CI personnel and the group as a whole. Each analyst met with Bill Mutell weekly, to set CI priorities. Analysts were evaluated on criteria such as:

- Development of their human-intelligence network.
- Quality of their reports.
- Ability to link recommendations to performance.
- Timeliness.
- Quality of interpersonal interactions.

The formal evaluations centered on how individual analysts and the group could improve their products and services.

Pulling together the variety of evaluations, the CI group next determined what types of activities would assist them in achieving their vision. At Compaq, their continuous improvement efforts included:

- Team-building activities.
- CI-skill development for analysts.
- Business-skill development.
- Personal growth goals.

The final step in the evolution process is to develop a set of goals for the future. Compaq's CI goals included:

- Expanding the group.
- Developing a better understanding of the business models of competitors.
- Emphasizing deeper dives in their projects.
- Enhancing their role in the strategy process.

The process described above (and illustrated in Figure 2) focuses attention on how the evaluation and evolution of a CI function can be managed. Some of the major take-aways of this lesson include:

- A vision for CI based on key drivers of business performance.
- Systematic assessment of both formal and informal feedback, to understand the strengths and limitations of the CI group.
- Development of a continuous improvement plan.
- Development of goals to achieve the vision.

SUMMARY

I began with a bold proclamation that CI is embedded into the fiber of businesses throughout the world. I was sure that many readers would be skeptical of my assertion. To support it, I developed four overarching lessons and contrasted "to do" lists with process maps as alternative methods for designing CI systems that produce actionable intelligence. Let me offer one additional piece of evidence to support my contention. The Appendix contains a list of the companies mentioned in this book. Approximately 115 organizations are identified as having some association with the field of CI. The list is impressive, and it doesn't extend to the numerous additional companies with CI operations that have been discussed in *Competitive Intelligence Review* or at SCIP conferences and symposiums during the past decade and a half. If we consider the alliance partners and strategic suppliers of these organizations who benefit from and participate in the CI processes of these organizations, there can be no doubt that CI is institutionalized.

We still have a lot of work to do. Our hope is that the lessons and articles in this book will have several results. Our highest priority focuses on the practicing CI professional. This book provides ample evidence of the value of CI, which can be presented to skeptical managers who provide funding and champion intelligence activities. A second priority is to encourage CI practitioners, vendors, and academics to continue to publish their latest concepts, frameworks, and cases to further advance the sophistication of CI. A third priority is to educate the general public regarding the legitimacy of CI. Recent incidents, such as the case involving Oracle and Microsoft (Brindis et al., 2000), are unfortunate because they illustrate some of the grey areas of our field. A final priority is the need to increase our attention to international CI topics.

We have a bright future, and companies that practice the principles of CI will have sustainable and profitable growth.

REFERENCES

APQC. (1999). *Starting a CI Program*. Houston: APQC. (www. APQC.org)

Brindis, Ted, Glenn Simpson, and Mylene Mangalindan (with Lee Gomes and Ted Clark). (2000). Search Engine: How Piles of Trash Became Latest Focus in Bitter Software Feud, *Wall Street Journal*, June 29, pp. A1, A6.

D'Aveni, Richard A. (1994). *Hypercompetition: Managing the Dynamics of Strategic Maneuvering*. New York: The Free Press, a division of Macmillan, Inc.

Directorate of Intelligence, Central Intelligence Agency. (1997). *A Compendium of Analytic Tradecraft Notes, Volume 1 (Notes 1–10)*. Washington, DC: Government Printing Office.

Gilad, Ben, and Jan P. Herring (eds.). (1996). *Advances in Applied Business Strategy, Supplement 2, 1996: The Art and Science of Business Intelligence Analysis. Part A: Business Intelligence Theory, Principles, Practices, and Uses*. Greenwich, CT: JAI Press.

Gilad, Ben, and Jan P. Herring (eds.). (1996). *Advances in Applied Business Strategy, Supplement 2: The Art and Science of Business Intelligence Analysis. Part B: Intelligence Analysis and Its Applications*. Greenwich, CT: JAI Press.

Griffith, Samuel B. (1971). *Sun Tzu: The Art of War*. New York: Oxford University Press.

Krizan, Lisa. (1999). *Intelligence Essentials for Everyone*. Washington, DC: Government Printing Office.

LeCarré, John. (1963). *The Spy Who Came in from the Cold*. New York: Ballantine Books.

Leana, C., and Rousseau, D. (2000). *Relational Wealth*. New York: Oxford University Press.

Nohria, Nitin, and Robert G. Eccles (eds.). (1992). *Networks and Organizations: Structure, Form and Action*. Boston, MA: Harvard Business School Press.

Nolan, John. (1999). *Confidential: Uncover Your Competitors' Top Business Secrets Legally and Quickly—and Protect Your Own*. New York: Harper Business/Harper Collins.

Prescott, John, and John H. Grant. (1988). A Manager's Guide for Evaluating Competitive Analysis Techniques, *Interfaces,* 18 (May-June), 10–22.

Scott, John. (1992). *Social Network Analysis: A Handbook*. Newbury Park, CA: Sage Publications.

Society of Competitive Intelligence Professionals/Rutgers University CEO Roundtable. (1996). Symposium: "Understanding the Competition: A CEO's Perspective," *Competitive Intelligence Review*. 7(3), 4–14.

Tao, Qingjiu, and John E. Prescott. (2000). China: Competitive Intelligence Practices in an Emerging Market Environment, *Competitive Intelligence Review* 11(4), 65–78.

PART 1

COMPETITIVE BUSINESS INTELLIGENCE: CORPORATE CASE STUDIES

Corporate Insights into Structures and Processes for Collecting, Analyzing, and Communicating Actionable Intelligence

In this initial section, we focus on how corporate leaders establish and maintain top-notch CI operations.

John Pepper was just ending his successful tenure as Procter & Gamble's CEO when he outlined the crucial role CI plays as P&G undergoes a fundamental restructuring to remain competitive in today's faster, globalized markets. Similarly, after seeing its competitive position erode substantially in the early 1990s, IBM discovered competitive intelligence. With the enthusiastic support of its new CEO, Louis V. Gerstner, Jr., Big Blue launched a pilot program to build a company-wide network of CI teams linked to a small core of corporate CI professionals who manage the overall operation.

The "convergence" CI and knowledge management is aptly demonstrated by Bret Breeding, then of Shell Services International, who offers a detailed description of how CI is made available to employees via the firm's intranet. Hans Gieskes, then-president and CEO of the Lexis-Nexis Group, provides insight into how this knowledge-focused firm monitors the competitive landscape and factors that information into competitive strategy. His frank discussion of the use of the firm's intranet, as well as "Rival Reports" and e-mail briefings to collect and disseminate competitor information, should inspire others to give CI the high priority we believe it must have in today's global "new economy."

Articles by NutraSweet's Robert Flynn and by Xerox's Judith M. Vezmar, as well as by Motorola's legendary Robert W. Galvin, deliver a surprisingly forthright look at CI in action at their firms. Kenneth Sawka and Stéphane Marceau address why CI is imperative for telecoms trying to survive deregulation. And how CI was used to guide the reengineering of Digital Equipment Corporation's computer systems division is described in a case study by Larry Kennedy that can serve as an example for applying CI to internal-process benchmarking.

The SCIP/Rutgers CEO Roundtable was a watershed event, bringing together many of competitive intelligence's leading corporate advocates. So that their insights could be shared with a wider audience, *Competitive Intelligence Review* published a symposium drawn from the day's panel discussions, an excerpt of which is included herein.

Evidence that competitive intelligence has become a fundamental corporate operation continues to be reported in surveys and samplings. Included is a comprehensive analysis of the American Productivity and Quality Center's "Competitive and Business Intelligence Consortium Benchmarking Study," coauthored by *Competitive Intelligence Review*'s executive editor John E. Prescott, along with Jan P. Herring and Pegi Panfely. The absolute necessity of CI as practiced at the companies that participated in the study—including Bell Atlantic, Eastman Kodak, Fidelity Investments, Ford, Merck, Pacific Enterprises, and Xerox—and the lessons derived from their experiences make this a "must read" article for anyone involved in corporate CI.

Conway L. Lackman, Kenneth Saban, and John M. Lanasa present the results of research conducted at Duquesne University in "Organizing the Competitive Intelligence Function: A Benchmarking Study." The authors survey how the market-intelligence function is structured at best-practice companies, including 3M, Kodak, and US West. Areas studied range from the use of multidivisional teams to gather intelligence to the critical role played by senior management.

Another groundbreaking study jointly conducted by SCIP and APQC examines how leading corporations, including Dow Chemical, Amoco, and Met Life, use "coordinating mechanisms" to deploy strategic and tactical intelligence for sales and marketing. Authors Cynthia E. Miree and John E. Prescott served as subject-matter experts for the project.

As a reminder that CI isn't only of benefit to the biggest corporate players, Amy Berger contributes her perspective on practical steps for conducting CI at medium-sized firms, especially it terms integrating sales reps into CI operations.

We wind up with Jan P. Herring's discussion of how Key Intelligence Topics (KITs) can help to identify and define intelligence needs—and hence the type of CI organization and activities that will best help a company leverage information into actionable intelligence for competitive advantage.

Competitive Intelligence at Procter & Gamble

John E. Pepper
The Procter & Gamble Company

EXECUTIVE SUMMARY

In the following keynote address to the 1999 SCIP CEO Roundtable, held April 1999 in Montréal, John E. Pepper, chairman of the Procter & Gamble Company, spoke of the evolution of CI operations at Procter & Gamble and the role business intelligence plays as the company embarks on the biggest change effort in its history, revamping its structures, processes, and culture simultaneously. CI at Procter & Gamble has developed from routine report generation to an activity embedded in strategy development. Organizationally, CI operations have moved from being both too highly centralized and too highly decentralized, to a "hub & spoke" structure. Chairman Pepper offers a series of "Old World" versus "New World" perspectives on CI activity.

I can't imagine a more appropriate time to be talking about competitive intelligence than right now, for I can't imagine a time in history when the competencies, the skills, and the knowledge of the men and women in competitive intelligence (or, as I'll be calling it, business intelligence) are more needed and more relevant to a company being able to design a winning strategy and act on it.

It's particularly timely for our company, because we're going through a major organizational change. And a structural change like this presents a fresh opportunity to reframe the linkages between business intelligence and our operational units. It certainly is presenting that opportunity for us.

Competitive Intelligence Review, Vol. 10(4) 4–9 (1999). © 1999 John Wiley & Sons, Inc.

I'd like to share some changes going on within Procter & Gamble (P&G) and show how these will particularly impact business intelligence, and how successful exploitation of those changes will depend on business intelligence.

First, a bit of background on the company. We were started in 1837. We were a family business partnership until 1890. We didn't have anyone other than a Procter or a Gamble lead P&G until 1932. Very few people have run this company. I make that point not to argue the value of age, but to underscore the importance of a very simple set of core values in our company, starting with a foundational commitment to the consumer through the products and, increasingly now, the knowledge and the service we provide.

We have over time had a history of growth, doubling our business every 10 years for the last 50 years. Our market capitalization over the past 12 years has increased strongly. Our success has been based on our brands, including those we have brought to the market to create whole new categories: Pampers was the first affordable disposable diaper, Crest the first fluoride toothpaste, and so on. These products renewed or reconfigured categories, if not creating them outright. We've also had significant success in being able to acquire and grow brands.

The foundation of that excellence has been our technology. We are a science-based company with a commitment to know the consumer—and I've referenced that because it will prove relevant to what we're now doing in business intelligence.

WHY CHANGE?

With all that strength, we have embarked right now, as many companies have, on what is clearly the biggest change effort in our history. This is much more than evolution. While we are certainly in no way losing our roots, our purpose, our principles, our values, and our commitment, we've placed everything else on the table. The reason: Our growth is too slow (about half the rate we really need), and our complexity is too high (with an organizational structure that evolved over time as we became a global company).

As many companies, certainly consumer goods companies, did, we started out in the United States. We then tended to create "mini-United States" of the regional and country organizations developed as we went into Europe, Latin America, and then Asia. As recently as 1986, our company could only reach about 1 billion consumers in terms of economies and political regimes allowing it; today that number is 4½ billion.

We had regions, functions, and, increasingly, global categories—a triple matrix. Some would say a quadruple matrix, with the fourth element being top management. It had become way too complex in terms of structure.

Our objectives in this change are to build and create leadership brands globally better than ever before—that is our business; to capitalize on the knowledge, capability, and commitment to our people beyond what we've ever done. This we are attempting to achieve through simplification of our organization structure and of certain processes, capitalizing on technology and changes in our culture. Although growing from our fundamental purpose and the principles and values of the company, this is a quantum change. It's one that involves changes in the structure, process, and culture *simultaneously*.

It won't be the big that eat the small; it will be the fast that eat the slow.

We're operating under the banner of stretch, innovation, and speed. Stretch is a mindset away from the incremental toward breakthrough (I'll return to this later). Knowledge-based innovation has obviously been the foundation of our company, but we're recognizing the need to innovate at ever higher levels. Speed hardly needs to be emphasized. Both in our structure and our culture, we need to improve speed to market by orders of magnitude of 3 and 4 to 1. If 10 years ago we could take 6 years to take a product global, we now need to do it in 18 to 24 months—and we're finding even at 18 to 24 months, we could be beaten in moving into global markets.

I can remember back in Europe a fellow who ran our baby-care business, Michael Allan, saying it won't be the big that eat the small, it will be the fast that eat the slow. Yet, as important as speed was then, it's even more so today.

With that as a context, I'd like to discuss business intelligence. Let me start with a brief review of the role over time of competitive intelligence at P&G. Prior to 1985 it was functionally focused. We had clear focus in R&D at a very early stage, and we had focus in marketing. In 1985, we started to bring in multifunctional examination of strategies. In 1988, we had our first global multi-sector analysis. Over the period of time since, under the leadership of Susan Steinhardt, our director of corporate competitive analysis, we've done much more in the area of benchmarking, which has been fundamental to our ability to know where we were too heavy in our administrative work. This has included benchmarking in terms of speed to market and benchmarking the structure of our organization as we went into this move.

As we've looked at how we should evolve, we've had three core premises in terms of what our business intelligence activity ought to be focused on:

1. How do we generate greater innovation to reach our goals?

2. How do we recognize our people, their knowledge, and their ideas and convert these into action?

3. How can we capitalize as fully as we can on emerging technologies in communications, both internally and externally, to make the best use of that knowledge?

In his book, *Business at the Speed of Thought,* Bill Gates writes, "I have a simple but strong belief that the most meaningful way to differentiate your company from your competition, the best way to put distance between you and the crowd, is to do an outstanding job with information. How you gather, manage, and use information will determine whether you win or lose. Information flow is the lifeblood of your company because it enables you to get the most out of your people and learn from your customers." Even allowing for some self-interest in that statement, I think all of us would buy into it. I certainly would.

OLD WORLD VERSUS NEW WORLD

I'd like to present a comparison of the Old World and the New World of business intelligence at Procter & Gamble, to shed some light on changes that we've made and our vision of changes we should undertake (see Table 1).

In the stylized Old World vs. New World of business intelligence, the basic truth lies in these comparisons. Next, I'll discuss how they relate to five issues involving business intelligence at P&G:

1. Reason for being.

2. Structure.

3. Access to information/role of technology.

4. Use of knowledge.

5. Culture.

Table 1   CI at Procter & Gamble

"Old World"	*"New World"*
• Static competitive analysis	• Dynamic competitive response modeling
• Routine report generation, reactive	• CI embedded in strategy development and option analysis
• Responsibility of CI analysts	• Everybody's responsibility
• Highly centralized and highly decentralized	• "Hub & spoke"
• Individually and functionally driven	• Team effort
• "Need to know"	• "Need to share"
• Limited and sporadic top-management support	• Top management deeply involved

REASON FOR BEING

We keep reminding ourselves it can be too easy at Procter & Gamble to be complacent about what the competition is doing and what their reaction will be to our initiatives. But it's important to think of this more broadly, in terms of business and market intelligence—not just the strengths and weaknesses of the competition and how they'll react, but of new business models they'll be developing in our categories or categories we might enter.

I've never seen a time when so many whole businesses have changed before our very eyes, redefining what constitutes success. Internet technology, to take just one transformative development, has changed not just how you reach consumers through commercial channels, but how you design products, how you test products, and how you communicate with consumers as to what they want.

In this environment, business intelligence must develop from collecting, analyzing, and disseminating knowledge and information to the point of helping organizations acquire and use information and knowledge to create winning strategies.

> I've never seen a time when so many whole businesses have changed before our very eyes, redefining what constitutes success.

STRUCTURE

We tended in the past to be either highly centralized or highly decentralized. We could be very centralized in some activities, but we didn't have much expertise or reach into the business units. Or we were highly decentralized. R&D, for example, was an extremely capable operation but quite decentralized. We're now moving to a "hub-and-spoke" that fits with our new organization structure. We're moving resources and people with competence to projects as they occur rather than have so many fixed in place. And we're shifting from an organization with information centers in multiple countries to a truly unified global information structure. Of course, technology is helping us do this in a material way.

We now have seven "global business units." In addition, we have market development organizations, which you might think of as regions, plus a global business service organization, which brings together services. We have representatives and linkages between our central corporate business intelligence unit with each of those, and we're seeking advantages you'd expect, both from what is in the hub and what's in the spoke.

The hub is important to provide the benefits of scale in purchases, to have a common mission across the whole organization, standardized

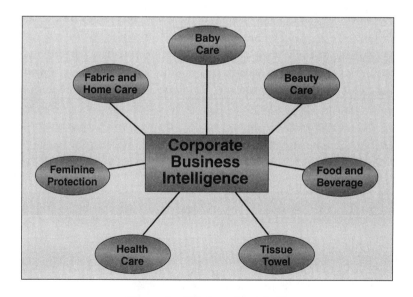

Figure 1   "Hub-and-spoke."

processes, and so on. At the same time, the spoke is terribly important for specific, flexible knowledge in the individual business units, and ownership of the activity in the individual business units. It's also going to prove important for the diversity of ideas, for different approaches that will come from our operations around the world.

INFORMATION/TECHNOLOGY

In the Old World, "information" and "technology" tended to be situated independently, often resulting in redundant individuals with personal competitive files having relatively little interaction. Studies were often repeated due to lack of retention. We are now moving to what we're calling a Global Knowledge Network, which will be available to all electronically. It's providing a venue for collecting data, sharing opinions, and disseminating analysis. All intranet content is registered, nearly all of it is open and accessible to everyone in the company; that's been a change for us. Electronic publishing is easy. It doesn't require special skills, and it enables connections to people that will have a tremendous benefit in fostering innovation.

USE OF KNOWLEDGE

In the Old World, there was too much routine report generation, and too many non-actionable requests. All of which tended to be too reactive, and too far removed from the core strategy and the key planning activity. In moving to a new organization structure, we are making an effort to get it right from the beginning by having the business intelligence activity embedded into strategy development in the line.

For example, our business intelligence group has been terribly important to Procter & Gamble in improving the quality of our options analysis. We tend to be people who want to get to a solution quickly. If we can avoid having to spend too much time thinking of a lot of different options, we'll tend to welcome that. So we benefit by having someone who holds our feet to the fire and says, "Slow down a bit to look at what the options are" so you'll have a really robust, competitively viable strategy. This has been a major contribution.

In terms of getting top management deeply involved, we're making real progress in that as well—it has been an area where we needed to. We're also more focused on setting our own winning strategy in the context of competitive strengths. We're moving from a static competitive analysis toward one focused on action, which includes competitive response modeling using multifunctional teams, and scenario planning that will better allow us to prepare for the competitive response.

CULTURE

If you're making change in an organization, you can only accomplish so much through structure. You can simplify and clarify roles and responsibilities, but then it gets down to how people interact and what kind of conversations are going on between individuals and within groups. While we have an extremely strong culture—we wouldn't be the company we are today without it—there are elements of our culture that we are seeking to strengthen and change.

Generally, the things you need to improve, the areas of relative weakness, turn out to be the flip-sides of your greatest strengths. Where we've had a tendency toward excessive perfection and risk aversion, we're moving toward promoting risk-taking, with victory defined as "stretch goals" and what may be possible and is worth trying, rather than what you know you can do, or have a 90 percent certainty you can do. P&G people are very thorough, with a commitment to do the job right. But, again, it can be taken to excess, which limits innovation.

Another cultural change is a more vigorous focus on coaching and sharing, promoting collaboration and candor, trust, and constructive confrontation. Have you ever heard of the moose on the table? It describes a phenomenon where you have people in a company who tend to come into a meeting and talk about the easier things, topics which can be approached without too much controversy. And then one day the group comes in and there's a huge moose sitting right in the middle of the table, and accustomed to their previous practice they look between the moose's leg and over it and nobody acknowledges "we've got a great big moose on this table and we'd better deal with it or it's going to kick us in the teeth."

We're moving away from the concept of sharing on a need-to-know basis, and assuming a need-to-share basis.

We now have this metaphor where if something is going on in any kind of a meeting in the company where we feel the real gut issue isn't being addressed—there's an area of basic disagreement that hasn't been surfaced and brought to a resolution—we say, "We've got a moose on the table," and it's a rather nice way to say stop and deal with it.

In that same spirit, there are culture changes we are applying in our business intelligence area. We are striving to counter the thought that competitive intelligence is the responsibility of particular specialists or analysts, and make it clear that it's everybody's responsibility. We're moving away from the concept of sharing on a need-to-know basis, and assuming a need-to-share basis. CI training, which before might have been made available selectively, is being made available to everybody who would benefit from scenario planning, from better strategic analysis. And from having the activity individually and functionally driven, we're moving toward more team efforts and seeing tremendous benefit from getting multifunctional teams involved in scenario planning and competitive reaction scenarios.

Not to be overlooked, we're also moving from limited and sporadic top management support for business intelligence, to having it become part of an embedded strategic and planning process.

OPPORTUNITIES

I'd like to conclude by reviewing what I would suggest are opportunities for business intelligence, at least looking through Procter & Gamble's eyes.

Let People Know What You Can Do

There hasn't been enough acknowledgement within Procter & Gamble of all the resources and the capabilities that exist. We have gone out and bought multiple reports and surveys, instead of using our internal resources. So we've got to do a better job of just publicizing what the capabilities are, and that has to be done down the line.

Know Who Your Customers Are and Link with Them

Again, this is a matter of relationships. And if your company is going through organization change—and it would be hard for me to imagine one that's not—a key point is knowing who the customers are in the new organization and establishing the right linkages and relationships, determining how the information is going to flow, and how to become involved in strategic planning.

Have a Clear List of Key Priorities and Measures of Success in Achieving Them

Know what really are the key issues that management wants to have addressed. It isn't just more data. For instance, how is the Internet going to change the way business is done in baby care? Or for women interested in health and nutrition?

Be Prepared to Say "No" to a Past Service in Order to Say "Yes" to a Bigger Future Priority

We have a very hard time taking stuff off the table, but we have to, or we won't move forward. Help your internal customers deal with information. Differentiate report generation from actionable intelligence. When I know it's coming from the heart, that helps me, and I can draw actionable conclusions or sometimes affirmations of what I believe from that.

The goal is to be able to come in and give a point of view, as our business intelligence group did last fall when they met with our 30-member executive committee and talked about the future. They laid out scenarios of what the future is likely to be in 2010 for our customers, what our channels are likely to be, who our employees likely will be, and trends regarding our consumers. That day changed the way we've operated since. We wouldn't have been able to reach those conclusions if somebody hadn't presented it very well. There were videos of thought leaders who were talking about these things, so that got our attention, thanks to the quality that went into the work and let us know in a riveting way the issues we needed to deal with.

HANG IN THERE

Any of these changes don't happen overnight. In getting those linkages started, the first audience may not be that pleasant, and people might not get the picture right away. And yet it's so important. You have to keep going back, it may take a 2- to 3-year effort, and it has to start with the CEO or the head of the business unit. It may require some tough, honest conversation. Recognize this is a corporate-wide effort, not only an individual corporate category effort.

I was with an ad agency the other day, one of our great agencies that does our Folger's coffee copy. I asked, "How do you keep going on this great campaign?" Because it's been kept going year after year. "Well," he said, "we're just in perpetual whitewater." I love that. Keep learning and thinking about what are the key trends and how to approach them corporately. It's a singularly important role that you play in the business intelligence area.

PERSONAL LEADERSHIP

Finally, let me end with a few words about the need for strong personal relationship. Everything big that I've seen done has come about because somebody has had passion about something they felt had to be done, and they were able to enlist others in it and then overcome obstacles and move it through to the solution. This area of business intelligence is filled with opportunity today because of the role of knowledge, the importance of speed, and the competitive world we're in. Getting the right systems, the right linkages and relationships with the right people in a corporation, opening the mind, recognizing the need for external knowledge, is going to call for a great deal of sustained personal leadership to achieve the results that we all need and want.

RELATED READINGS

CI of "singular importance" says Procter & Gamble Chairman. (1999, July–September). *Competitive Intelligence Magazine,* 2(3), 5–7.

Face to face with: John Pepper and Susan Steinhardt. (1999, October–December). *Competitive Intelligence Magazine,* 2(4), 35–38.

ABOUT THE AUTHOR

After serving nine years as president of Procter & Gamble, John E. Pepper was elected as P&G's ninth chairman and chief executive in 1995. After retiring as CEO in January 1999, he continued as chairman of the board until that September, when he became chairman of the executive committee of the board. In June 2000, he returned from retirement to again serve as chairman of the board. Mr. Pepper also serves on the boards of Motorola and Xerox.

Shaping a Corporate Competitive Intelligence Function at IBM

Lynn Behnke and Paul Slayton

IBM CORPORATION

EXECUTIVE SUMMARY

Losing more than $14 billion during the period 1991–1993, combined with the arrival of new CEO Louis V. Gerstner, Jr., changed the way IBM thought about customers and competition. As IBM began to reshape itself in the 1990s, its traditional emphasis on customer satisfaction broadened to include a renewed focus on competition. In 1993, IBM revised its approach to competitive intelligence, which had previously been isolated within business units. This article summarizes experiences in shaping a corporate competitive intelligence operation at a large multinational company. Under a pilot project, rival information technology vendors with whom IBM's customers planned to do more business were identified. For each of these competitors, a senior IBM executive was assigned as the resident "expert," responsible for ensuring that strategies throughout IBM addressed the competitor and led to appropriate actions in the marketplace. "Virtual" CI teams were established, consisting of the assigned executive, peer executives representing various IBM business units, a small core of CI professionals, and representatives from functional areas such as manufacturing, development, marketing, and sales. A small corporate team was formed to manage the overall program, while day-to-day competitive analysis was performed by teams located throughout the company. Lotus Notes-based systems provided teams with online discussion databases, and provided executives and analysts with global access to CI databases and updated competitive assessments. The teams also used IBM Internet technology to access sources outside of IBM, and IBM intranet technology to post updates within IBM. Lessons learned from the pilot project were assessed and the program refined, as competitive intelligence became ingrained in IBM's corporate culture.

Competitive Intelligence Review, Vol. 9(2) 4–9 (1998). © 1998 John Wiley & Sons, Inc.

J ust over four years ago, the chief executive of one of IBM's leading competitors said in a keynote address to a user's conference, *"We get up every morning and think about killing IBM."* Figuratively speaking, of course. But the implications to IBM under new Chairman and CEO Louis V. Gerstner, Jr. were clear: IBM's customer base was at risk, and sales lost to competitors meant loss of market share, less profit, reduced investment funds, and the decline of the enterprise.

In his own way, Mr. Gerstner had been delivering the same message to the IBM work force: *"We are too preoccupied with ourselves and not concerned enough with the outside,"* he told employees. By *"outside"* he meant not only customers, but also competitors. IBM needed to strengthen its relationships with customers and to sharpen its focus on competitors—quickly.

This article summarizes our experience in shaping the corporate competitive intelligence operation at IBM. We believe that our observations will help others in the profession, especially those in large multinational companies who have a similar responsibility.

> IBM needed to strengthen its relationship with customers and to sharpen its focus on competitors—quickly.

ACKNOWLEDGING A BLINDSPOT

Years of being the undisputed leader in the worldwide information technology industry, coupled with prolonged antitrust scrutiny by the US Department of Justice, created an environment at IBM in which management did not feel required or compelled to use actionable competitive intelligence as input to business strategies, product plans, marketing programs, and sales tactics.

Losing more than $14 billion during the period 1991–93, combined with the arrival of a new CEO from outside of IBM, brought a crisp change to our thinking about customers, markets, and competitors. When Mr. Gerstner was brought in to lead IBM in 1993, he focused from the start on two topics—customers and competition. Mr. Gerstner and the market were telling IBM that our lack of attention to competition had become, to use Benjamin Gilad's term, a *"business blindspot."*

As IBM began to reshape itself in the early 1990s, our traditional emphasis on customer satisfaction quickly broadened to include a renewed focus on competition as well.

How to Start?

Competitor analysis and the use of competitive intelligence have a fairly long history at IBM. For example, in the early 1990s IBM conducted several internal conferences on competitive intelligence and offered classes by leading academics to help analysts develop their skills. For most of this time, however, competitive intelligence was largely isolated within various business units, with marketing, product development, and finance units each hosting their own competitive analysis or business intelligence function. These functions operated in a parochial fashion and were rarely linked. In 1993, IBM revised its approach to competitive intelligence.

The new approach was very simple. We identified a dozen or so premier vendors of information technology. These were vendors with whom our customers planned to do more and more business. For each of these competitors, a senior IBM executive was assigned to be the resident "expert," responsible for ensuring that strategies throughout IBM addressed the competitor and led to appropriate actions in the marketplace.

Most of these executives established "virtual" competitive intelligence teams that assessed their competitor's actions and strategies. The ideal virtual team consisted of the assigned executive, peer executives representing various IBM business units, a small core team of competitive intelligence professionals, and representatives from functional areas such as manufacturing, development, marketing, and sales.

A small corporate team was formed to manage the overall program, while day-to-day competitive analysis was performed by teams located throughout existing organizations. These teams were expected to think and act with the overall best interests of IBM foremost in mind, rather than thinking and acting first in the interests of their individual business units. Requiring team members to extend their point of view was one of the objectives in assigning senior executives to be IBM's resident experts on competitors. In other words, the new competitive intelligence program aimed not only to improve our competitive intelligence, but also to help change the culture of IBM.

Requiring team members to extend their point of view was one of the objectives in assigning senior executives to be IBM's resident experts on competitors.

LESSONS FROM THE PILOT PROJECT

With the core structure in place and a mandate to act, the corporate team ran a pilot project that focused on a single competitor. We learned several important lessons from the pilot:

Each virtual team requires a visible "intelligence leader." A prominent, full-time intelligence leader raised the visibility of the pilot team's work and provided direction that bridged business unit boundaries.

Cross-functional teams work well. A mix of backgrounds such as development, marketing, and service on a team led to more complete and insightful views of the assigned competitor.

The frameworks and methods IBM had used in the past to evaluate competitors still worked, but communication was a weak link. For example, we discovered that executives often find it difficult to communicate the questions about competition that keep them awake at night. We learned that we needed to work closely with our executives to develop the questions worth answering if we intended to leverage competitive intelligence for strategic purposes. These questions are what Jan P. Herring calls Key Intelligence Topics, or "KITs," as shown in Figure 1.

Consultants, SCIP, and other outside sources of expertise can jumpstart an intelligence operation. Initially, program leaders used an outside consultant to interview key IBM executives to elicit what they really wanted to know about competition. An experienced consultant calling on key decision makers proved to be effective in surfacing strategic questions quickly. We also learned to use SCIP as a source of energy and ideas for people within IBM who were just learning about the practice of competitive intelligence.

A code of ethics simplifies life for the team. IBM's *Business Conduct Guidelines* are similar to SCIP's Code of Ethics. In the long term, such a code helps protect the company from the consequences of unethical conduct. In the short term, a code helps to remove debates about what

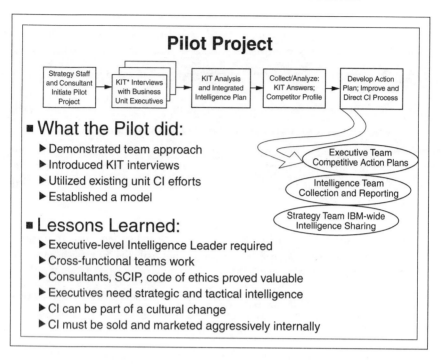

Figure 1   Overview of pilot project.

is and what is not acceptable conduct in dealing with competitors. A relevant excerpt from IBM's *Business Conduct Guidelines* is presented in Figure 2.

"Should we be strategic or tactical?" is a misleading question. We learned to recognize that the audience for competitive intelligence ranged from senior executives to sales representatives, with a corresponding range of requirements for competitive intelligence. The question for the team evolved from *"Should we be strategic or tactical?"* to *"How can we be both?"* The competitive intelligence program now contributes to the development of strategy and also recommends near-term tactics.

Competitive intelligence is hard work. Competitive intelligence, the team rediscovered, consists of more than just formatting information into attractive charts. It requires the additional effort of drawing implications and suggesting outcomes that executives can consider and act upon. As such, it requires a deeply felt commitment to the work. Achieving measurable results against the competition helped the team

IBM on the Ethics of Competitive Intelligence

Acquiring and Using Information about Others

In the normal course of business, it is not unusual to acquire information about many other organizations, including competitors. Doing so is a normal business activity and is not unethical in itself. In fact, IBM quite properly gathers this kind of information for such purposes as extending credit and evaluating suppliers. The company also collects information on competitors from a variety of legitimate sources to evaluate the relative merits of its own products, services, and marketing methods. This activity is proper and necessary in a competitive system.

There are, however, limits to the ways that information should be acquired and used, especially information about competitors. No company should use improper means to acquire a competitor's trade secrets or other confidential information. Illegal practices such as trespassing, burglary, wiretapping, bribery and stealing are obviously wrong; so is attempting to acquire a competitor's confidential information by hiring the competitor's employees. Improper solicitation of confidential data from a competitor's employees or from IBM customers is wrong. IBM will not tolerate any form of questionable intelligence-gathering.

Source: IBM Business Conduct Guidelines, May 1995 version

Figure 2   IBM's guidelines on acquiring competitive intelligence.

develop this commitment, and a belief in the value of the work helped to sustain the team when the team's messages met resistance.

Competitive intelligence is partly a cultural issue. The pilot demonstrated that successful competitive intelligence often requires a change in the behavior of people. First, members of the competitive intelligence team had to learn to view a competitor from IBM's point of view, not just from the point of view of their particular business unit. Second, everyone developing and using the competitive intelligence had to learn—or remember—to present and to evaluate bad news objectively.

Establishing a competitive intelligence program requires internal sales and marketing. We learned that, because competitive intelligence required some change in the culture of IBM, the program needed a director who could *"sell"* the program throughout the company. In other words, the competitive intelligence program needed an evangelist. When the program was first starting, the intelligence director spent only 20 percent of his time with the team, and 80 percent with other people in the company demonstrating the value of competitive intelligence to IBM.

MOVING BEYOND THE PILOT PROJECT

By early 1995, an expanded competitive intelligence operation was broadly implemented. To link competitive intelligence with strategy, the Corporate Strategy group began to lead the program by providing a framework, methodology, and tools to each of the virtual intelligence teams. This helped to keep competitive intelligence visible to executives while they were developing IBM's strategies.

Currently, virtual intelligence teams focus on approximately a dozen corporate competitors. In addition, teams from individual business units assess their particular competitors as well as emerging technologies. Figure 3 illustrates the essentials of the expanded competitive intelligence program.

> Currently, virtual intelligence teams focus on approximately a dozen corporate competitors. In addition, teams from individual business units assess their particular competitors as well as emerging technologies.

Figure 3   Overview of current program.

Team members now communicate and collaborate by using IBM's own technology. Lotus Notes-based systems provide teams with online discussion databases, and provide executives and analysts global access to various competitive intelligence databases and to competitive assessments as they are completed. Information suppliers from outside IBM provide information in Lotus Notes format for easy access by the teams.

Teams use IBM Internet technology to access sources outside of IBM, and use IBM intranet technology to post updates within IBM. One of the teams developed a set of intranet applications unique to its own needs, then linked these applications to the broader Notes-based application set. By using such a roll-your-own approach instead of buying off-the-shelf applications, teams can tailor applications to their needs.

The competitive intelligence teams have begun to systematically integrate a wealth of internal and external information that previously was scattered among market research and competitive analysis reports, press clippings, observations from trade show visits, customer surveys and consultant studies. The teams are also capturing the personal knowledge that IBM executives have of competitors. By linking a wide range of resources and concentrating the information for executives, we are striving to make IBM more proactive in the marketplace and more effective in specific competitive situations.

We've achieved this progress in a very cost-conscious environment with a corporate budget that provided only for a small core team. The program was able to leverage existing resources by focusing corporate-wide competitive intelligence efforts on key competitors and key threats, and by providing tools to raise the level of collaboration among competitive intelligence teams.

SELF-ASSESSMENT

Results from our collective efforts have been positive. We give ourselves good marks over the last two years for bringing together the global resources of IBM to be more effective against the competition. Even the industry press has remarked on the new, more competitive IBM. We are redeploying sales resources to attack competitors' weaknesses and rallying various parts of the IBM company to address specific competitive threats cohesively. Competitive intelligence has become more ingrained in IBM's product development processes.

We are redeploying sales resources to attack competitors' weaknesses and rallying various parts of IBM to address specific competitive threats cohesively.

We have not reached journey's end, however. Aspects of the program that we continue to refine include:

- Maintaining human intelligence networks inside and outside of IBM.
- "Professionalizing" competitive intelligence within IBM by developing education and career paths for competitive intelligence practitioners.
- Strengthening the links with competitive marketing and with strategy development.
- Managing requirements that range from identifying long-term strategic intents to assessing the morning's events.
- Delivering actionable intelligence.

CRITICAL SUCCESS FACTORS

Five factors have been critical to IBM's success in increasing the effectiveness of our corporate competitive intelligence function:

1. A new CEO brought a MANDATE and directed executive participation. Having the CEO's sponsorship helped move the program along quickly.

2. The declining financial condition of the company, combined with the arrival of a new CEO, intensified everyone's FOCUS on competition.

3. We sought the ADVICE of external experts and consultants to supplement IBM's own best practices. We had no time to tolerate a "not invented here" syndrome.

4. The VIRTUAL TEAMS coalesced to meet competitive challenges to the business. Team members recruited from various business units and drawing upon a variety of skills and backgrounds fed each other information, insight, and energy.

5. By delivering timely updates, objective analyses, and thoughtful rec-ommendations, the competitive intelligence teams earned CREDI-BILITY with senior management.

So What?

Actionable intelligence is the goal of our competitive intelligence operation. We learned that to deliver actionable intelligence, users and developers of competitive intelligence must continuously ask, *"So what?"* Asking *"So what?"* reveals that information and analysis are inert, but focused intelligence can precipitate action—action that leads to competitive advantage.

So what? The competitive intelligence operation provides IBM with an advantage in the daily battle to be the best at satisfying our customers in the global marketplace.

That's what.

References

Behnke, Lynn. (2001). Virtual CI Teams. *Competitive Intelligence Review,* 12(1).

Fahey, Liam. (1993). *Analyzing the Competition,* IBM internal education.

Gilad, Benjamin. (1994). *Business Blindspots,* Chicago: Probus Publishing Company.

Griffin, Robert J. (1997). *Just Do It: Establishing a Corporate Business Intelligence Function at IBM,* Proceedings, SCIP 12th Annual International Conference and Exhibits, Vol. II, 123–133.

Herring, Jan, and The Futures Group. (1994). *Results,* IBM internal project.

International Business Machines Corporation. (1995). *IBM Business Conduct Guidelines.*

Society of Competitive Intelligence Professionals, various proceedings and publications.

About the Authors

Lynn Behnke is a competitive analyst at IBM Corporation, and a member of a team whose mission is to raise the effectiveness of CI throughout the company. He has co-authored an IBM White Paper on CI, taught classes in various topics on CI within IBM, and contributed to the definition of IBM's strategic imperatives. Mr. Behnke became a competitive analyst after a career in product publications, where his assignments included technical writing, publications planning, and management.

Paul Slayton is a program director at IBM Corporation, where he is involved in CI and market analysis programs worldwide. He has been a CI practitioner at the division and corporate levels, and a SCIP member since 1993. Prior to that, he held various engineering, marketing, and management positions in IBM's server divisions. He holds master's degrees in the management of technology and in computer engineering.

CI and KM Convergence: A Case Study at Shell Services International

Bret Breeding

SHELL SERVICES INTERNATIONAL, INC.

EXECUTIVE SUMMARY

This case study looks at how competitive intelligence activities at Shell Services International (SSI) have been impacted by the extensive use of knowledge management (KM). The case study begins with the corporate processes influenced by CI. It then details the four activities that CI analysts perform, focusing on the progression of moving from lower to higher value-added activities. The CI/KM system that SSI currently uses (including the intranet-based CI KnowledgeHouse) is then examined in terms of automating many of the tasks that the CI group performs on a daily basis. A taxonomy of this CI/KM system is introduced with a "tie-back" to the corporate processes influenced by CI. It is demonstrated that by using the CI/KM system the analyst has more time devoted to higher value-added tasks such as simulation/strategy. Finally, a "lessons learned" section discusses some of the highlights and pitfalls encountered in implementing KM for SSI's CI practice.

The Shell Services International Group of Companies (SSI) was organized on January 1998 to combine the information technology (IT) and business services practices of several Royal Dutch/Shell Group entities. Providing greater efficiency, coordination, and cost-effectiveness, SSI became the primary IT services provider for the Royal Dutch/Shell Group. Its current focus is to deliver services to other Shell companies, but SSI also markets to non-Shell customers to develop commercially

Competitive Intelligence Review, Vol. 11(4) 12–24 (2000).

viable solutions and services. SSI operates throughout the world with more than 5,000 employees and a range of strategic relationships.

One of the companies that made up SSI was Shell Services Company (SSC)—an entity that provided IT services for mostly US-based Shell operating companies. This was the company that I joined after working for almost a decade at EDS. Upon joining SSC, I found an environment where there were no existing standards or methods in place for examining the competition. This was not entirely surprising as SSC had been in business only a short time. With not many competitive analysis methodologies in place, we termed the environment a "green field site." Still, CI was a necessary component of doing business. The main goals (as they still are today) were: helping to protect and increase market share within the Shell Group of Companies while competing against Andersen Consulting, EDS, and IBM, as well as beginning the process of winning business outside of Shell when those same companies were the competitors.

One fact was certain: We wanted the SSI competitive intelligence function to be as "proactive" as possible. One of the lessons learned from previous work experiences was that CI departments were constantly battling the perception that they were reactive in nature and would always have to go find information, apply analysis, and communicate to the sales and strategy teams after requests were made. Virtually every request happened in this fashion. We felt that the ideal state was for the users of the information to "self-service" the information themselves, then call the CI department and ask for extra or needed information and analysis.

To reach that state of "proactiveness," many shorter-term milestones would have to be reached, and this effort is what makes the SSI CI case study a valuable lesson in how a CI department can apply technology (and a bit of gamesmanship) to make a transition from a state of reactiveness to one of proactiveness. With this goal in mind, we set out to create the vision for SSI and its Competitive Intelligence Group:

> Take SSI to a position of thought leadership in the application of competitive information and knowledge sharing to enable responsiveness.

PROBLEMS/ISSUES BETWEEN CI PRODUCERS AND CI USERS

Many companies have CI departments, and most of these groups serve a given set of users. Often, however, there are inherent disconnects between the users and producers of intelligence. In many of the seminars I've conducted, we set out to identify audience members who are the users of intelligence and the producers of intelligence, and we engaged them to openly discuss some of the issues they face. Many times, they repeatedly talk about the same problems.

Users of CI characterize the information they're receiving in terms of the following attributes:

- *Information is too shallow.* The information doesn't have much depth and mostly contains the public relations viewpoint as reported by the media or by the competitor.

- *Credibility.* The information and analysis were assembled by a 25-year-old MBA who has little work experience in the industry. How can such a person possibly know more about what's going on with a key competitor than a 20-year industry veteran?

- *Timeliness.* Many users need the information *today.* If it takes a couple of days to assemble an intelligence report, it may be a couple of days too late.

- *Focus.* Users feel they should not be brought in at the last moment when the report is needed. When they make the intelligence request, they should have some say on how the report is assembled. The last thing they want is a 200-page report when all they are looking for is a couple of pages.

- *Whom to send intelligence to.* When people on the front lines have intelligence that they would like to share, they often don't know anyone in the intelligence department who should receive the information. And the users don't know how to participate in intelligence-gathering activities.

Producers of information face the following dilemmas with the users they serve:

- *No clear objectives.* Users often won't share with the CI group exactly what type of decision they want to make with the information they'll be getting. This is basically like going to buy a car and expecting the car dealership to help you, but not telling the salesperson the kind of car you want.

- *Not enough time to satisfy all the users.* When a CI function adds real value, it soon becomes very popular with its constituency. Users then send a deluge of requests, and they ultimately become too much for the CI department to handle.

- *Different needs of multiple users.* Some users want more in-depth information (deep divers), and some want high-level information (skimmers).

- *Too much information to get through.* With all the information available on the Internet today, as well as all the subscription-based services from third-party research bureaus, the flood of information is simply too much for the analysts to wade through.

- *No sharing of information.* Users find it difficult to obtain information from the field. The axiom "Knowledge is power" holds true to form. Users fear that if they have to share what's in their heads, they'll lose any career positioning advantage within the company.

- *Organizational barriers (whom to call, no follow-up).* Company structures are becoming more complicated; many are moving to matrixed organizational charts. As a result, accountability and responsibility are compromised at the expense of moving closer to the customer. This also creates problems for the CI group. As CI practitioners attempt to get close to their users, they have trouble determining who their users should be.

- *Poor identification of who the customer is.* Who should the CI group be serving? Should it be the salespeople? The strategy group? The top 20 executives in the company?

- *Lack of feedback.* Often, when work is performed and a report is given to a user, that's the last the CI group hears about the work it has delivered.

- *Low budgets.* Many companies focus on the bottom line rather than the top line. The CI group is viewed as an overhead function requiring funds that, if cut, could enhance the bottom line. Ultimately, when cuts occur, the CI group is forced to handle the same or an increasing workload with fewer resources.

- *Tough to get on executive schedules.* Executives lead busy lives and often cannot fit the CI function into their schedule. These same executives are privy to all sorts of excellent CI information because they often visit with colleagues and lawyers from competitors, partners, and customers.

At SSI, we wanted to confront these challenges head-on, but, over time, we realized that the issues could never be fully eliminated. Therefore, we set out to implement an approach that would attempt to minimize the occurrence of these issues.

CORPORATE PROCESSES AFFECTED BY CI (AUDIENCE IDENTIFICATION)

It is a fact of life that many companies have convoluted organizational structures. This ultimately complicates the task of identifying the audience that the CI group serves.

Before setting out to determine an appropriate audience for the CI group to interact with, it's important to address the value of CI when it rests in isolation.

When examined as a process, CI in and of itself cannot lead to end results. In other words, a company may have a great CI function, but if it doesn't interact with other corporate functions, its value is severely limited.

In any organization, CI must be viewed as an input to other corporate processes. Regardless of the organizational model employed, it is fairly simple to classify the users in the company as being in one of the process categories shown in Figure 1. For example, instead of examining multiple sales teams that sit in different business units, the SSI CI group treats all salespeople, regardless of where they reside, as part of the Sales and Marketing process.

Many companies begin their initial CI efforts with a focus on the Strategy process and/or the Sales process. Both areas are obviously affected by CI. SSI was no different when we started back in 1997. At the time, the main goals were to support users at the business development level (i.e., Sales and Marketing process). However, over time, other processes were factored in as well. The goals changed from supporting users at a business-development level to supporting users from a broad set of disciplines and core corporate processes. To add value at SSI, we discovered that CI must offer input into the following:

- New product development.
- Strategy (with mergers and acquisitions).
- Sales and proposals.

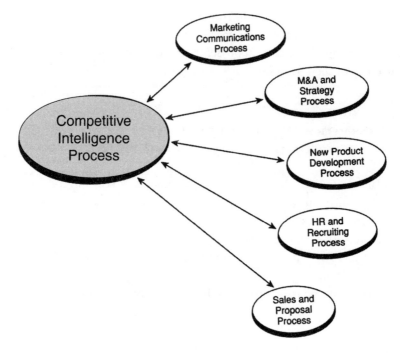

Figure 1   The CI process at SSI.

- HR and recruiting.
- Marketing communications.

It was fairly easy to classify groups of users into one of these core processes. Then the issue became: How can we best affect and communicate to a core process? Bearing this in mind, each of the groups became a potential audience for the CI analyst at SSI. Throughout the remainder of this case study, all of these groups are referred to as *the core audience.* Every action taken by the CI group focuses on affecting one of these core processes.

ACTIVITIES PERFORMED BY CI ANALYSTS

Once we've addressed the audience we want to serve, the next issue becomes: Exactly what do we want to do for that audience? In my experience, most CI analysts perform many of the same activities on a daily basis, differing only in the amount of time they spend on each activity. The goal is to work most on projects that lend the highest value-added to the company, and spend less time on the more mundane, less analytical projects.

Given this premise, we organized the tasks that CI analysts perform on a periodic basis into four different categories. Each had a corresponding level of value-added, as shown in Figure 2 and described below.

AD HOC REQUESTS

The first—and often the only—task that many CI analysts perform is answering ad hoc requests. Typical items requested include:

- Demographics and statistics.
- Company financial comparisons.
- Journal and news article searches.
- Emerging market overviews.
- Investment analysts' reports.
- Executive biographies.

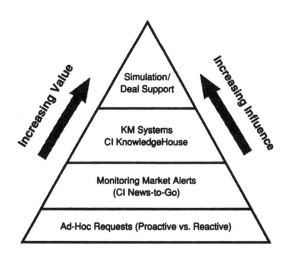

Note: The higher value-added activities cannot be performed credibly without first performing the lower value-added services.

Figure 2 Activities performed by CI analysts on a periodic basis.

- Studies and research reports.
- Competitive information.
- International business research.
- SEC and other public-entity filings.
- Economic indicators.

At SSI, the first thing the CI group does every day, upon arriving at the office, is answer phone calls and e-mails—almost 7,500 each year (around 35 a day)—and perform research on information that the core audience requests. These requests range anywhere from:

> We are competing against IBM. Can you tell me anything about IBM's oil-and-gas IT practice?

to:

> We are in Egypt. We're considering partnering with a small local company, and we need information.

An executive might call and say that he or she is having lunch with an executive from Texaco and needs to have a biography of that person before their meeting. The point is that these requests vary a great deal. At SSI, we classify all of these in terms of being *proactive* versus *reactive* requests.

Basically, proactive requests are those we already have the answers to before the user calls. Reactive requests require us to do research. Two facts are certain: (1) We definitely prefer proactive requests, but (2) CI analysts can never get away from reactive requests. We simply can't have, beforehand, the answer to every request that comes in.

When a request is received, the CI function should typically raise two key questions:

1. Before undertaking the project: "How is the information going to be used or what type of decision are you wanting to make?"
2. After completing the project: "What else do you need to know?"

This gives the CI analyst insight as to what the user specifically is looking for, so no wasted information is produced. As for finding the information, there are several excellent places to begin looking. Many companies use pay-for-use services such as Dow Jones, Hoover's Company Data Bank, Standard & Poor's, NEWSEDGE, and free information sources such as company Web sites, SEC Edgar, and corporateinformation.com. When time is constrained or we simply cannot find the information, we contact the appropriate market research librarian in a certain geographic region.

Extensive follow-up is essential when performing ad hoc research in that it ensures a high level of customer satisfaction and enables relationship building. In addition, the CI analyst may provide information that meets some but not all of the users' needs, and this provides an opportunity for add-on work that has higher value-adds. Finally, maintaining this kind of contact with the core audience expands the CI group's network and feedback mechanism, and enables the CI function to interact with the core audience at any time to discuss other important issues. For these reasons, when we finish work on a project, we contact users with the report findings and ask what else they may need to know.

If the CI group effectively answers its ad hoc requests, it's sure to be swamped with even more requests from throughout the company. Many articles have been written about the process a CI group should go through to handle this. Suggested steps include setting up workflows to tackle the volume of requests, and setting priorities among the core audience. Regardless of the process for answering ad hocs, this type of information gathering can be a time-consuming, low-value-add activity. Often, the requests involve looking up simple information that could have been answered by the requestor. Still, it is important to note that a CI group can never get away from answering ad hoc requests, if for no other reason than it's an important aspect of building a relationship with the core audience. At any point in time, if CI practitioners need information from the field, it makes their job much easier if they've built solid relationships.

EXTERNAL ENVIRONMENT
MONITORING/MARKET ALERTS

To add higher value, the CI group should be performing other tasks, such as monitoring the external environment and regularly reporting news to the core audience. At SSI, the CI group produces a weekly report that we have branded *CI News-to-Go*. When assembling the materials, the CI analyst examines multiple sources, spending about 30 minutes each day scanning news articles on the competition. From these sources, the CI analyst will

extract stories and summarize the contents. *CI News-to-Go* profiles stories on SSI competitors in the IT-services marketplace, new areas of technology that could impact our positioning, information on alliances, mergers
and acquisitions (M&A) among our competitors, and trends that third-
party research organizations (e.g., Gartner, Yankee, Meta, and so on) see
occurring in the industry. Competitive implications are added to some of
these stories, based on the analyst's insights and experiences while tracking
this industry. At the end of each week, all stories are summarized and sent
to users in the core audience.

Providing this service accomplishes several goals. First, it's a time-
saving mechanism; the core audience receives news about the competition
that is pushed directly to their desktop without having to do any searching
through newspapers, Web sites, and so on, on their own. Second, it height-
ens awareness about the competition; users become aware of the competition in many of their day-to-day activities. Third, and most importantly,
it creates an awareness of the CI group among the core audience. One of
the problems in many companies is that people in the field do not have
awareness of the CI function; or, even when they do, it's not top-of-mind
awareness. By pushing the news to the core audience's desktop on a periodic basis (at SSI, once a week), users must consider the competitive environment at least once a week. Often, when events occur on the front lines,
these same users automatically think of the CI function and know to communicate what they have heard to the CI group. When members of the
core audience need competitive information to help them make decisions
on a day-to-day basis, there is no question about whom they'll call.

Finally, in an effort to measure the ongoing effectiveness of *CI News-
to-Go,* the CI group should periodically (approximately every six months)
survey the core audience and request a response to the quantity/quality of the
information provided and to how it meets the needs of the user community.

KM Systems

Up to this point, it may seem that these two tasks would consume a great
deal of time. However, another important function of the CI group is to
identify, research, and analyze competitors. At SSI, we try to maximize
efficiency by automating not only competitors' profiles, but also the information uncovered while doing ad hoc requests and researching *CI
News-to-Go.* The SSI approach is to take all the deliverables discussed thus
far and disseminate them through the construction and maintenance of a CI

system (we call ours the CI KnowledgeHouse) that resides on the SSI intranet. The CI KnowledgeHouse is supported for approximately 8 to 12 hours each week to ensure content and strategy are always fresh. Answering requests from around the corporation requires only about one or two hours each morning (instead of being a full-time job). Many of these same requests can be answered proactively, based on projects already completed in the KnowledgeHouse.

The keys to this system are its information reusability and self-access features. Once the information is compiled, it is sent to a central place (where it is constantly updated) and is ready to be accessed a second, third, fourth . . . time. Each additional time it's accessed, the cost to assemble the information is virtually nothing. Also, every time a member of the core audience accesses the system, that is, for the most part, one less request the CI group has to answer. Finally, there is the issue of knowledge sharing. When the audience can view what the CI group knows (via viewing profiles or other information in the system), they become confident in their ability to share information *with* the CI group. We'll discuss the taxonomy of the SSI CI KnowledgeHouse in the following section. The main point here is that by automating the basic information, communicating the accessibility to the core audience, and enabling the self-service element of the information, the CI group is free to perform the higher value-added activity of simulation and deal support.

SIMULATION/DEAL SUPPORT

In an ideal setting, the CI group should spend anywhere from 25 percent to 50 percent of its time providing deal support. This is where the CI group adds the most value; still, there is no way the CI analyst can get away from providing the activities described above. There will always be ad hoc reports; there should always be development and maintenance of competitor profiles, and so on. However, for the CI function to justify the expense that management outlays, it must be involved in the business development process contributing to key wins.

> The CI group should spend from 25 to 50 percent of its time providing deal support. This is where it adds the most value. For CI to justify the expense that management outlays, it must be involved in the business development process that contributes to key wins.

At SSI, the CI group works on deals that involve simulating the antici-pated competitive responses of SSI's competitors. The CI group, through its experienced people who have observed competitors' movements year in and year out, should engage members of the core audience in scenario planning when working on key deals. They accomplish this by using information they have compiled through the years. Working with a member or two from the deal team who is familiar with customer requirements, this small subgroup can then craft a response that a particular competitor is likely to make if a specific set of events should occur. Essentially, instead of simulating a com-petitor's moves, the CI group is attempting to determine the competitor's ca-pability and developing a response that positions our company in a positive light relative to the competition.

THE CI KNOWLEDGEHOUSE

SSI's CI Knowledge Management System, or CI KnowledgeHouse, actu-ally grew out of the fact that the Internet is a critical part of SSI's business system. Residing on the SSI corporate intranet, the CI KnowledgeHouse is a knowledge management system with an in-depth view of SSI's com-petitors and markets. Specifically, this site profiles competitors—their products and services, strengths and weaknesses, market focus, sales ap-proaches, and tactics that SSI can reference in competitive scenario plan-ning. Central to its value is the issue of enabling responsiveness on the part of the core audience. When armed with knowledge on how to find and use information contained therein, they are able to make decisions more quickly, and can more efficiently use the CI group's time.

First, a word about security. Because much of the information is con-sidered sensitive, access is available to SSI staff in a secured environment. Access can only be obtained by contacting the CI group and making a case for access. The CI group maintains the passwords and controls who does and doesn't gain access. To keep matters simple, the access list for the CI KnowledgeHouse is in sync with the same people who receive *CI News-to-Go*. In short, a person who has access to the CI KnowledgeHouse will also receive weekly CI newsletters.

On entering the CI KnowledgeHouse, users find that it contains three major components and, overall, 16 modules. The three main levels are:

1. *Level-set components*—sections where users can obtain a working knowledge of CI. Modules include the Knowledge Broker and The

Gloss (modules are described in detail below). Users are encouraged to have this basic knowledge before using the other components of the system.

2. *Research components*—information in these modules originates from secondary research or published information. The modules include Executive Themes, Competitor Profiles, Yellow File, and the HR Manager. When constructing the CI KnowledgeHouse, information was drawn from over 100 published sources.

3. *Knowledge Management components*—in these modules, the core audience, in some form, shares its knowledge. Modules include the CI Community of Practice, the IT Landscape, The Pursuit/Deal Tactics, and RequestNet.

Now, on to each of the modules (see Figure 3).

Figure 3   SSIs intranet-based CI KnowledgeHouse.

LEVEL-SET COMPONENTS

The *Knowledge Broker* module functions as a toolkit for using the CI KnowledgeHouse. Inside, users find an electronic newsstand that lists the sources for most of our information. These include such Web sites as SEC Edgar and corporateinformation.com. Users also find a Competitor Portal that lists all competitors on whom we've conducted research, with links to their Web sites. Also included is a Best Practices for CI section that details each of the four activities the SSI CI group performs, with accompanying process detail that CI analysts are required to perform on a periodic basis. This allows new SSI analysts to accelerate their personal learning curve with a referenced guidebook, even if they are located far away from headquarters or have not received training from the centralized CI group.

The module entitled *The Gloss* (for glossary) contains all the definitions used throughout the CI KnowledgeHouse. In this module, we detail how the CI group classifies its competitors into Tier-One Competitors, Emerging Competitors, Regional Competitors, and Niche Competitors. Other terms include Strategy and Scenario Definitions, Proactive versus Reactive Research, and Yellow File, which contains stories about competitors and their inability to deliver solutions to customers.

> The Yellow File contains stories about our competitors' inability to deliver solutions to customers, and the Executive Themes module encapsulates the market and SSI's competitive positioning.

RESEARCH COMPONENTS

When we are examining the core audience, we often interact with executives in each of the core processes. The *Executive Themes* module profiles competitors from a broad-based perspective, thus encapsulating the market and SSI's competitive positioning. For example, one area contains information on the competition—its headquarters, growth rates, revenues, and employees. Another focuses on the major IT-outsourcing megadeals that have been signed in the industry during the past 15 years. Other features include market sizing and market trends, as well as information on how contracts are structured.

The *CI News-to-Go* module contains all information mailed out to the core audience via the *CI News-to-Go* newsletter. This is the area where the information is archived weekly. Numerous times each week, the CI group is contacted by users requesting information from the past year that was pushed out via the newsletter. Because we archive each of our newsletters, the CI group is able to use the CI KnowledgeHouse search function to quickly and easily find information that has been published in previous news alerts.

The *Competitor Profiles* module is the heart of the system. Every CI group has competitor profiles, whether they buy them from an external vendor or create their own. At SSI, we create our own profiles and classify our competitors into four different categories: Tier-One Competitors, Emerging Competitors, Regional Competitors, and Niche Competitors. The definitions of these four classifications reside in The Gloss module.

Tier-One Competitors are companies such as IBM, CSC, EDS, Andersen Consulting, and Cap Gemini. They all have a global presence and sizable IT services practices for the energy industry, and they compete against SSI in most if not all of our global practice areas.

Tracking Emerging Competitors is important as well. Companies such as Hewlett-Packard, the Big Five, Oracle, and SAP, which derive a large percentage of their revenue from areas other than IT services, could, over time, leverage those relationships into the IT services market. IBM, in the early 1990s, had IT services revenue of $2 billion to $4 billion. By leveraging the relationships it had in hardware, software, and other core areas into IT services, its revenues rose to over $35 billion by 1999.

Regional Competitors exhibit characteristics similar to those of Tier-One Competitors, but they conduct business mostly on a regional basis. Niche Competitors are those that compete against SSI in only one or a few of SSI's solution areas. Such is the case with Schlumberger Geoquest in seismic processing. Regardless of the size of these companies (some are larger than SSI), they compete against SSI in only one of our lines of business.

The *HR Manager* module features information on the competition from a slightly different perspective. The HR Manager profiles competitors for their HR policies, organization charts, layoffs, hiring areas, staffing, and training. This can be an invaluable source of information in that it sets benchmarks detailing the best and the worst HR practices of competitors, as well as how they attract and retain their people. One example of how the HR Manager can help the HR department is in the effectiveness of hiring people. The labor market for technology is currently very tight. If the CI group is able to detail where our competition has had mass layoffs, it might enable our HR department to advertise for job openings in those geographic areas, thus enabling us to find some very good people at lower hiring costs than might otherwise be possible.

The *Yellow File* module details competitors' inability to deliver solutions to their customers. Judicious use of Yellow File is encouraged at all times. Yellow File is always best used by examining competitor stereotypes or areas of weakness that competitors consistently demonstrate to prospective customers. By highlighting these stereotypes, a company can set traps for the competitors to fall into. Once a competitor falls into a trap, the Yellow File can be used to bring out areas where the competitor has lost business that relates to the trap and that has eventually cost customers millions of dollars. It is always recommended that before the core audience begins to use Yellow File on a competitor, they should contact the CI group to discuss the most appropriate way to present this information.

The *marcom@competitor.com* module contains information on how competitors communicate to the external marketplace. Detailed in this module are competitor advertisements and ad campaigns, annual reports, press releases, community affairs, brochures, success stories, and so on. By detailing such areas as competitor advertisements, the SSI Marcom function can observe specific competitors' messages to the marketplace and craft a message that is effectively differentiated and offers more than a "me-too" statement.

KNOWLEDGE MANAGEMENT COMPONENTS

The *CI Community of Practice* module details a "yellow pages" list of SSI people who are providing CI activities in some form. Also in this module are listings of employees who have come over to SSI from outside companies (most often, competitors). These people participate in providing information about the IT services industry as well as input on deals involving certain competitors, as long as they do not violate previously signed noncompete agreements.

The *Pursuit/Deal Tactics* module represents the strategies and tactics that SSI's Tier-One competitors employ, and the competitive countertactics that SSI can use to combat them. This is where the CI group shares its knowledge of the competition with the organization. Over time, the members of the CI group should be talking to employees who have worked for the competition at one time, have relationships with people from other competitors, and participate in seminars and best-practice events, in which they observe certain tendencies that competitors exhibit, given a competitive scenario.

Depending on the scope and parameters of a given deal, a competitor may use one of several different sales strategies that are discussed in depth in this module. Each competitor is analyzed from the viewpoint of whether it has product or service superiority and, if not, how it might change the buyer's criteria to give itself an advantage.

This becomes critical input for the CI group in performing deal simulation and support. The deal team will look at the profile of the competitor it is facing and will attempt to position itself in a certain way. The CI analyst, along with a few members of the deal team, will attempt to simulate what they feel the competitor is likely to do. This role playing is extremely valuable. It forces the deal team to consider the competition and craft a response to the prospective customer that positions our company in a positive light. Not every competitor is going to have a "playbook." Only the major competitors that the CI group has followed through the years, observing how they compete on deals, will be profiled in this section.

The *Private Discussions* module represents a place in the CI KnowledgeHouse where users can input or discuss information pertaining to competitor issues they are hearing about on the front lines. Many times, there is a disconnect between the knowledge of the people in the field and their ability to share that knowledge. We've all heard the axiom: Knowledge is power. The task of CI analysts is to bridge the gap between information sources and the decision makers. They must develop the CI group into a central point where competitive information and knowledge are input, analyzed, and communicated as intelligence for making decisions.

The *Benchmarking* module examines benchmarking from several different perspectives. It features benchmarking competitor and industry information around four key areas:

1. Competitor Pricing.
2. Customer Satisfaction/Quality/SLAs.

3. Human Resource Capabilities.

4. Macro-Level Industry Indicators, such as oil/gas IT benchmarks for departments.

The IT Landscape module seeks to profile all of the prospective customers and the competitors that are doing business with those prospective customers. Areas that are profiled here are: the projects the competitors are working on, whom they are partnering with to deliver the services, when each project is set to end, the status of their relationships with their customers, and so on. Often, this becomes an excellent area for the sales executives to generate new business because they are able to look for synergies between projects being currently worked on and SSI offerings to enhance those projects. This module will always be a work in progress, and the starting point consists of information that can be pulled from publicly available sources. To make it truly valuable, the CI group must work closely with the sales executives who serve each account, and document projects that competitors are working on at customers' sites, as discovered by the account executives.

The *3rd Party Research* module details the vendors that provide information on the IT services market. Often, these analysts have access to the inside workings of SSI competitors or, in the case of companies such as TPI, may actually influence prospects in the decision-making process. Moreover, all the reports that SSI purchases are listed in this section. Where online rights to publish materials have been granted, we try to put those full documents on the CI KnowledgeHouse. Otherwise, the reports are listed in this module, and the core audience is encouraged to contact the CI group if they need the report.

The *Conferences and Events* module details conferences that might possibly interest the core audience, including conferences sponsored by IT analysts. These events are great places for making contacts and discovering new ideas and trends. Besides providing information on which conferences to attend, this module seeks to capture written reports from the core audience members who have attended conferences. Information in these reports might include: Whether any of SSI's competitors were present. If so, did they have a booth? Did they speak at the conference? Were they sponsors? Did you pick up any brochures? What was the organization level of people who attended? Is this something that SSI needs to sponsor, have a booth at, speak at? Having this information enables our Events Planning group to make better decisions as to the conferences at which SSI should appear.

The final module, *RequestNet,* features all ad hoc projects that were requested from SSI personnel. Not only is it an excellent tool for tracking which projects the Competitive Analysis function performs for SSI, but it's also a source for reusing information for new projects. Besides the actual research compiled, the module features the person who requested the project and the date of the request. This is important because, many times, several people request the same project. The CI group, besides using the same information, can bring the previous and current requesters together to discuss outcomes of the earlier research efforts.

CI KNOWLEDGEHOUSE IN PRACTICE

Here's a typical example of how KnowledgeHouse can be used. Let's say that a group inside SSI is facing a competitor on an SAP deal. The group can get information on the competitor's SAP capabilities from the Competitor Profiles. Next, they can visit the Yellow File module and see where the competitor has had problems with SAP deals. Then they can visit the Pursuit/Deal Tactics module to figure out which strategies the competitor is likely to use on the deal. At that point, they should contact the CI group to come in and actually simulate responses the competitor might attempt.

It is important to remember that intranet-based communications with the core audience certainly do not replace the need for face-to-face contact. Rather, the idea is to use the intranet to free up the CI group to solve more complicated problems and provide better service on those tasks.

CI ASSESSMENT

One task the CI group should keep "top of mind" is: continuous evaluation on the effectiveness of its activities. There are many evaluation methodologies on the market, and whichever one a company uses is dependent on the circumstances and preferences of the CI group. At SSI, we use a 24-item evaluation model described previously in *Competitive Intelligence Review.*★

★ Jan P. Herring. (1999). "Key Intelligence Topics: A Process to Identify and Define Intelligence Needs," Competitive Intelligence Review, 10(2), Second Quarter, pp. 4–14. See also Herring's book, Measuring the Effectiveness of Competitive Intelligence (SCIP Publications, 1999).

This methodology is particularly useful because, independent of new technologies in the marketplace, it maps the activities the CI group should perform to add value to core processes, and it sets a measuring stick for areas where we are weak and need to improve. But whatever evaluation method is used, the focus must be on the continuous improvement of the CI function. No CI function should be content to revel in its past successes; rather, it should continue to develop new ideas and techniques that can improve the competitive positioning of the organization. The evaluation method used should not only reveal and communicate areas of achievement, but recommend areas where the CI group can make future improvements.

CI AS A COMPONENT OF BUSINESS INTELLIGENCE

Set in isolation, competitor intelligence is of little or no value. If an organization knows nothing of its markets, customers/prospects, technical abilities, and so on, its chances of winning business are very slim. At SSI, we have integrated our approach to CI and the CI KnowledgeHouse within the larger concept of business intelligence (BI), which we conceptualize as an umbrella that spans each of five different types of intelligence. The SSI Business Intelligence KnowledgeHouse examines five different types of intelligence, as pictured in Figure 4 and described next:

1. *Competitor intelligence*—the current and proposed activities of competitors, as detailed above.
2. *Customer/prospect intelligence*—information and analysis focusing on current and prospective customers, with emphasis on relationship building between these entities.

Figure 4   SSIs intranet-based BI KnowledgeHouse.

3. *Market intelligence*—broader market issues from a macro perspective, examining vertical industry groupings or countries/trade organizations, as well as social, political, economic, and environmental issues.

4. *Technical intelligence*—internal technical competencies within the organization, functioning as a liaison among the product marketing, strategy, and product development functions.

5. *Partner intelligence*—profiles of proposed alliance partners, covering areas such as Discussion Progress between SSI and the proposed partner, biographies on key people in the partnering organization, the customer base of the proposed partner, competing partnerships, and so on.

SUMMARY/LESSONS LEARNED

In closing, it is important to review a few key learnings gathered in our implementation of the CI KnowledgeHouse.

1. Do Not Have an Elegant Plan

Do the smart, obvious thing (i.e., start with competitor profiles, a competitive tactical playbook, a news module) and then fix it up as you go. It is important to remember that your best ideas come from people in the field. However, they will not be able to contribute unless your CI group can share with them some of the basics. After assembling these basics, the CI group should schedule seminars where you select a small subset of the core audience and conduct a system demonstration. You'll find that these users will give you the best ideas to incorporate into the system. After you rework the first set of ideas and incorporate them, go to another group and conduct another seminar. After five to seven iterations, idea generation will slow and your system will begin to take form. Still, every year after conducting larger-scale seminars, you'll find that several modules will change or new ones will be added.

For SSI, the CI KnowledgeHouse has been on annual road shows to our locations in Europe and the United States. More than 500 members of our 850-member core audience have viewed the KnowledgeHouse seminar. We use these demonstrations to incorporate user feedback and ideas into the structure and content of the CI KnowledgeHouse, and to monitor the usefulness of the CI group's activities.

Another part of continuous improvement is paying close attention to the type of ad hoc requests the CI group performs. At SSI, common themes among ad hoc requests help drive the design of the CI KnowledgeHouse. Common requests can often become major modules within your CI systems. Remember, the idea is to automate the most common requests for information, thus freeing up time for the CI group to perform high value–added activities.

> Common themes among ad hoc requests help drive the design of the CI KnowledgeHouse. Remember, the idea is to automate the most common requests for information, thus freeing up time for the CI group to perform high value–added activities.

2. Relationships with Members of Your Core Audience Are a Critical Success Factor

The CI group can build credible relationships over time by simply performing reliably in the area of ad hoc requests. Trust in knowledge content is built, over time, by repeated demonstrations of reliability and quality. It is important to find a good set of users who believe in your group's mission and can help evangelize CI within their own groups. At SSI, we feel that our top 10 customers may not be the 10 highest executives in the company; our best customers are the ones who provide us with the most constructive criticism about projects we are undertaking and the deliverables we are providing. We can get a large number of users to consistently contribute their knowledge from the field because we have done an outstanding job of nurturing relationships via ad hoc requests, demonstrations of the CI KnowledgeHouse, constant awareness building from *CI News-to-Go,* and so on.

3. The Major Benefit of Any CI Knowledge Management System Comes in Self-Service

As the number of people in your core audience increases, it is natural for the number of your ad hoc requests to increase. Without a mechanism in place to handle such increases (as the popularity of the group increases and CI is used more), there will be no way to reduce the overall workload, and the group will never get away from doing anything but ad hoc requests.

4. A Promotional Plan Has Been the Most Critical Factor Contributing to the Success of the CI KnowledgeHouse

During my seminars, I often ask the following question: Is anyone in the room familiar with Bob Arum? Typically, only a few people in the room raise their hand. I then ask the question: Is anyone in the room familiar with the name Don King? Typically, everyone raises their hand. Both Don King and Bob Arum are highly successful boxing promoters who have made millions of dollars in their careers. However, what sets Don King apart from the others is his promotional plan.

At a Don King event, one gets to experience the prefight weigh-in, the prefight press conference, media events in the tents outside the hotels, merchandising, post-fight press conferences, and so on. It is truly an event like no other, and at the center of it all is Don King. He makes himself and the event larger than the fight and the fighters themselves.

I like to think there's an important lesson to be learned from Don King and his boxing promotions. By making CI larger than life (and other processes in the company), it can become an integral part of the corporate culture. By using a regularly distributed news function, by conducting regularly scheduled seminars at key locations, by working with the corporate communications group to get the CI group featured in company literature and newsletters, the CI group can begin to position itself as an important and integral part of the company. The key point: If you don't believe in your group enough to promote yourselves among your core audience, how can you expect them to believe in your group?

ABOUT THE AUTHOR

Bret Breeding joined Shell Services International in 1997 as program manager for competitive intelligence. In this role, he was responsible for SSI's competitive intelligence efforts and maintained the CI KnowledgeHouse—SSI's competitive intelligence/knowledge management tool. While at Shell Services, he traveled to many locations all around the world to conduct seminars on CI. In addition, many SSI customers have heard about the company's CI capabilities and inquired how they could get their own CI practice up and running. He also worked with the American Productivity and Quality Center (APQC), speaking to groups of executives regarding CI and participating in an APQC study focusing on best practices in CI. At SCIP's

15th Annual International Conference, in Atlanta, in March 2000, he gave three presentations centered around CI, including a widely attended discussion entitled "CI and KM Convergence." Prior to joining SSI, Mr. Breeding was employed at EDS in a variety of areas within the energy business unit. During his tenure there, he worked in the competitive intelligence, strategy, and planning unit for the Asia/Pacific region, and in sales support for critical deals. He graduated with honors from Oklahoma State University with a double major in management and marketing, and a minor in geography.

Bret Breeding is currently the worldwide competitive intelligence manager at Compaq Computer Corp.

Competitive Intelligence at Lexis-Nexis

Hans Gieskes
LEXIS-NEXIS GROUP

EXECUTIVE SUMMARY

Hans Gieskes, president and CEO of the Lexis-Nexis Group, described the importance of competitive intelligence (CI) to his company and the ways in which CI is used in his rapidly evolving online information market, in a keynote address to the Society of Competitive Intelligence Professionals' 4th Annual European Conference and Exhibit (held November 4, 1999, in Amsterdam). Some 10 full-time CI professionals are based in various Lexis-Nexis business units, and the sales and marketing staffs, in particular, are used to collect competitor data. CI is conveyed through a number of vehicles, including "Rival Reports" and e-mail briefings, as well as through the corporate intranet. CI activities at Lexis-Nexis include (1) profiling and monitoring the activities of "traditional" and "nontraditional" competitors, (2) assisting sales by identifying product advantages vs. competitor's offerings, (3) product development support, and (4) alliance and acquisition support. Structured information tools (including the Lexis-Nexis database) are employed in conjunction with the corporate intranet to make CI accessible to all employees. At a strategic level, forecasting and scenario analysis are considered key to remaining competitive.

If CI isn't part of a corporation's strategy, then it's just an interesting exercise. In my organization, nobody has time just for interesting exercises. Ours is an industry where almost every day new products arrive, new regulations are voted in or changed, and new market segments open

Competitive Intelligence Review, Vol. 11(2) 4–11 (2000). © 2000 John Wiley & Sons, Inc.

Table 1   The Lexis–Nexis Database

- 2.5 billion searchable documents
- 24,871 sources
  - 18,871 news and business
  - 6,000 legal (Lexis)
- 10,700 databases
- 3.9 million documents added each week
- 1.8 million subscribers
- 18 million searches per month

up. As a market leader with a significant revenue base to protect, we certainly understand the value of competitive intelligence.

Before discussing how CI operates in our organization, it would be helpful to give a bit of background about our company. A source of real-time and archival information for 26 years, with 1998 revenues of $1.3 billion, the Lexis–Nexis Group provides customers with highly structured information tools. Our mission is to be the preferred provider of decision support information and services to professionals in legal, business, and government markets. We are comprised of companies operating either within Lexis Publishing (for the legal profession) or the Nexis business unit (serving business, government, and academic markets). Our brands guarantee access to information from authoritative sources, enriched with enhancements such as indexing, linkages, and segmentation.

We're a large, global organization with about 8,000 staff in 63 locations, and all 8,000 staff members have access to our CI tools through our internal corporate intranet, as I will discuss below. We have 1.8 million subscribers, excluding the two-thirds of the U.S. undergraduate student population that have full access to Lexis–Nexis via their campus networks.

About half our business is online and half offline—books, CD-ROMs, newsletters, and so on. We provide access to some 2.5 billion documents, which is probably equivalent to between 5 and 6 billion pages in Web-size measures, or about 28 terabytes of searchable data online (Table 1). We store these on a dozen large mainframes.

CI IS INTEGRAL

For our company, CI is an integral part of our strategy development (Table 2). I'd like to stress an earlier point again: CI is not just an exercise.

Table 2   Competitive Intelligence at Lexis–Nexis

Services include:
- *Monitoring.* Tracking the activities (and related impact of these activities) for a defined set of competitors
- *Profiling.* Creating composite of information regarding a defined set of competitors and/or their respective leaders
- *Developing game plans.* Assist sales by identifying product advantages vs. competitor's offerings
- *Product development support.* Customer input, competitive products, timing
- *Ad-hoc requests.*

Products include:
- In-person updates and product demonstrations
- Rival reports
- E-mail briefings
- E-mail hotline

Benefits include:
- Provides forecasting/scenario analysis
- Alerts the business to competitive plays
- Explores growth and market opportunities
- Underscores product/market strengths
- Identifies product development ideas
- Provides support for alliances and acquisitions
- Reduces financial risks
- Keeps employees smart

What are the trends in our business? We're moving from being an aggregator of information to being a full-service provider of decision-support information and services, and there's quite a difference between those two. We've also expanded our reach over the last few years to include not just departmental users, information professionals, and CI professionals, but also end-users within enterprises. As we start serving broader and deeper markets, it would be a big mistake for many of our customers, including ourselves, to simply think that since end-users in our organizations have access to information, they can now do their own CI. As you know in your own organizations, and as I know as a beneficiary of my own CI professionals, we can't just depend on our own research. The best of both worlds is always the best solution.

Let me give you an example. Day and night from my hotel room in Amsterdam, I can access our intranet and check on my competitors. When planning a major acquisition, if I want a weekly or quarterly update of competitors, I'll have a briefing done by my people; I won't do it myself. But I can also access all of the systems and find information if I need to.

> It would be a big mistake to simply think that because end-users have access to information, that they can now do all of their own CI.

STAYING COMPETITIVE IN TWO MARKETS

As noted above, the Lexis-Nexis Group straddles two markets: legal information and business information. Looking at the online business information market, the customers are changing. Again, as noted, end-users are beginning to conduct their own searches. Companies have intranets. Some also have "extranets" where they link their customers, their suppliers, and their staff in one seamless way.

We compete in a portion of this business information market, valued around $1.4 billion in total, which obviously is only a very small corner of a $24-billion corporate information market. There are 3 major players: ourselves, Dow Jones, and Dialog.

As you would assume when you have 3 major players, competition gets rather hot and steamy, and competitive intelligence becomes extremely important. The Web and new Web players are certainly making inroads in these markets, sometimes causing traditional players to partner, to review their products, and to decide how they can make the best use of the Internet for their customers and for themselves.

The U.S. legal information market is also very interesting. Less than 5 years ago there were about 7 substantial players. After industry consolidation, there are now just 2 large players (ourselves and the Thomson/West Group). This market is about $3.5 billion per year. It's growing at about 5 percent to 6 percent annually, and the competition between these two 800-pound gorillas is intensifying every day, which again makes CI extremely important.

Both the Lexis-Nexis Group, with an Anglo-Dutch parent (Reed Elsevier, plc), and the Thomson/West Group, based in Canada, have over the last 10 years strengthened their position in the U.S. legal information market through a long path of acquisitions. Last year we bought Matthew Bender and SHEPARD's, which was a $1.6-billion acquisition. CI has played a major role in the acquisition process, as I'll touch on a bit later.

CI Keeps Us Competitive

Competitive intelligence is any information or knowledge about the marketplace that keeps our company competitive, including:

- Customer intelligence.
- Product development.
- Brand values.
- New technologies.
- Sales/marketing intelligence.
- Regulation/legislation.

We capture information on our competitors as well as on what's happening in the industry, and we try to use it to our advantage. We collect CI in many ways, as I'll discuss next, and while I can't divulge all of our secrets, I can certainly say our ways are aboveboard and ethical.

> Competitive intelligence is any information or knowledge about the marketplace that keeps our company competitive. We capture information on our competitors as well as on what's happening in the industry, and we try to use it to our advantage.

People and Systems

At the Lexis-Nexis Group, CI is basically people, and of course systems. It's nice to have the availability of good people and good systems to give you up-to-date competitive information. I can't stress the importance of the people. Although computers can search overnight all those 14 million new documents from yesterday and find out if anything is relevant for our own competitive intelligence purposes, it's people that make the assessments of how relative the data is, and it's people who link that data to existing data and existing views.

We employ about 10 people in competitive intelligence. You're going to say that's not a lot out of a staff of 8,000, but these are 10 very important people, and they're within the business units. I do not have a central competitive intelligence unit for my own purposes; I make use of these units on a project basis.

Basically, we do two kinds of competitive intelligence:

- *Tactical (product) CI.* Primarily supports the needs of product managers and the marketing and sales organizations.
- *Strategic CI.* Primarily supports the needs of management (for short- and long-term decision-making).

I myself don't see a lot of the tactical competitive intelligence because it's very detailed: it's about products, prices, and assessments of emerging competitors. My own interest is on a strategic level. We like to analyze our competitor's capabilities on a continuous basis, in terms of financial systems, organization, and so on.

Last year, when we acquired Matthew Bender and SHEPARD's, we spent quite some time analyzing the depth of our main competitors first. We knew it was a two-horse auction with Wolters Kluwer. And in a frenzied world where companies are being sold through auctions, you have to make sure that apart from analyzing the company you'd like to buy, you also know how far the other guy can go financially, because if you get that assessment wrong, you're going to be making the wrong bid.

We spent a good deal of time analyzing their balance sheets, lending history, and other factors that could indicate the company's pain threshold. We were absolutely "on the dot" in the end. You must have this kind of data available, and you must have tools to analyze it. Again, you must have good people—in this case, both financial people and CI people—to assess where you think your competitor's pain threshold is.

We use CI to decide on funding for product development. We do that by asking, "What is the competition doing?" and, in particular, "What are the nontraditional players doing?"

We do a lot of *SWOT* (strengths, weaknesses, opportunities, threats) *analysis* on our competitors. Basically, I like to have quarterly briefings on our updated SWOT analysis as our competitors would see themselves, and the level of "threat" with which they view us. We update these frequently. We do *scenario work,* looking at what our competitors might do if we take the following steps. Their strategic intent is extremely important to analyze and correctly assess.

If you look at the size and scale of the leading telecomms and other big players, Reed Elsevier is only a small $5-billion corporation in relative terms. We need to know what they do, and what will be the power plays coming from the Internet. We need to make scenarios. Two years out, we would like to know *who the players will be, what their strategies will be, and how that could impact our business.* We no longer plan 3 or 5 years ahead because 18 months is a long planning horizon in the Web world.

When we plan how we will design future projects, we like to analyze competing products and to assess why our competitors have made certain moves, or why not, and build that into our own design plans.

As usual, CI professionals sadly suffer from a lot of ad hoc requests, where they're suddenly asked to drop everything because we need to know this or that.

ACTIVE MONITORING

For active monitoring, we use our own Lexis-Nexis updating services, and CI consultants help to collect primary source intelligence discreetly and ethically. Our employees, especially our sales and marketing personnel, are a major resource. We have over a thousand people in sales; they meet with customers every day, and they pick up information about our competitors from our customers who will say, "Have you heard this, have you heard that." And we need to collate that information, filter it, validate it, and make sure we have access to it. We do a lot of profiling on competitors. We develop game plans; some of that is fun, and some of that is scary, but it's very important so that nobody winds up saying, "Yeah, I guess we could have known that, but we didn't." That is not an acceptable answer in my organization.

We have *incentive programs* that help us find and gather useful bits of information that we can then use in our competitive analysis. At our annual sales meetings and regional sales meetings, there's always a combination of learning and playing. People can earn "casino money" for an internal game. But aside from monetary and other prizes, I know that most of our staff are extremely interested just in seeing the company act upon the intelligence they find out in the field. If you are a sales rep and your home base is in Nebraska, the head office is very far away and you don't always understand how decisions are made. So I think the reward is already there when they get feedback saying, "That was very useful. It has helped us to make the following decision."

SHARING INFORMATION

Probably my biggest single concern about competitive intelligence in my organization is how do you share that information? If you have a large organization with hundreds of people in various locations making important decisions regarding customers, product design, product management, and you have all this valuable data, how do you make sure the information is leveraged for the benefit of your organization? You need to use technology as well as face-to-face meetings where senior management receives briefings on competitors and situations in the market. We do *e-mail briefings* to staff. I'm very pleased about how well that works. We have a monthly *"Rival Report,"* which is electronically circulated internally to key managers worldwide. The Rival Report includes all our competitors, both at the parent company level and within a company's business units. Although by the time I read it I've already seen many of these findings based on overnight briefings through Lexis-Nexis trackers, it pulls together what's happened to our competitors in the last month. It's a very useful tool to have.

THE CORPORATE INTRANET AND OTHER TOOLS

We have on our Web site an *intranet* area, accessible only to internal staff, that focuses on competitors (Figure 1). It's available to all our employees. Now you can argue that if you work in the mailroom why would you need access to this information, and I guess they don't use it a lot. But we want all of our staff to be very much aware of what our competitors do and what's happening out there in the marketplace so they better understand why we take the course we take at particular times. We have an *e-mail hotline* especially for the sales force. They can send in information that they've found in the market and that they think may be relevant. We can collate it and integrate it rapidly into our decision making.

People can select any competitor and access data about them, or they can access a listing of competitors by products or by area. They can see what's in the news about our competitors. This is updated frequently, and

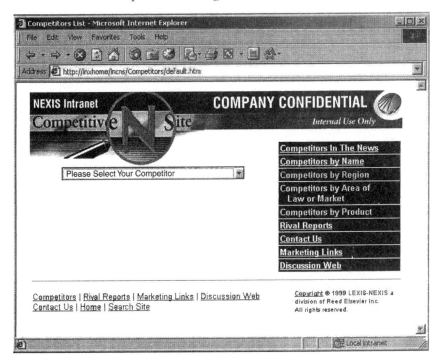

Figure 1   The Nexis intranet.

it's an extremely useful internal tool to have. The Lexis-Nexis Group intranet site is accessible to all 8000 employees anywhere in the world. We have our own network going around the globe, and we use the AOL/CompuServe nodes as well, so I can be in a small village in Holland, where I actually might be this weekend, and I can access the intranet and see what's happening.

Smart Tools.   We also have what we call Smart Tools. We not only use them ourselves, but we also make Smart Tools available to our customers. And increasingly customers are applying our Smart Tools to link in all of their staff to particular paths or databases.

Smart Tools provide a daily tracker on all of our competitors and where we've been in the news ourselves. So overnight, after a company gets mentioned in the Dutch press, French press, U.S. press, or trade journals, it's all collated and every morning you can see what was said about our company in the press worldwide, or about our competitors, or about our parent company. It's quite useful. The Smart Tools work in a very simple way. We have our CI consultants craft the searches. These searches are run overnight against the updates in our systems and the next morning provide the briefing on the intranet. The CI consultants may select some particular news items for finer analysis, which they may send by e-mail to a particular decision-maker, saying, "You may have seen such-and-such article this morning, but you should really look at this particular part for the following reasons."

Again, people have no excuse to say, "I didn't know what happened in the market. I didn't know what our competitors did." Of course they could have known. It's available to them day and night.

Company Dossier.   Another tool which we have been using internally, and which is now available to customers, is our Company Dossier. A Company Dossier provides a dynamic overview of a particular company—a snapshot of who they are, where they're headquartered, number of staff, financials, and so on. It gives news, both as an archive and an update, on that particular company. You can collate the information by region, by topic, or by publication. We created one for Microsoft earlier this year. You can find out about Microsoft in Europe, or about MS Office, or about what has been said in the U.K. press about Microsoft. You can collate it, slice-and-dice it in any way. It provides a key business analysis, giving a list of all the competitors and all their brands and products. In terms of financial analysis, it provides 10K or 10Q income statements, M&A reports, and so on. It provides access to all the analysts' reports that we store on Lexis-Nexis as well, bringing all this information together under the company name.

In addition, a Company Dossier provides an update on a firm's legal situation. It will tell what litigation a company is currently involved in and what litigation they've been involved in over the last five years (which in intellectual property cases is of particular interest). Have they been involved in patent cases over the last few years? What was the outcome? What is still pending? Especially when you are about to acquire a company, you'd like to know if they have legal history that is pertinent.

As regards intellectual property, the Company Dossier will list all the patents, all the trademarks and copyrights owned by the company. And again it's dynamic. If they file a new patent, that will be on the system updated on the same day.

CI FOR PRODUCT
DEVELOPMENT AND POSITIONING

So these are the tools we have at our disposal. Now, what do we use them for? I want to give a couple of examples. When we launched our Web product for the business markets—Internet Solutions—we used CI to decide how to position it and to learn what were the key elements in the product that customers would like to have. The market need for Smart Tools and Intranet Solutions has been supported by competitive intelligence as well. In this case, not looking at what our traditional competitors do, but looking at what our *nontraditional* competitors are doing: the IT consultants, the Ernst and Youngs, the IBMs and Microsofts—what they're working at in providing information tools to companies.

We created a new brand last year, Lexis Publishing, as an umbrella for all our legal brands. We did analysis on competitors' brands: why they were created, how they're being perceived in the market, and so on.

And, of course, proposed alliances and acquisitions are supported by analyses provided by our CI professionals.

> We are not just looking at what our traditional competitors are doing, but at what our nontraditional competitors are doing: the IT consultants, the Ernst and Youngs, the IBMs and Microsofts.

AN INTEGRATED APPROACH

As CEO of the company, I strongly believe it's important not just that we have good CI resources and systems, but also that we try to merge CI with what I call business intelligence.

As I define the difference, *business intelligence* largely comes from our own systems, out of our own customer data. *Competitive intelligence* comes from our people and from lots of external data. Our systems contain not just data on revenue about customers, which is very interesting, but about usage patterns. We know at what time people search, and we know what they search. It's extremely important to start using that data from an active marketing perspective.

The excitement about Amazon.com is not over whether it will make a profit in the future, but the fact that it has such good, integrated knowledge about what its customers are doing with their marketing systems. The company can use that information to create better products for its customers.

This kind of business intelligence is as important as competitive intelligence, and to be successful businesses will have to merge the two.

Knowledge management is another buzzword, another Holy Grail. Knowledge management to me means that you combine everything you know from your own staff with external data collected from databases and other source collections. At a law firm with 600 partners, there's so much knowledge gained by people who have done similar cases for similar customers. All that may be stored in WordPerfect files, maybe on hard drives, or on a server within the law firm. Large corporations and other big players such as the Big 5 professional consulting firms increasingly want to connect that past experience with data from all kinds of resources. We are interested, and I think well positioned, to have our search engine, our tools, and our indexing capability apply to their internal data as well. As to whether that means storing their data on our systems, or having our indexing tools index their data for them, or having our search engine behind their firewall, these are all options.

Over the next five years, there's going to be an off-the-shelf tool rapidly developing, and Microsoft is very actively working in that direction. I think that might be very good for certain smaller organizations. But larger organizations will need to have it customized, because their own internal data is so big and so complex.

From a scale point of view, if there are 800 million pages on the Internet, and some 6 billion pages available in private database organizations like ourselves, then there are probably 5 billion pages locked away in organizations' hard drives and filing cabinets. Ultimately, if you can connect those three with the right tools and the right people, you become a very powerful organization.

KNOWLEDGE MATTERS

We need to know a lot of things. We need to know them very fast. In the past, our environment has created a need for competitive intelligence. Now things are moving so much faster than the need is to have this information available in real time, accessible 7 days by 24 hours. The rapid economic, competitive, political, and especially technological changes in our markets require that we increasingly find better ways to filter information, to organize it, and to use it to our own advantage. If we don't, we'll be in trouble.

> CI, especially when used for forecasting and scenario analysis, alerts us to competitive plays that are happening or about to emerge in our markets. It helps us to explore growth and market opportunities. It keeps employees smart, and it pays to have smart employees.

CI, especially when used for forecasting and scenario analysis, alerts us to competitive plays that are happening or about to emerge in our markets. It helps us to explore growth and market opportunities. It keeps employees smart, which I always like, because it really pays to have smart employees. In rapidly changing and consolidating industries, you're managing chaos—lots of input happening all the time. You need a well-articulated marketing strategy based on sound market research, sound competitive intelligence, sound business intelligence, benchmarking, and metrics (Figure 2). CI is a vital element for finding the right strategies, and for executing the strategies right. With the appropriate resources, there's no reason why companies can't continue to grow in markets that are changing rapidly.

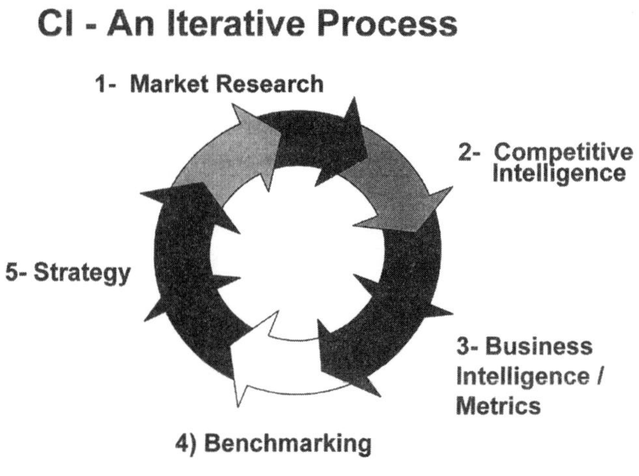

CI - An Iterative Process

Figure 2   The Lexis-Nexis CI cycle.

RELATED READING

CI not just an "exercise," says Lexis-Nexis CEO. (2000). *Competitive Intelligence Magazine,* 3(2), 5–7.

ABOUT THE AUTHOR

Hans Gieskes joined Lexis-Nexis as president and CEO on December 1, 1997, and for three years guided the largest business-to-business online information service in the world. Mr. Gieskes worked for Reed Elsevier, the parent company of Lexis-Nexis, for 19 years. Previously, he served as vice chairman of the company's legal division, which operates 14 legal publishing companies in 12 countries. He is currently the president of Monster.com.

CI at Avnet:
A Bottom-Line Impact

John H. Hovis, Ph.D.
Avnet, Inc.

Executive Summary

John Hovis, senior vice president responsible for global strategic planning at Avnet, Inc., one of the world's largest distributors of electronic components, describes the evolution of his firm's CI operations in the following keynote address to SCIP's 15th Annual International Conference and Exhibit, held in March 2000 in Atlanta, Georgia. Although Avnet's formal CI program has been in place only since 1997, it has already had a major impact on the firm's operations. CI is now embedded as part of the company's Strategic Management System, where it is linked with global strategic planning, budgeting/performance measurement, and investor relations functions. The firm's Business Information Office (BIO), its eight-person CI team, plays an important role in growing shareholder value, in part by helping senior management understand what it must do—both strategically and structurally— to compete effectively against direct and indirect competitors in the fast-changing New Economy. In addition, the CI team is expected to make recommendations and offer guidance—a step often lacking in the traditional CI process.

S trategic control is "hitting what you aim at." CI "lights up the targets." CI must be a functional part of the strategic management system. In fact, in my mind I don't separate the two. Competitor intelligence is part of the structure of strategic planning inside of Avnet.

To better understand the role of CI at Avnet, I'd like to briefly provide an overview of the company.

Competitive Intelligence Review, Vol. 11(3) 5–15 (2000). © 2000 John Wiley & Sons, Inc.

Avnet is, globally, the second largest distributor of electronic components, computer hardware, peripherals, software, and related services. In North America, it is the market leader with 25 percent of market share (as a result of the acquisition of the 6th-ranked Marshall Industries). Avnet has a primary competitor, Arrow Electronics Inc., which has 24 percent of the market. The next closest competitor is German-based VEBA Electronics with 13 percent of the market.

Phoenix-based, with 10,000 employees worldwide at 250 locations in 60 countries, Avnet has 40-plus years in the electronics industry, and is listed on the New York Stock Exchange. The company had 1999 annual sales of $10 billion (proforma).

Avnet's global Business Information Office (BIO), which is what we call our CI team, is managed by Andre Gib, a past member of SCIP's board of directors and one of the top CI professionals in the country. The CI team has a big responsibility: to keep our senior executive team, located all over the world, informed of what our key competitors are doing on an ongoing basis.

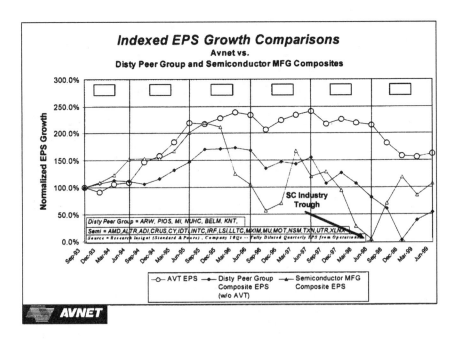

Figure 1   Avent EPS performance versus rivals.

Globally, Avnet is structured into three key operating groups:

1. *Electronics Marketing Group.* Leader in supply chain management services.
2. *Avnet Applied Computing.* Shaping the emerging market of embedded computing.
3. *Computer Marketing Group.* Profit leading in midrange enterprise server market.

Avnet Applied Computing is a new operating group for Avnet, and it is a result of the strategic thinking process and the CI process that we employ within Avnet. The job of our BIO is to help create and find new value propositions, such as Avnet Applied Computing.

Our competitive intelligence team, structured over these three operating groups, has a significant responsibility in tracking all of the varied competitors—not just our direct competitors but all the peripheral competitors that have a potential to impact our ability to create value.

We're also a consolidator pursuing a "growth by acquisition" strategy, with 35 acquisitions since 1991. One of the things we are about is finding new acquisition candidates, and of course our competitive intelligence unit is very much involved with our acquisition team in helping to profile potential acquisition candidates.

Avnet's vision statement calls for us to "provide the highest value relationships to our customers, suppliers, employees, and shareholders, globally." Can CI make a difference to the shareholders of your company? If you have competitive advantage, it makes a serious difference to the shareholders of your company.

When our CEO goes on the road, whether he's talking to Wall Street or talking at a supplier conference or a customer event, the presentations he's providing are to a large extent created and crafted by our CI team. Why would the CI team be involved in doing that? For one thing, it's an opportunity for them to get noticed because they have the information that we need on a continuous basis that our CEO is going to want to talk about (e.g., our market share). CI is a strategic group for us, and we do strategic group analysis inside of Avnet. Andre takes that responsibility and we utilize this analysis in our strategic long-range planning meetings.

Aside from our "historical peers," there are also a large number of small competitors that are niche players and have at one point in time or another created competitive issues for Avnet. So we track these companies on a continuous basis. Even more so the peripheral competitors.

For Avnet to succeed, we need two things: strategic effectiveness and organizational effectiveness. We've got to have good strategy, and part and parcel of that is competitive intelligence lighting up the targets for us and helping us to understand how we're executing our strategy.

However, the purpose of our BIO is not only to understand whether we're being strategically effective from a benchmarking perspective, but also to look inside the organization and compare what we think Avnet is really good at organizationally to those things that our competitors are really good at. In this New Economy, in the era of the Internet, a role of CI is to help us understand what we must do *internally* and *structurally* to compete with those competitors that have not been on our radar screen. If we can be strategically and structurally effective, it will create the right kind of financial and operational performance that will maximize shareholder value.

Our CI activities, our analytical activities inside Avnet, are focused around growing earnings per share (EPS). Why are we growing EPS? Why are we not growing as fast as we need to, compared to our industry peers? Are we maximizing returns on capital employed? What is the returned on capital employed in the industry as a whole? It has everything to do with shareholder value. As that information gets moved into my area and I have the opportunity to explain, through our investor relations efforts, why Avnet is performing so well, then hopefully we'll also be able to increase our stock price and the PE multiple over a period of time by effective communications with The Street.

> In this New Economy, CI helps us understand what we must do *internally* and *structurally* to compete with those competitors that have not been on our radar screen. If we can be strategically and structurally effective, it will create the right kind of financial and operational performance that will maximize shareholder value.

GROWTH OF CI AT AVNET

I didn't come into Avnet with an existing competitive intelligence team. When I started in 1997, I had a total of one person on my team—me.

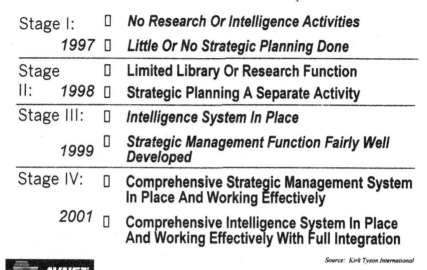

Figure 2 Evolution of a strategic management process.

There was literally no research or intelligence activity being accomplished inside Avnet, and there was no strategic planning being done to speak of either. A multibillion company without any strategic planning being done. Today, it's a totally different story.

In 1998 we moved into Stage 2. We had a limited library/research function. Strategic planning just began to get nurtured when my boss came to me and said, "I'd like you also to take over a strategic planning function." As I was selling CI to him on a day-in, day-out basis, we kept coming back to strategy over and over again. It seemed natural to pull these two things together. We had the opportunity to create the strategic planning role for CI.

In 1999 we were in Stage 3, where we really had the competitive and strategic intelligence system in place, largely due to Andre. If you're stalled in your CI activity, consider figuring out how to bring someone in who can take it to a whole other level.

Stage 4—to have a comprehensive strategic management system in place and working effectively—is still in front of us. We have a strategic management system in place today; I don't think it's necessarily working effectively. Again, I think we have a comprehensive intelligence system in

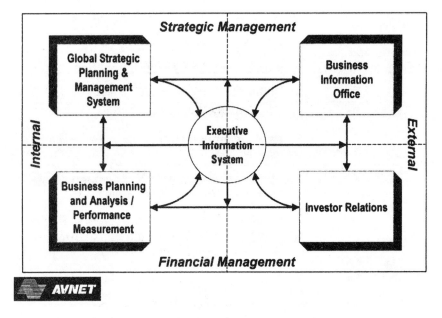

Figure 3   Avnet's strategic management system.

place but it's not fully integrated with our strategic thinking and strategic planning process, at least to the extent that I want it to be. So we still have some work to do.

What is the strategic management system at Avnet? It has four pieces:

1. *Global Strategic Planning and Management System.* Avnet's strategic thinking and planning process. It's globally deployed, and we are automating the system for 7 × 24 access over the corporate Intranet.

2. *The Business Information Office.* The function of the BIO in our planning process is to very clearly understand what the strategic imperatives are of our group-operating presidents. Strategic planning feeds BIO, and BIO is very much a part of feeding the strategic planning system.

3. *Business Planning and Analysis/Performance Measurement.* Operation budgeting is connected into the system. It's the audit mechanism of our strategic planning process. All the great thinking that comes out of the global strategic planning system gets audited

through our performance measurement and operational budgeting process.

4. *Investor Relations.* IR's role of IR is to communicate outside of Avnet with investors and potential shareholders about how we're performing strategically and whether we are achieving competitive advantage and generating return on investment.

All of this then flows into an *Executive Information System* (EIS), which uses the corporate intranet. We drive all of our operational planning data into the EIS, giving group presidents and the CEO a "dashboard" that they can look at on a day-to-day basis and understand how we're executing our strategic plan.

THE BIO STRUCTURE

When I started, it was just me, the director, sitting at the top. I then moved out of that role and Andre Gib had the opportunity to come in. A $10 billion

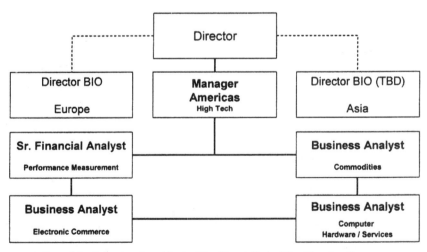

Figure 4   BIO structure.

organization, and we've got seven people involved in it. It's not enough. We are hooked up on an everyday basis just trying to get all the requests for information and intelligence to our operating groups, and that's a great position that you want to find yourself in. Under Andre's direction, we now have a manager in the Americas responsible for working with all of the analysts. We have financial performance measurement, and an analyst who's looking at commodities. We have a focus on how we're performing in different areas of technology. And there's a brand new position that we just brought in for e-commerce.

We've embedded CI into the organizational fabric itself. The requests for information out of our BIO continue to grow on a daily basis. As an economist, I have an appreciation that information is power. We have a strategy for our own team to be the information providers inside of Avnet. If you become *the* information provider inside of your organization, it becomes very difficult to dislocate you. It's part of the infrastructure; it's part of our strategic planning process as well.

CI AND THE STRATEGIC PLANNING PROCESS

What is the role of competitive intelligence in our planning process? Every strategic long-range planning meeting that we have, every quarterly review that occurs inside of Avnet throughout the globe, happens with data and information provided by our CI team. Relative to our long-range planning, Andre brings his team in and takes us through a full environmental. We look at all our market opportunities as well as the competitive threats. We analyze these against our core competencies, and come to understand our competitive weaknesses.

Another important role I see out of the BIO gets back to competitive advantage. If Avnet has strategic leverage inside of the markets it chooses to operate in, it's because it has been able to successfully harness some kind of competitive advantage. There are limiting forces and there are direct forces that work against Avnet from our being successful. Andre's job is to help us to understand, in the limiting-forces arena, the intensity of the indirect competition that's occurring. Every quarter we have a staff meeting where I am responsible for talking to the senior executive management team specifically about indirect competitors. You can see in the upper left corner of Figure 6 it says EMSI, which signifies contract manufacturers for

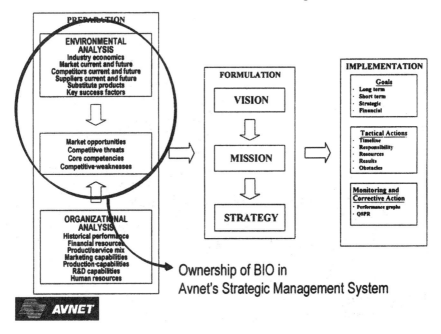

Figure 5   Role of CI in Avnet's planning process.

the electronics manufacturing services industry; we view them as peripheral competitors and we're always giving an update on where contract manufacturing is. We're also giving an update on where the state of the Internet or e-business is, as this also is reshaping our industry, as it is reshaping yours.

As regards the threat of entry by new or peripheral competitors, one of Andre's responsibilities is to help us understand if there are any competitor moves in the last quarter that would change our view of the competitive landscape and help us understand contract manufacturing and three PLs, which are third-party logistic providers, or 4PLs, large consulting organizations that have the ability to come in and play a competitor role in our marketspace. And then Internet metamediaries, as we call them. All of these things are happening not only in our industry, but also in yours. And you need to have them on your radar.

There are also pressures on our supplier base and the things that suppliers are doing relative to working with our competitors. And then, of course, there are always the micro- and macroeconomics of the environment in which you are operating.

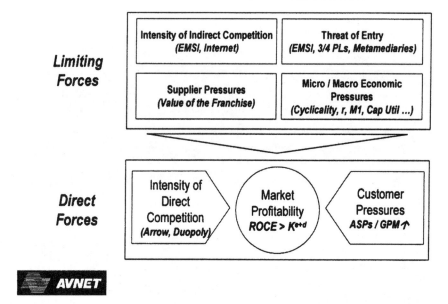

Figure 6   Discover the determinant factors of Avnet's strategic leverage.

We're a cyclical industry, which presents difficulties—especially in the area of creating shareholder value. One of the things that Andre does is very carefully understand, monitor, and forecast the cyclicality of our marketspace. Then there are the direct forces, including the intensity of direct competition and customer pressures that we are under on a constant basis, and the overall market profitability in our industry.

RECOMMENDATIONS AND GUIDANCE

What is successful CI? It facilitates "alignment." By "lighting up targets," helping us to understand who, what, where, and when, it helps us to achieve alignment in our strategic plan. It keeps the executives informed as a key element in decision-making. It needs to be more than "competitor" intelligence. It needs to be market intelligence. I don't mean market research; I mean market intelligence. I rely on Andre to tell me what's going on in the markets in which we're competing, and to help me to understand so I can communicate this to the executive team.

A couple of points here: You have to be creative. You have to be innovative. And you have to be a risk-taker. I'm an economist. I have a quantitative background. I'm an analyst. Sometimes it's hard for you as an analyst to take a risk, but you will never have an impact in your organization unless you do. You can be as creative as you want, and you can be as innovative as you want. You can take all these tools and techniques and still not make an impact because you failed to do one thing, which is to take a risk. When you take a risk, that's when you really add value.

What is adding value? What do executives look for in competitive intelligence? It all comes down to basically one thing—guidance. Do you know what your boss, or your boss's boss, or your chief executive officer, is doing every day? Do you think they are sitting in their office scratching their head and wondering what they are going to be doing strategically tomorrow? Absolutely not. When the CEO comes in and asks the secretary, "What's on my calendar?" the response is, "You have a meeting at 8 o'clock with Joe supplier. And at 10 o'clock this customer called and he wants you to call him back because he's got a big gripe." Then the CEO meets with the rest of the staff over specific tactical issues that need to be decided to run the bases forward day to day. Then, all of a sudden, somehow along the way, during this time of being tactical on a day-to-day basis, they have to figure out how to be strategic. There's the competitive intelligence person running in with this great document, and it says, "These are some of the things that we think we need to do." And the executive says, "Okay, that's great." And then he or she is sitting there and looking at you and one important question comes into their mind: "Tell me what you think I should do." What is guidance?

First, tell them what they already know, because that way you establish credibility—but be brief about it. One of the mistakes that CI practitioners make is that we major on telling what we already know. The objective is not to go out and pull a lot of information together and repackage it and present it to the chief; that is not the goal. The objective is to tell them very quickly what they already know but then get to the nonobvious point. Tell them what they do NOT know. And that's where you need to elaborate. That's where your creativity and your innovation come into play. Then comes the third part, where the risk-taking occurs: You've got to tell them what it means for the company. You've got to make a recommendation, without telling them what to do. Good analysts, good CI practitioners, get to what it means, and they make a recommendation.

The conventional CI process has three pieces: collect your data, analyze it, and distribute it. You probably spend one-third of your time at least distributing what you've put together, which is really a nonvalue-add activity—which is why you need to harness the power of the intranet for your organization and disseminate information that way.

But this three-step process, as described earlier, is inadequate. The winning formula is getting to impact, which means there's another necessary step: You've got to make the recommendation. You've got to put yourself on the line and tell the senior staff, or whoever you are articulating the message to, the "so what." This is the winning formula for a CI process.

> The winning formula is getting to impact, which means there's another necessary step—You've got to make the recommendation. You've got to put yourself on the line and provide the "so what."

One of the tools we use at Avnet is a Strategic Leverage Matrix (SLM), where we literally plot our competitors in a 2 × 2 matrix, charting their return on working capital and sales growth. I ask our CI team to do that because I want to understand how Avnet compares to its competitors in its

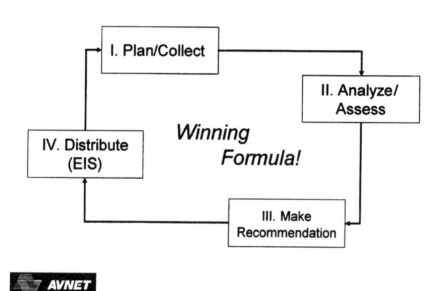

Figure 7   CI process → Impact!

ability to create economic value. And return on working capital is a close approximation of economic value added. This gets back to our governing objective of creating shareholder value inside of Avnet. We're looking at ability to grow sales and ability to create return for shareholders. We conduct that analysis and we literally report that every quarter in our CEO staff meeting.

These tools and techniques can be used to conduct analysis and make assessments. But you've got to get to the recommendation. Again, you can't just rely on the wizardry and the sophistication of these tools. We need to create credibility for our profession. We've been around for four years inside of Avnet, and we're just now beginning to build credibility. Early on, if I walked into my boss's office with this really cool vulnerability analysis or TOWS analysis or whatever, he would look at that and say, "Uh-huh, that's great, next." If I don't get to the recommendation, if I don't make it meaningful to him, I've lost the opportunity to add value. Take a competitor. Let's assume that we've begun to understand that the competitor has changed its strategy. Its current strategy looks different or is articulated in the press in some way, shape, or form that this is a direction in which it's moving. We want to begin to understand: Is this strategy sustainable? Is it significant for us? What's the probability of its succeeding? These are the types of questions that lay the groundwork for the next step—making a recommendation, or getting to the "so what" that provides your senior executive team with guidance.

After all, what is intelligence? It's actionable information. In other words, it's giving your decision-makers inside your company the opportunity to look at a body of information and take action. But you'll never get them to take action unless you tell them what it means. Because they don't have time often to sit down and really figure it out. When you start to provide actual guidance, you then begin to make an impact.

MAKING AN IMPACT

There are two levels to strategically positioning competitive intelligence within the corporation. The first is looking at how to *play the game better*. You focus on what exists today, your strategic competitive position, and you try to help the senior executive team to improve it. But if you're in a fluid industry, an industry that is under change like Avnet is today, you

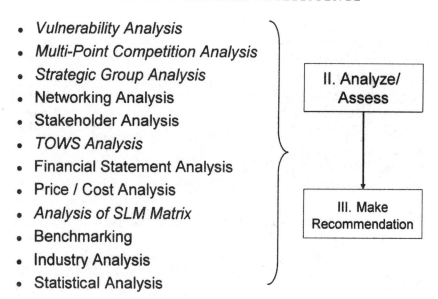

- *Vulnerability Analysis*
- *Multi-Point Competition Analysis*
- *Strategic Group Analysis*
- Networking Analysis
- Stakeholder Analysis
- *TOWS Analysis*
- Financial Statement Analysis
- Price / Cost Analysis
- *Analysis of SLM Matrix*
- Benchmarking
- Industry Analysis
- Statistical Analysis

II. Analyze/ Assess

III. Make Recommendation

Figure 8   Tools and techniques of impact analysis/impact assessment.

can't just look at what currently exists at this point in time. You've got to figure out how to help your senior management team to *play the game differently,* which is to identify new customers, new suppliers, and new markets to enter. In other words, what are the new targets that you're lighting up on the radar screen for us to begin to think about and plan for? To be successfully, you have to be able to do both.

We had a great CEO who was a champion. As I reflect on my reading and some of the things we've talked about at SCIP, there's this idea of whom we report to. If I don't report to the chief information office, if I don't report to the chief executive officer, how can I really have the impact that you have at Avnet? That's a good question. We were lucky. Our CEO had a vision, he gave us a charter, and we made that part of the strategy and structure of Avnet. And there's something else we did—we worked really, really hard. We had an attitude of excellence. Working smart, we used tools and technique, but we also worked really hard, again. Then we hired well; from the very outset I had in my mind that no one on our time would have less than an MBA. (And today, one person has less than an

MBA but he's enrolled in an MBA program.) Our analysts are going to have structured thinking, and the way you get structured thinking is through the course work. And the last thing we did that led to our success at Avnet? We worked really hard. There is an expectation that we not only have to turn out quality work, but we have to do it like clockwork and turn it around quickly, because information is vapid. You don't have the luxury of sitting around and thinking about something for weeks.

You have an opportunity, more than many others in the company, to make a significant impact at the senior executive level. But to do that you have to be creative, you have to be innovative, and you have to take risks. And you have to work really hard.

Achieving Credibility

How can you get noticed inside the company? Oftentimes there's a gate-keeper between you and the CEO. One of the things you've got to do is get to that gatekeeper. And that's what networking is all about. You need to create influencers within the organization. If you don't work for the CEO, you need to find a champion. And the best way that you can do that

Play the Game Better

Focus on our *existing* strategic/competitive position and try to improve it, incrementally. Practices such as profiling competitors, SWOT analysis, financial statement analysis, daily/periodic intelligence briefings.

Continuous Improvement

versus

Play the Game Differently

Identify new / un-exploited customer segments *(a new "who")*; new customer needs that no competitor is satisfying *(a new "what")*; new ways of producing, delivering, or distributing your firms products and services, *(a new "how")*. Use tools and techniques of impact analysis.

Discontinuous Innovation

To be successful, Competitive Intelligence must be able to do both!

Figure 9   The strategic positioning of competitive intelligence.

is by making somebody that you think will respect your work and your effort a hero. The way you make him or her a hero is by giving them all your information and allowing that individual, if he or she has contact with the person you want to influence, to influence them through your analysis. Over a period of time, as you're funneling information through this influencer, that CEO is going to sit there and say, "You know Chris, where are you getting all this stuff. Because I know you and you don't think this way." Chris, being a true champion, will say, "Well, that's the work of the CI team." Now you've begun to build a relationship that ultimately turns into a direct relationship because over time that chief executive will become reliant upon your information.

At Avnet, I get jazzed when I'm standing in my office and I watch the CEO walk right by my office and go down to the guy who runs the CI team.

Credibility is hard to get. It's extremely hard. But the traits of a good CI practitioner are very simple. You work hard. It means long hours. You need to read voraciously. How much do you read outside your industry? You need to be a work creator not a work processor. If your boss is telling you what to do on a day-in, day-out basis, guess what you are. I don't need to go into Andre's office and tell him what to do. Andre's responsibility is to come in and tell me what he's doing.

You've to get to what it means. You've got to apply your analytical tools and then you've got to take risks, and this means getting to actionable intelligence. It requires you to take a stand and make a recommendation. It's okay to make a mistake. When you make a recommendation, you make it based on what you know in a still uncertain environment and things can change. Things will happen so that when you make a recommendation to management based on this or that, you may be wrong. But that's okay. That's an error of commission. You gave it a shot, you were doing your job. (The objective, of course, is to not make too many mistakes.) But an error of omission is because you never tried, you never got there.

You've got to build credibility, and it's hard to get. We're still building credibility in our organization. Networking is an important secret to that. We've been doing this for four years now, and I think it takes that long for any of you to ultimately build credibility in your organization. And it's easy to lose. Andre says that one "oh, gee" wipes out a whole lot of "atta boys."

Last point: You're an analyst, yes, but you've got to be a salesperson. Especially in CI. Especially with the newness that it has for strategic planning and thinking in the markets today. You've got to sell, sell, and keep selling.

You sell through the analysis that you do. You sell through your contacts and networks. And you've just got to keep coming back like the tide, day in and day out.

ABOUT THE AUTHOR

John H. Hovis, Ph.D., is senior vice president and director of investor relations and corporate planning, Avnet, Inc. In this capacity, Dr. Hovis reports to the chairman and CEO of Avnet, and is responsible for the global strategic planning and management systems, which includes strategic planning, a global budgeting system, a performance measurement system, and the global business information office, Avnet's CI Center. Before joining Avnet, he was an economics consultant and professor of economics at the University of Maryland. Dr. Hovis holds a Ph.D. in economics from the University of Wyoming.

Competitive Intelligence at Xerox

Judith M. Vezmar
XEROX CORPORATION

EXECUTIVE SUMMARY

Xerox, renowned for its quality products and with a reputation for technological innovation, nevertheless found itself blindsided by competitive challenges beginning in the 1970s. In response, the company established a competitive intelligence operation that works globally, nationally, and locally to help decision makers anticipate and counteract competitor moves. Benchmarking is a major focus, and includes service leaders outside the office-equipment field. Xerox's Competitive Evaluation Lab keeps company engineers informed about competitor product developments. Its sales and service reps have a Competitive Hot Line to phone in information. And Xerox continually surveys current and potential customers regarding the perceived strengths and weaknesses of the company and its competitors. All this information is fed into a national competitive database, accessible to the company's sales force via their laptops.

In the 1960s, Xerox Corporation introduced the first office copying machine, the Xerox 914. It changed the way people did business, and Xerox "owned" the copier/duplicator marketplace for more than a decade. Then the Japanese taught us a lesson about the necessity for competitive intelligence.

When the Japanese first introduced their copiers in the 1970s, we didn't care. After all, we invented the technology. We were the biggest guys on the block. We were the only game in town. What we really were was so arrogant that we didn't see the competition coming. By the early 1980s, we

This article is adapted from a presentation by Ms. Vezmar at the SCIP/Rutgers CEO Roundtable. *Competitive Intelligence Review*, Vol. 7(3) 15–19 (1996). © 1996 John Wiley & Sons, Inc.

found we were rapidly losing market share so we analyzed Japanese products and prices. It was a shock to discover that the Japanese were selling machines for what it cost us to make ours.

At first we told ourselves that the product quality must be poor. But it wasn't. We were defensive and said, "For such low cost, they can't be making any money." Wrong again. In fact, the Japanese were getting to the market in half the time, with one-quarter the design changes, and one-third the expense. From 1976 to 1982, our market share was cut in half. When we closed the books on 1982, our earnings had dropped 50% in one year.

That got our attention when it came to competition.

In an effort to get back on track, our former CEO, David Kearns, went to our Japanese affiliate, Fuji Xerox. Learning from their success, he benchmarked the Japanese quality processes and became a quality convert. On returning to the United States he launched our own quality strategy, which helped us regain market share and lead the industry.

Competitive benchmarking is still helping us today.

Back in 1989, our competitive intelligence information showed that we had to improve customer satisfaction and quality. But how? Our answer was a revolutionary idea: a Total Satisfaction Guarantee. Our CEO, Paul Allaire, said let's give customers a money-back guarantee. In the past, if a customer had been unhappy with a Xerox machine, we'd let them complain about it for months. Eventually, we'd take it back. In the meantime, we lost our customer's confidence. To determine how to fix the problem our competitive intelligence people conducted focus groups. They uncovered an interesting thing: Our customers didn't want a *money-back* guarantee. They wanted a strong, simple *replacement* guarantee. They just wanted Xerox to stand behind its equipment.

> Competitive intelligence showed we had to improve customer satisfaction and quality. Focus groups uncovered that our customers didn't want a money-back guarantee. They wanted a strong, simple replacement guarantee. They just wanted Xerox to stand behind its equipment.

Again, we benchmarked. But we didn't study office equipment manufacturers. We went to Land's End, the company that's known for standing behind its products. We hammered out a guarantee that says, in essence, if at any time within three years you are not satisfied with your Xerox equipment, then Xerox will replace it without charge. Some said, "Don't do it! You'll lose your shirt! Customers will take advantage of you."

On the contrary, inspired by the guarantee, 80,000 customers inquired into Xerox products and services. And we replaced very few machines. Our customers were happy with us again. We can all learn a lot from companies that are the best in their business. Value and quality transcend industry lines.

> When Southwest Airlines wanted to cut its service time, it didn't go to competing airlines. Instead, it went to leaders in service and refueling efficiency—the Indy 500 pit crews.

Southwest Airlines found similar benefits in benchmarking. According to management consultant, Dr. Price Pritchett, who addressed a Xerox Worldwide Employee Obsession Symposium last year, Southwest Airlines is *the* most successful airline in business today. It's one of the few making money. When Southwest wanted to cut its service and refueling time, it didn't go to competing airlines. It didn't look at American Airlines or even United, the biggest in the business. Instead, it went to the leaders in service and refueling efficiency—it went to the Indy 500 racing pit crews.

As a result, Southwest cut its "pit stop" time in half. They knew that improving their efficiency was the way to satisfy customers. In the end, that's our focus, too: Satisfying our customers is the most important factor of all. It's the only way to succeed. The best defense is a good offense.

But we also know that we have to *remain vigilant* to keep our edge. And so we do competitive intelligence on three levels:

Globally, our Xerox Business Divisions develop products and services for a specific customer segment. They listen and watch for information that could affect our long-term or strategic plans.

Nationally, U.S. Customer Operations gathers and uses competitive intelligence.

Locally, we have 37 Customer Business Units sprinkled across the country. They gather and interpret local data via their individual marketing managers, who understand the pricing strategies of the distributor down the block. But they wouldn't be involved in looking down the road at the possible implications of a new Canon offering. That information is gathered by the Business Divisions.

We see competitive intelligence as a cycle with four steps. We gather the information, organize it, analyze it, and put it into action. Almost all of the information we gather is in the public domain. At Xerox, we have analysts who surf the net, use online search services, attend trade shows, review competitors' press releases and listen to their executives' speeches and public statements.

Our analysts also use technical information from our library facilities and commission research from secondary resources with industry knowledge. When we get information, we bucket it into four main categories: companies, products, channels, and the marketplace.

All four give a picture of what the competition is doing in their day-to-day business. We ask, "What are our competitors up to? What patents have they filed for? What mergers and strategic alliances are they engaging in?"

Legal decisions also make a difference in the way we compete. And price announcements can be good indicators of market activity. We also look at "traditional" indicators such as competitive products, services, profit, market share and customer satisfaction. We do this every week. We sort the information and see if the pieces fit together.

Sometimes we even use the information we've collected to draw a competitor's organization chart. You can see what a company values by how close it is to the chairman's desk.

> Sometimes we use the information we've collected to draw a competitor's organization chart. You can see what a company values by how close it is to the chairman's desk.

We also look at the physical locations and acquisitions of our competitors. We follow every deal that Alco or Danka makes. But while it's important to look at what a competitor says, just as important is what it doesn't say. Recently Kodak chairman George Fisher said that his vision of Kodak's future was the digital camera—a graphic link to the PC. The possible applications for the camera are huge, and we think it will be Kodak's lead product. What George didn't talk about is the role of Kodak copiers in that overall strategy. So Kodak's subsequent announcement of changes that could result in the sale of its copier division didn't surprise us; we already suspected it.

Competitors are also a terrific source to help you better understand your customers and their requirements. Sometimes, competitors can spot trends and other market phenomenon that you'll have to contend with.

> Our Competitive Evaluation Lab carefully examines competitive products. We purchase them, tear them down and issue reports to the engineering community. We try to understand every strength and weakness, point for point.

We have a Competitive Evaluation Lab to learn everything we can from competitors. That's where we carefully examine competitive products. We purchase them, tear them down, and issue reports to the engineering community. We try to understand every part, every feature, every strength, and every weakness, point for point.

But if you think taking apart copiers is tough, try an airplane. When Boeing came out with the 707 jetliner in 1958, Air France bought one. Then they flew it to Toulouse, France and took it apart, piece by piece. It was not to copy the technology, but to learn from it.

And today, we gather data about our competitors and their breakthroughs, not to imitate but to learn in order to lead the market.

I can't overemphasize the importance of knowing your competitors. New players are coming into our markets all the time. Companies that weren't competitors a few years ago are now major players, while some of our former competition has faded away.

> In our early years, we saw IBM as our greatest threat. Meanwhile, Kodak was branching out from photographic items into copiers because they were both ways to image.

Some examples: In our early years, we saw IBM, *the* business machine giant, as our greatest threat. Meanwhile, Kodak was branching out from photographic items into copiers because they were both ways to image.

Years ago, we never saw Hewlett Packard, a computer hardware company, as a threat. Now, it's a formidable competitor. Hopefully, we've gotten better at this game and have learned to keep our eyes on the big picture instead of just single pieces of the puzzle. On the horizon, there's a certain software giant that we believe could turn out to be our next big competitor, since it plays a major role in the proliferation of document creation and management. You can bet we're keeping an eye on Microsoft.

We're not just worried about software giants, of course. We're also concerned about the local office equipment dealers who provide fast response and flexible pricing. We have to watch out for them as well.

> How can you keep ahead of the trends? Go to the experts, the people who know more about your marketplace than anyone else—your sales reps and your customers.

Think about how much our marketplace is changing. The way we do business is evolving. Who would have bought a computer off the shelf 15 years ago? You'd call up IBM and make an appointment with a person who knew hardware and software. Today, you can walk into Office-Max, grab a box off the shelf, go home and plug it in.

How can you keep ahead of the trends? You can go to the experts, the people who know more about your marketplace than anyone else. Who are these experts? They're your sales reps and your customers.

At Xerox, we have a Competitive Hot Line for our sales people to phone in competitive information. We use our sales force to identify where the competition is located, who our potential customers are, what industries they're in, what applications they have and even why they bought from the competition.

Here's an example of how important these "eyes and ears" are. Early last year we received competitive information indicating that a competitor was planning, for the first time, to offer service on Xerox products. One of our competitor's service reps told one of our service technicians that he was being trained to service our products. Our service rep went to his manager and that information was passed up through the channel into the Competitive Intelligence group.

We verified the information with about three additional clues, one of which was rather obvious—an ad the competitor had placed in the classifieds for people with Xerox product experience. This allowed us to announce a counter-strategy as the competitor was about to announce its new service strategy.

But it's not just our employees who give us this valuable information. We rely heavily on our customers. We survey approximately 5 million establishments in the United States—all current or potential customers—and ask them what they value, what they do or don't like about our current competitors, and what they see as our strengths and weaknesses. We then load the information into a database that our sales reps across the country can access. If a customer cancels their contract for our machine, we ask that customer why. That reason is coded and kept with the machine record. You'd be surprised at how frank your customers are willing to be with you.

We have several thousand competitive units in our competitive database. Since all of this data goes into a national database, we can look at any part of the country and see that Canon has this market share or that Ricoh has that market share in that area. When a new product is launched by one of our competitors, we load that into the database. Our sales force can use their laptops to tap into this information about the product and its features. They can even sort their customer base and find which ones would be vulnerable to the competitor's new product. We can tell the reps about customer awareness of our brand in a particular market: how much market share we have against our competition's, and a particular customer's predisposition to buy or *not* buy from us. We can even tell our reps which customers are the early adopters of technology.

> Since all this data goes into a national database, we can look at any part of the country and see that Canon has this market share or that Ricoh has that market share. When a new product is launched by a competitor, we load that into the database. Our sales force can use their laptops to tap into this information and sort their customer base to find which ones would be vulnerable to the competitor's new product.

Armed with that information, our marketing managers can develop local strategies, and sales reps can anticipate their customers' needs.

Xerox and other U.S. firms that want to stick around will make competitive intelligence an integral part of day-to-day business. I believe that support needs to come straight from the top. As Jan Herring predicted in the early 1990s, "Until senior executives become more interested and involved in the use of business intelligence, the competitiveness of U.S. companies

Xerox Competitive Intelligence Recognized as Benchmark in Study "This Isn't Cloak-and-Dagger Stuff"

ROCHESTER, N.Y., March 17 / PRNewswire/ — Xerox Corporation (NYSE: XRX) has been selected as among the best at keeping tabs on the competition — a critical strength in a fiercely competitive global marketplace.

The company's competitive intelligence program has been selected as one of the best in the country by members of the non-profit American Productivity and Quality Center, who identified and evaluated the best practices and key trends in the area of competitive intelligence.

"This isn't cloak-and-dagger stuff," said Warren Jeffries, manager of customer services benchmarking for Xerox. Employees gathering competitive intelligence must conform to rigid ethical standards. At Xerox this involves the effective use of publicly available information and depends on a decentralized network that meets monthly to share information across business units."

Xerox uses intelligence gathered on competitors to better anticipate trends and develop counter strategies so its people are better prepared to develop and market Xerox products and services more effectively. The result is added customer value that distinguishes the company from its competition.

For instance, in the late 1980s, competitive intelligence reported that customer satisfaction was slipping largely because of slow problem resolution. After a series of focus groups and benchmarking, the solution became apparent: the Total Satisfaction Guarantee.

It stated that if, within three years, customers were not satisfied with their Xerox equipment, the company would replace the machine without charge. As a result, Xerox received 80,000 inquiries from customers, replaced very few machines, enhanced customer satisfaction ratings, and gained a competitive advantage.

Among the best practices the APQC found at benchmark companies are:

— Decentralizing intelligence networks to leverage experience, expertise and resources across the company;

— Incorporating information technology to help collect, sort, organize and disseminate the vast amount of publicly available information;

— Interrelating customer needs, feedback evaluation and implementation to maximize the impact of competitive intelligence;

— Using analytical frameworks to test hypotheses and develop recommendations.

The study, entitled "Competitive and Business Intelligence: Leveraging Information for Action," will be available this July from the American Productivity and Quality Center, which is based in Houston.

SOURCE   Xerox Corporation

CONTACT: Sandy Mauceli of Xerox Corporation, 716-423-4336, or Sandy_Mauceli@mc.xerox.co / For more information about The Document Company Xerox, please visit our website at http://http://www.xerox.com. Xerox news releases are available via fax retrieval by calling 1-800-758-5804, and entering the code "XEROX-1" (937691).

PR NEWSWIRE
home
(Today's News) (Company News On-Call) (Feature News) (Automotive)
(Entertainment) (Health/Biotech) (Technology) (Financial) (Energy)

Figure 1

will be limited by their inability to understand and out-think global competitors" (Herring, 1992).

Executives in the United States are beginning to make headway. More business schools are offering formal competitive intelligence studies—there's even a CI course on the Internet offered by the University of Pittsburgh.

My recommendation: Make competitive intelligence a part of your marketing function. Link it to every operation in your business that can be affected by competitive actions. Once you have the information in hand, use it. Be sure the right data gets to the right people at the right time. Above all, find ways to add value for your customers; it remains the best way to distinguish you from the competition and ensure success.

REFERENCES

Herring, Jan P. (March/April 1992). Business Intelligence in Japan and Sweden: Lessons for the US, *The Journal of Business Strategy*.

ABOUT THE AUTHOR

Judith M. Vezmar served as vice president and general manager of the Long Island Metro Customer Business Unit of Xerox Corporation's U.S. Customer Operations. Before joining Xerox in 1979, she held numerous sales, marketing, and management positions in Chicago, Rochester (headquarters), and New York City.

NutraSweet Faces Competition: The Critical Role of Competitive Intelligence

Robert Flynn
THE NUTRASWEET COMPANY

Yesterday you had the good fortune of listening to Michael Porter's ideas about the value of competitive intelligence. I know he thinks information is a key part of innovation and improvement—particularly information that you have and your competitors don't.

General Norman Schwarzkopf also understood the power of information, and used it to great advantage in the Persian Gulf War. People gave a lot of credit to our weapons technology. But an equally important advantage was our superior *intelligence* operations. Largely through our surveillance aircraft, we knew more about Saddam Hussain and his military operations than we have ever known about an enemy. We knew:

- The size of his army division—when they were building up and when they were shifting from defensive to offensive formations.

- The desert terrain—the weather and light patterns, the best and the worst times to strike.

- The make-up of his arsenal and the possibility that chemical weapons would be used.

- That one of Saddam's greatest weaknesses was his lack of modern surveillance technology.

This article is based on Mr. Flynn's keynote address at the SCIP Ninth Annual International Conference in Boston on April 29, 1994. *Competitive Intelligence Review,* Vol. 7, Supplement 1 S25–S28 (1996). © 1996 John Wiley & Sons, Inc.

We knew the enemy perhaps better than he knew himself; so much that we beat him on his own land.

The role information played in the outcome of the Gulf War provides a good lesson for corporate executives. The way Schwarzkopf used competitive intelligence to protect his own position and prepare his willing strategy, is a model for effective corporate behavior.

At the NutraSweet Company, we certainly have been in our competitors' sights. In the late 1980s, we had several potential competitors who knew a lot about us. Frankly, they would have had to keep their heads in the sand not to. NutraSweet had a high brand awareness in the U.S. and our trademark Swirl appeared on thousands of consumer products around the world. It was no secret who we were, or who our customers were. It was also quite well-known that in December, 1992, our U.S. patent for aspartame would expire.

It seemed like every chemical company in the world was considering going into the aspartame business, and getting their share of *our* business. The margins were attractive enough to interest many people.

As we looked toward a postpatent world, we needed to know who our likely competitors would be:

- Who had enough money on an ongoing basis?
- Who had the marketing ability?
- Who knew how to satisfy the regulatory requirements?
- Who had the skills in applied engineering?
- Among the likely competitors, what would their probable cost positions be?
- What rate of return would their parent company or their investors expect?
- How long would they be willing to put money into the operations without taking any out?

At the same time, we had the opportunity to expand the use of aspartame out of the diet category. In many areas of the world, we were looking to market aspartame as an *economic* alternative to sugar and high fructose corn syrup. What would be the barriers to entry in those markets?

- An entrenched sugar lobby?
- Regulatory resistance?
- A medical position that would require years of new tests?

The stakes were high. In the United States, erosion of our traditional customer base would be very costly. Globally, sugar substitution could be a major revenue opportunity. In both cases, we were not in control of the outcome. Many different competitors would influence our ability to succeed. We defined our competition broadly:

- Companies who would choose to enter the aspartame business.

- Mainstream sweeteners of sugar and high fructose corn syrup.

- Alternative sweeteners that were still in new product pipelines or seeking regulatory approval in various regions of the world.

- Those who would have a say in whether our products received regulatory approval.

As the NutraSweet Company approached the expiration of our patent at the end of 1992, all our chips were on the table. Our postpatent objective was to establish a competitive position by driving costs down and providing customer service to remain the favored supplier to our customers around the world.

So far, we have succeeded due to the efforts of our company teams: sales and marketing, technical applications, manufacturing, regulatory, and competitive intelligence (CI). Our intelligence-gathering capability is a major contributor to our competitive advantages in marketing, manufacturing, organizational structure, and financial backing.

In marketing, we use CI to understand:

- What are our competitors doing with their promotional and advertising campaigns?

- How are they pricing their products?

- What do they have coming in new product introductions?

- How are their existing products perceived in the marketplace?

- How are they doing in customer satisfaction?

- What kind of value-added initiatives are they working on?

- What are the potential alliances and joint ventures?

In manufacturing, CI tells us what kind of production capabilities we are up against, productivity levels we have to beat, global inventory levels, and who might be building a state-of-the-art production facility that would shift the competitive balance.

Organizationally we use CI to get a sense of the organizations that want to take market share from us, to judge the impact of structural changes in competing companies, and to predict the effect of leadership styles and other cultural issues that we run into in the global marketplace. Financially, CI helps us monitor strengths and weaknesses:

- Who can afford to build a world-class facility?
- Who can make the investment to serve the global needs of our key customers?
- Who has the staying power to challenge our low-cost produce status?

In each of these areas we demand four things from our CI effort. First, it must provide up-to-the-minute *information*. That information must be in a form that is easy to use and easy to translate into actions. We are in a *race* with our competitors to meet the demands of customers and consumers around the world. The faster we receive information and the more decisively we act on it, the sooner we can get a head start on the competition.

Second, CI must provide an "insurance policy" against being *blindsided* by our competitors or the external business climate. It has become a cliche to talk about the rapidly changing global marketplace. But it has never been harder to keep up with all the forces at work on a global level, and doing so has never been more important to the success of our business.

Third, CI must be a source of *unfiltered, unbiased news.* Schwarzkopf was relentless when it came to the accuracy of information. He has served in Vietnam where the U.S. military had been regularly criticized for sugar-coating information to please the President. And he had seen the President make decisions based on bad information. He was determined not to repeat that mistake. Every shred of information he reported would be accurate— even if it was not what the President wanted to hear.

We have all seen information lose its edge in corporate staff groups— people telling their higher-ups what they want to hear and confirming bad ideas. Our intelligence people must do their job in the field, getting a first-hand view of the global competitive environment. Because they work outside company walls, their information is free of political or operational bias. They have no incentive to give us a rose-colored view of the world. And they are good at bringing back details that an experienced executive might overlook or disregard.

The fourth requirement is the highest *legal* and *ethical* business practices in the gathering of our CI. We are very fortunate to have top professionals in charge of our CI function. I know they have given a lot to SCIP and have gotten a lot back in return.

In these four ways, CI keeps us from operating in a vacuum. It keeps us from sealing ourselves off from the real value of our business in the marketplace and the real threats to our success. For example, what if Schwarzkopf did not know how big the Iraqi forces were, did not know where they were coming from, did not know the size and strength of their arsenal? How would the war have turned out?

It sounds crazy to talk about a general going into battle without sizing up the enemy. But people in business do it all the time. Companies launch new products without checking out the competition, without knowing if there is a consumer need, or if the market will support it. Then they fail and wonder why.

In today's world, you have to know your competitors and your markets, and you have to know them on a global basis. You have to know what your competitors are charging on the other side of the world, what their raw material costs are, how good their quality is, and what they have in the new product pipeline. If you don't know all that, and more, you are no better off than the general who orders his troops into a minefield, without knowing about the mines.

To get the kind of competitive information we need, we must have a formal organization that is responsible for nothing else but the professional gathering, organizing, analyzing, and circulating of information about competitive activities. CI is important enough to be someone's full time job.

You need to put a little distance between them and the rest of the company. We all know how easy it is for people in an organization, especially in a successful organization, to protect the status quo, to make quick judgments that something will or will not work, to fall back on the comfortable ways of doing things. The CI function needs to be separate from that way of thinking and be the antidote to it.

As a separate function, CI can provide a fresh look at the effectiveness of our own sales and marketing strategies versus the competition. They can offer ideals for improving the value we can bring to our customers and their consumers. As a separate organization, CI can provide checks and balances to the things we hear from our managers in the field. If what we are hearing from our managers is the same as what our CI people are saying, it is a pretty sure bet we are on target. If the stories are inconsistent, it is a red flag. We need to take a closer look.

I am a firm believer that CI has helped us make more good decisions at The NutraSweet Company, and fewer bad ones. I can even put a price on it. CI is worth up to $50 million per year to our company. That is a combination of revenues gained and revenues "not lost" to competitive activity. I believe in CI, our senior managers believe in it, and together we have created a corporate culture that supports it. That is the only way competitive intelligence *can* provide value—with the complete backing of the company's decision makers.

As professionals in the CI field, you can do several things to encourage management buy-in by your organizations. The two biggest ones are:

- Become well grounded in your company's business plans, marketing plans, tactical plans, and contingency plans.
- Relate your findings to management in those terms.

There will always be executives skeptical of the information you provide because they do not think you understand the business. It is up to you to show them that you do understand. It is your job to package the intelligence you gather in terms *your customers*—the management of your company—can relate to and act on. It is in fact your obligation to win over the skeptics in your organization. The day is gone when the service you provide can be treated as an option. It is now a necessity. If you fail to make that understood, you are contributing to the ultimate downfall of your own company.

Technology is adding to the speed of communication. It is multiplying the amount of information available. Business is rapidly becoming a game of "What did you know?" and "When did you know it?" In this game, serious, professional, strategic intelligence gathering and analysis is a *requirement* for success. It is a *prerequisite* for survival. The winners of this game will be those who know the most, know it first, and are the quickest to turn knowledge into action.

With those needs always high on my priority list, I am very thankful for the CI professionals who serve in my company. I didn't train them. I didn't teach them how to do what they do. I didn't provide their high professional standards. I am just the beneficiary of their capabilities and their professionalism. For that, I think I owe a lot to your society. You have established the kind of ethical standards that are a great comfort to people like me, who employ people like you. And you do an outstanding job of self-education.

So let me take this opportunity to say thanks, to the Society of Competitive Intelligence Professionals, for providing a most valuable service. Let me end with a quote from General Schwarzkopf:

It doesn't take a hero to order men into battle. It takes a hero to be one of those men who goes into battle.

As the chairman of a company that does its daily battle with competitors around the world, I take none of the credit for our success. The real credit goes to all the men and women who go into battle every day. I wouldn't think of sending them out there unprepared. In my book, they are *not* prepared without the best competitive intelligence we can provide them.

ABOUT THE AUTHOR

Robert E. Flynn served as chairman and CEO of The NutraSweet Company.

Competitive Intelligence at Motorola

Robert W. Galvin
MOTOROLA, INC.

EXECUTIVE SUMMARY

At the SCIP/Rutgers University CEO Roundtable on Competitive Intelligence, held in February 1996 in New York City, some of the CEO participants advocated establishing dedicated competitive intelligence units staffed by CI professionals and headed by a Competitive Intelligence Officer. Others favored more loosely structured efforts, such as simply having operating departments and staff contribute information into an accessible database. Robert W. Galvin, the chairman of the Executive Committee of Motorola, Inc., and one of the pioneers of modern corporate competitive intelligence (Motorola's Business Intelligence system is recognized by many as the most advanced operation of its kind), listened to the discussion and then took the podium, where he spoke adamantly in favor of CI as a professionally staffed effort, with an intelligence program that is both centralized and widely disbursed throughout the company. Provided here is an excerpt of his remarks.

Some 25 years ago, while serving on the President's Foreign Intelligence Advisory Board, I developed an understanding of and an appreciation for what professional intelligence people could do. I learned that intelligence agencies collect information. They sense indicators. They make analysis. They prepare estimates and they make net assessments, along with alternate estimates and assessments. In the early '70s, I realized that as with national security, we couldn't devise good

Competitive Intelligence Review, Vol. 8(1) 3–6 (1997). © 1997 John Wiley & Sons, Inc.

corporate strategies without good information, good analysis, and good estimates. It takes professionals to do that kind of job on behalf of the government. And I am strongly biased in the direction that it takes the bringing together of trained professionals to do the job for a corporate intelligence department. Intelligence, in my estimation, cannot simply be derived from your traditional business practices.

> It takes professionals to provide national security intelligence on behalf of the government. And it takes professionals to do the job for a corporate intelligence department. Intelligence, in my estimation, cannot simply be derived from your traditional business practices.

Our intelligence department at Motorola collects information that our sales people, engineers, and operating personnel can't get—honorably, overtly, they just know how to go out and get it. All of our people bring intelligence to the job, but the intelligence department brings an increment not supplied by wonderful engineers, wonderful sales people, vice presidents, or chief executive officers. We're not trained to do their job, and we lack the benefits they acquire as professionals dedicated to competitive intelligence.

STRATEGY COUNTS

Our determination to have a professional intelligence department coincided with my concern that our fundamental understanding of strategy was weak. We had people who were using the word "strategy" continually because it sounded so important. It made their statements seem authoritative, but it was totally irrelevant. "My strategy is to be number one," they'd say. That's not a strategy. We therefore set out to recast the meaning of strategy.

To us, a strategy is a timely and effective application of available resources. The use of those resources generates a distinctive competence that provides a benefit to our customers that our competitors cannot generate, at least not in a timely fashion or in a profitable manner. But it takes a lot of information to synthesize the thinking out of a particular strategy and to make that function work.

FOCUSING ON THE CUSTOMER

The focus must always remain on the customer. I heard an awful lot [during the Roundtable panel discussion] about being "competitive." The implication is that you're competing to serve the customer. But sometimes that fact gets lost. To us, we want intelligence that assists us, ultimately, in serving our customer. We may be doing that with no competitor, because the history of our company is one of creating industries. So we go out and create customers. And then once we've got the customers, we generate some competitors.

> In being "competitive," the implication is that you're competing to serve the customer. But sometimes that fact gets lost. Intelligence should assist us, ultimately, in serving our customer.

Our aim is to process information in a way that helps us to anticipate the creation of an industry, and therefore provides us with an opportunity to be a dominant player. Moreover, the driving thrust of our corporation is renewal. We renew everything as fast as we can. One of the things we try to do is to put ourselves out of business. That's the most dramatic renewal you can do. Well, if you're going to do that, then you really have to have a horizon that is 360 spherical degrees. You must be looking way outside of whatever your competitors are doing and ask yourself how you write new rules for new games, for new markets, for new customers whom you never ever thought would want to be a market for what you might be able to create for them.

A PROFESSIONAL APPROACH

I'm delighted to be standing literally shoulder to shoulder at this Roundtable with Jan Herring, Motorola's former director of intelligence who, following a distinguished career as an intelligence officer at the CIA, oversaw the firm's development of a pioneering business intelligence system based on national security principles. Jan personified the professionalism I wanted to bring into the company. My associates did a wonderful job of recruiting him.

Jan was obviously the opening wave in our company. It was not an easy task for him. He was not "a businessman." That happened to be something I liked very much about him. He could bring something very fresh to the institution, and he did. But if you're going to start an intelligence department, you will need to take some growing steps, and these will vary from company to company. My guess is it will take 10 years to establish a well-accepted professional intelligence function and department in almost any normal corporation. We've been at it a little longer than that now, and it's magnificently accepted. But it wasn't accepted to begin with.

When I first announced our intention to my associates some 15 years ago, the reaction was, "Well, it's kind of an interesting idea, Bob, but remember 'overhead'. . . . You can't spend any money. . . . It's another corporate function," and so on. And I said, "We cannot be good at strategic thinking if we do not have in the balance all the information to do the job, plus we've got to train ourselves to be better strategic thinkers." Which is to say, it was critical for strategy and intelligence to be wedded.

That this was not accepted early on didn't make any difference to me. Every new thing we've done wasn't accepted at first. Eventually, our strategy office came round and said, "Bob, we think you're on the right track."

> Every new thing we've done wasn't accepted at first. Eventually, our strategy office came round and said, "Bob, we think you're on the right track."

ORGANIZING THE INTELLIGENCE FUNCTION

How is the staff structured and disbursed? We have a core department that numbers circa 10 people. It's a part of the corporate strategy office. It's not there for the chief executive officer. It's there for the corporation. It's a service to the corporation and to the thousands of leaders in our company.

We have a central entity of specialized professionals who can do something better than anybody else can do—acquire information and then process it in an intelligent way. But it's disbursed in the sense that they have caused the elements of the corporation, whether we call them divisions, sectors, or what have you, to discover that they benefit by having one, two, or three of their own people who are responsible for interfacing with the intelligence department. And so the intelligence *activity* of the corporation probably numbers somewhere between 25 and 30 people. We are a hybrid, with a centralized yet widely disbursed intelligence program. And there's mobility built into this system. There are some experienced general-business people at Motorola who do fit into the intelligence department from time to time, becoming competent as intelligence professionals.

> We have a core intelligence department that numbers circa 10 people. But the divisions have discovered they benefit by having one, two, or three of their own people who are responsible for interfacing with the intelligence department, so the intelligence activity of the corporation probably numbers between 25 and 30 people. We are a hybrid, with a centralized yet widely disbursed intelligence program.

Now, the functions that are covered: Our intelligence department engages in some formal benchmarking for the company. They are not *the* benchmarkers for the company, but they do very special benchmarking when we have identified a certain target "affector." We are a technology company, so our intelligence professionals must speak the language of technology. They're very conversant with processes—business processes, technical processes, and manufacturing processes, to a substantial degree.

They are constantly searching out information to try to understand what resources our competitors have that they can offer our customers. We're always analyzing the subtleties of the other person's strategy. But the primary focus remains *customer* understanding—knowing the customers and how best to satisfy their changing wants and needs. We presume nothing is adequate. Nothing is complete. We avoid presuming that we already know enough. We've avoided the pitfall of not knowing what we don't know.

Our intelligence department is a benchmarkable source of information. Its credentials have now been established over a number of years, and based on experience we know that what they tell us is almost always proven to be correct. Thus, we have an enhanced confidence level and face less ambiguity in confronting new situations.

None of this reduces the responsibility that falls on the rest of us. We must be our own intelligence officers. We must act intelligently. We must do the job of leaders. Parenthetically, to us, the most distinctive quality of a leader is someone who takes us elsewhere, often into uncharted seas. And when we prepare for such a course by first running a scenario exercise, our intelligence department is one of the first places we go in order to, in effect, engineer the process.

In other words, an intelligence department can be seen as a professional entity that supports, or stimulates, or once in a while hits home runs, or most of the time gets some pretty good bunts in to help move along the more fundamental culture and character of the institution.

An Anthropological Perspective

I'll leave you with just one other word that will increasingly play a key role in intelligence and/or leadership: anthropology. A truly thorough understanding of the cultural anthropology of the world can explain the factors that underlie a particular nation's conduct. And it is likely that grasping and conveying anthropological knowledge will fall to intelligence departments as we expand our awareness of this very complex, multi-faceted world.

> It is likely that grasping and conveying anthropological knowledge will fall to intelligence departments as we expand our awareness of this very complex, multi-faceted world.

As an example, in attempting to break into the Japanese electronic market we came to realize the extent to which the Japanese respected power, in contrast to the deferential polite mannerisms of the more apparent culture. And when we finally realized that, we knew what to do. We used every piece of legitimate political power that we could—from the Senate Foreign Relations Committee right up to the President—to break down the market barriers put up by Japan. Eventually, Motorola opened up the Japanese electronics market and the Japanese respected us for it and responded by purchasing our products. They respected power. That's an anthropological principle, and a very significant piece of intelligence.

About the Author

Robert W. Galvin started his career at Motorola in 1940. He held the senior officership position in the company from 1959 until January 1990, when he became chairman of the executive committee. He continues to serve as a full-time officer of Motorola. Mr. Galvin, a SCIP member since May 1996, has been awarded honorary degrees and other recognitions, including election to the National Business Hall of Fame and the presentation of the National Medal of Technology in 1991. Motorola was the first large-company winner of the Malcolm Baldrige Quality Award, presented by President Reagan at a White House ceremony in November 1988.

Competitive Intelligence in Business Process Engineering: A Study at Digital Equipment Corporation

Larry Kennedy

DIGITAL EQUIPMENT CORPORATION

EXECUTIVE SUMMARY

Businesses undergoing reengineering efforts must rely on analytical data and management insight to design and implement processes that most effectively address market needs. These design efforts require endorsement and support by the most senior management and require a fundamentally different approach to market success than past business models and information would dictate. Therefore, competitive and externally-generated analysis is key to understanding the opportunities, risks, and potential investment profiles that will move a changing organization toward competitive advantage in dynamic markets. This article references a reengineering design process successfully implemented within Digital Equipment Corporation's Computer Systems Division in 1994–1995. In moving from a functional to a product-oriented business model, Digital employed competitive intelligence (CI) to analyze and evaluate new organizational designs and business process systems by defined market segments and competitors, and by projecting accepted economic principles. CI research efforts included information on competitive positions, potential shifts in product line positioning, trade off scenarios from one system type to another, pro forma investment, and market share analyses.

Competitive Intelligence Review, Vol. 8(2) 28–33 (1997). © 1997 John Wiley & Sons, Inc.

BACKGROUND: DYNAMIC MARKET
CHANGE FORCES REENGINEERING

The reengineering of Digital Equipment Corporation's Computer Systems Division in 1994–1995 involved changes in organization and decision-making, which required use of competitive intelligence (CI) different from that traditionally employed by the firm. Syndicated market research, customer focus groups, and competitive business analysis all had been focused on integrated computer systems issues. Shifts in the market and adoption of open standards, however, contributed to a disaggregation of the components of computer systems in ways that opened opportunities for smaller competitors and those focused on narrower product and service lines. Those companies were appealing to the customers' evolving view of offering values.

As a result, Digital needed to revise its efforts to access new and better intelligence sources aligned with business model changes being undertaken in a reengineering effort. To do so, Digital's staff conducted scenarios workshops together with customers, partners, and academics. These workshops tested potential product and service strategies necessary for success in ways that the market could understand, identified the kinds of information necessary to support the implementation of newly structured businesses, and engaged the support of influential managers in order to guide the implementation plans.

> Digital needed to revise its efforts to access new and better intelligence sources aligned with business model changes being undertaken in its reengineering effort.

Senior management involvement was critical. During the redesign of the organization, the executive staff was called upon to make decisions based on information presented to it in new ways. Reengineering an organization and strategy on this scale required flexible information sourcing to support a critical business turnaround during the early stages and a shift toward new processes that could create competitive advantage in the marketplace for the future.

APPROACH AND DESIGN: USING NEW FORMS OF INTELLIGENCE

The basis of competition had shifted in the computer systems market. Competitive information most readily available, and most trusted by management, centered on markets for integrated computer systems. And yet competitive threats were rising in components and subsystems. Open standards allowed customers to buy products and services from several vendors and connect them, thus changing dramatically the basis for competition. Rather than focus its CI efforts on a few large companies that offered integrated systems to the market, Digital needed to learn about companies offering competitive products and services that competed with the individual elements and with combined elements of a product set.

Figure 1 shows a typical computer system architectural "map" of the technical layers of major computer systems. Leveraging on the new open systems standards, companies were entering the market competing with products and services that provided value at individual layers, sometimes joining in strategic alliances to create a stakehold for one set of products or functions. In doing so, they broke the architectural franchise once held by major systems vendors and secured by proprietary technology. The battlefield became one of individual and combined subsegments, and the opportunity to generate profit shifted to understanding the interdependencies of the layered

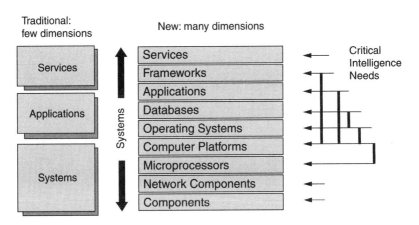

Figure 1   Shift in competition: the basis of using competitive information shifted.

technologies in an open environment. Understanding competitive strategies for this environment—including technology investment, product positioning, distribution options, and alliances—required Digital to research each sub-segment to identify current and future dominant players.

> Leveraging on the new open systems standards, companies were entering the market competing with products and services that provided value at individual layers, sometimes joining in strategic alliances to create a stake-hold for one set of products or functions.

The business design team identified the sustainable competitive differentiators and mapped them to market opportunity information by defined product and service type.

The design team used several types of external data as guides, all of which were key to influencing the reengineering effort. The Product and Service Business Unit models relied on industry practice market segmentation by product type and geographic area, using syndicated data to align product development organizations with target markets. Channel business models relied both on external data for channel coverage through distribution partners and on Digital's relationships with those companies. Information that best served to test the segmentation and design exercise included competitive distribution relationships and patterns. Charging a new Business Unit with market targets required understanding the competitive presence in each product and service area geography, including present distribution coverage. Internal financial data that was most familiar to senior management did not match these new organizations' expected revenues or resource needs for budgeting purposes. The team segmented available financial information to match the new, smaller organization units to then test for profitability and cost assumptions.

The design team created a messaging program to engage the support of employees, while maintaining daily operations to keep customer and partner orders flowing. This program was essential to assure the continued support of senior management for two reasons: the reengineering engineered structure was foreign to their company experiences and, at the same time, their time and energies were focused on keeping the company running during this major transition.

IMPLEMENTATION: BENCHMARKING
NEW FORMS OF VALUE

The team also created a framework for intelligence based on decision types and tested it using "points of excellence" or benchmarked criteria. One challenge faced throughout the process was the need for intelligence on business processes to gauge the competitive landscape. The team addressed the need by articulating the perceived changes in its own customer value proposition and discussing them with customers and partners to generate intelligence.

MOVING TO ADVANTAGE

The competitive landscape for business processes was changing rapidly as larger vendors found the need to leverage channels and channel partner relationships at the "extended enterprise." The rapid change in customer and partner needs required the development of product and service quality initiatives, "ease of doing business" initiatives and problem resolution initiatives that transcended the new product organizations and provided

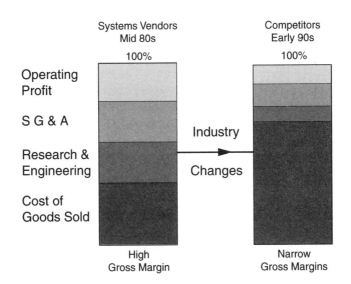

Figure 2   Cause and effect: Business models changed dramatically.

competitive response. At the products and services themselves gravitated toward commodity status in the changing computing market segments, these processes became more critical as differentiators. CI information became critical to help coordinated cross-organizational workteams understand the service levels necessary to be competitive, to identify the specific actions necessary to solve problems, and to understand the longer term expectations of customers and partners to "set the bar" for moving to advantaged positions in the market.

Figure 3 depicts the longer term direction for this process work as refocused workteams implement competitive process changes. The x-axis maps positioning in the marketplace, starting with a disadvantaged position, moving to a steady competitive position and then rising to an advantage position. The y-axis measures relative satisfaction by customers and channel partners. As satisfaction rises, the position improves. The work teams have recognized the criticality of competitive intelligence and the changing nature of its content. Again, senior management's commitment is necessary to affect cross-organizational change during reengineering efforts, and the changing nature of benchmark information creates difficulty.

The implementation teams worked closely with channel partners to test the viability of business process changes and to surmise the potential market advantages of their implementation. This partner involvement has

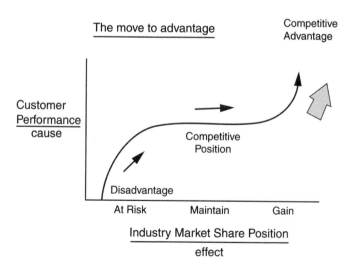

Figure 3   Moving to market share advantage.

built credibility with senior management that these actions will pay off in the long run.

> CI information became critical to help coordinated cross-organizational workteams understand the service levels necessary to be competitive, identify the specific actions necessary to solve problems, and understand the longer term expectations of customers and partners to "set the bar" for moving to advantaged positions in the market.

Some examples of CI information used in these efforts included examples of new software tools and methodologies for transactions, that is, order processing and tracking, new tools for providing complex product information to salespersons and partners, business modeling of the financial impact of new distribution methods, and industry information on employee empowerment and training methods.

MAINTAINING ADVANTAGE IN DYNAMIC MARKETS: NEW TYPE OF CI INFORMATION

All the efforts described so far support reengineering in order to rebuild and maintain position within specific segments as well as within the overall computer systems market. That market is constantly facing dynamic change, however, as the use of systems is becoming intricately tied to other markets and allied technologies (convergence). Leadership companies must understand tangential markets and the means by which vendors will collaborate and compete in them. In this case, the reengineering workteams have considered industries that offer potential opportunity and risk for computer systems vendors in the next few years as customers change their ways for using information. These industries include telecommunications, consumer products, business transactions and entertainment to varying degrees.

> The market is constantly facing dynamic change as the use of systems becomes intricately tied to other markets and allied technologies (convergence). Leadership companies must understand tangential markets and the means by which vendors will collaborate and compete in them.

Communications

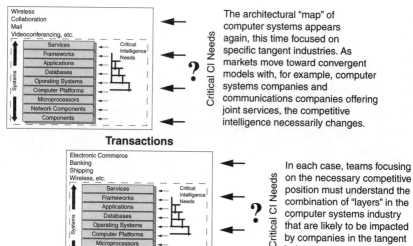

The architectural "map" of computer systems appears again, this time focused on specific tangent industries. As markets move toward convergent models with, for example, computer systems companies and communications companies offering joint services, the competitive intelligence necessarily changes.

Transactions

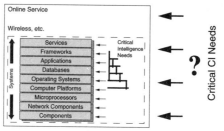

In each case, teams focusing on the necessary competitive position must understand the combination of "layers" in the computer systems industry that are likely to be impacted by companies in the tangent industry and by competitors' alliances with those companies.

Information Services

Participating companies in those industries can develop market opportunities by targeting individual layers or combinations of them. These are just four examples of industries whose participant companies and whose customers appear likely to impact computing markets.

Entertainment

The segmentation and principles used in re-engineering efforts, by focusing on market rules with identified customers, competitors, and economics, are used to identify opportunities and risks in these combinations.

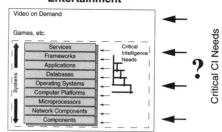

Figure 4   CI supporting future advantage: Convergence.

Figure 4 depicts the same architectural map shown earlier as a proxy for the computing systems markets that have been "de-layering," but then mapped to critical information necessary to understand the convergence issues that may arise with each of these tangent industries.

Summary: The Continued Challenge for CI in Dynamic Markets

Digital has undertaken some continued initiatives to support its positioning in competitive markets. The strategic information dimensions on which it is redesigning its business processes present continued challenges to building customer satisfaction and loyalty in newly segmented systems markets and in new segments that emerge from the convergence of information-driven markets. For some parts of the business, the most influential information on competitive values is more oriented toward business processes than to competitive product features. That information traditionally comes from the installed customer base, yet market success requires new customers from whom this critical information is available.

Thus, Digital and other systems companies must invest in new forms of primary research to support executive decisions that focus on those market segments that experience dynamic change. These needs include information necessary to track changing trends in user styles and business models, for example, the Internet as a source or a selling mechanism and information on the changing positions of competitors in the form of strategic partnerships in the marketplace.

Related Reading

Kearney, A.T. (May 1996). *Strategic Sourcing Study.*

CMP Publications. (April 23, 1996). *Trends in Big Six Consulting.*

Deloitte & Touche. (Spring 1996). *8th Annual Deloitte & Touche Survey of CIOs.*

Finely, M. (1996). Michael Hammer Reengineers Reengineering, *The Masters Forum.*

Kotter, J. (March–April 1995). "Leading Change: Why Transformation Efforts Fail," *Harvard Business Review.*

Rao, Srinivasa K. (March 1966). Looking Beyond Reengineering, *The Hindu.*

ABOUT THE AUTHOR

Larry Kennedy served as manager of strategic planning for Digital Equipment Corporation's corporate strategy group. He brought to this role several years of experience in strategic and operational planning, engineering management, and market research. Mr. Kennedy's work has included market segmentation and business consulting that contributed to the reengineering of Digital's systems business. Previously, he managed organizations that performed primary market research for product strategy and for technology assessment. Prior to joining Digital, Mr. Kennedy headed product introduction teams for several consumer products at The Gillette Company.

Understanding the Competition: The CEO's Perspective

EXECUTIVE SUMMARY

In February 1996, SCIP and Rutgers University co-sponsored a CEO Roundtable in New York City. This historic gathering, which brought together a group of distinguished corporate leaders to discuss the evolving role of competitive intelligence as practiced by their companies, was organized by Professor Ben Gilad, a SCIP Meritorious Award winner, and produced by SCIP board member Jean-Marie Bonthous, president of JMB International. Provided here is an excerpt.

LINKING STRATEGY WITH REAL WORLD INFORMATION . . . AND BUILDING A SUPERIOR ANTICIPATION CAPACITY

Moderator:

Max Downham, vice president of Mission & Strategy, The NutraSweet Company, Deerfield, IL.

Panelists:

J. Norman Allen, president of New Products and Technology, Duracell International, Bethel, CT.

Gary Costley, former president and chairman of Kellogg USA; dean of Babock Graduate School of Management, Wake Forest University, Winston-Salem, NC.

Robert Flynn, former chairman and CEO, The NutraSweet Company, Deerfield, IL.

Competitive Intelligence Review, Vol. 7(3) 4–14 (1996). © 1996 John Wiley & Sons, Inc.

Ben Gilad, associate professor of Competitive Intelligence, School of Management, Rutgers University, New Brunswick, NJ.

Thomas M. Gorrie, Ph.D., Worldwide Franchise chairman, Johnson & Johnson Medical Inc., New Brunswick, NJ.

Lorry Hathaway, president of Best Foods Grocery Products/CPC International, Inc., Angelwood, NJ.

Jan Herring, senior fellow, The Futures Group, Glastonbury, CT.

Robert C. Mauch, president and CEO, AmeriGas Propane, Inc./UGI, Valley Forge, PA.

Dorothea Coccoli Palsho, president of Business Information Systems, Dow Jones & Co., Inc., Princeton, NJ.

David Thomas, general manager, IBM North America, White Plains, NY.

Willis Wood, Jr., chairman and CEO, Pacific Enterprises, Los Angeles, CA.

Mr. Downham: There is no secret that the complexities and pressures of global competition and the need for competitive intelligence is increasing. Yet, this is not necessarily perceived by many chief executive officers and other senior-level managers. There are several reasons for this.

1. The concept of competitive intelligence is not adequately explained to them. They are not shown how intelligence is distinct in uniquely useful ways from the flood of information that they already receive. They are not shown, in particular, how business intelligence will help them achieve direct bottom-line performance objectives.

2. Knowledge of competitive intelligence has not been part of the business education or career backgrounds of most senior managers. They have little prior experience with the uses and benefits of professionally analyzed intelligence.

3. Competitive intelligence is not considered a fundamental corporate function. It does not have the same importance or status as sales, marketing, research, and production. Competitive intelligence relates to all of these functions but does not easily fit into them.

I would submit to the panel that to be effective the competitive intelligence function must be independent and it must report at a high level.

Many U.S. companies still don't have full-scale competitive intelligence functions, yet most American corporate leaders realize that success depends on looking ahead and moving more quickly than the competition. So the result is a management paradox.

Many U.S. companies still do not have full-scale competitive intelligence functions, yet most American corporate leaders realize that success depends on looking ahead and moving more quickly than the competition. So the result is a management paradox. They know that they must develop long-term competitive strategies, but they also increasingly know that they must respond swiftly to potential opportunities and threats. Those are high-stake responses, high-stakes decisions. If they make the wrong move it can not only cost the company reduced sales and profits, but perhaps the corporation in its entirety.

CAN YOU GIVE US AN OVERVIEW OF YOUR COMPANY'S INTELLIGENCE ACTIVITIES?

Mr. Wood: The business world has changed dramatically, and it has caused Pacific Enterprises to look differently at the need for competitive intelligence. We have begun slowly, setting up a two-person intelligence unit. In fact, their office is one door removed from mine. They don't report directly to me in the line, but they have complete access to me and I see them all the time.

This unit is critical not just in terms of setting up a network within the company that helps us gather intelligence on what's going on with our customers and with our competition. But also in changing the way that the whole organization views competition.

The intelligence effort provides me with information I otherwise would not receive that can change our strategic direction if need be. I get tremendous amounts of information and we disseminate it horizontally throughout the organization.

Mr. Allen: At Duracell, we've established a competitive intelligence network with the operating divisions, and we assign teams of people to accumulate information from the marketplace. This includes everything from divisional input on pricing, promotions, and advertising copy. We look at manufacturing, expansion plans by competition, organizational structures, reorganizations, changes in personnel, changes in distribution strategy. We look at all the areas of public information that you might expect—SEC filings, analysts reports, conferences, meetings, general media. We also collect information resulting from our participation in industry forums and panel discussions where competition is present and try to get a debriefing out of that.

All this information is collected in a standard format using Lotus Notes. It is boiled down and shaped into a financial analysis of the competitor's situation and, hopefully, insights into what might be their objectives with their profit and loss situation, where might they go, and how does that compare to our strategy.

We use this information as the basis for quarterly presentations to top management. We also do special presentations when they're merited, when we come across competitive intelligence that indicates one of the key drivers for our business might be at risk.

Ms. Palsho: Competitive intelligence for Dow Jones is not an event, it's a stream. It's dynamic. You want the information fast, and you want it from trustworthy sources.

We very broadly define competition. We obviously include our current competitors, who've been re-energized based on all that's happening on the information highway. We look at large, well-financed firms that are coming into the online information industry. We look at small firms that have no market at all to protect and are popping up all over Silicon Valley and Route 28 in Boston.

We look at business models. We look at pricing. We look at technology, information, customers, marketing, distribution, and we follow our partners.

We also look outside of our industry because we can apply lessons based on what's happened in other industries, such as consumer products goods.

Dr. Gorrie: Most of our intelligence at Johnson & Johnson Medical comes through our interaction with our customers and through our field forces searching the literature, looking at changes in management, partnerships, licenses, and so on. In the medical advice area we look at FDA approvals for products, patents, and technologies that are getting attention. We spend a great deal of time in the academic area to see what is going on.

While our individual companies focus on specific competitors, as a corporation we use benchmarking to assess our internal performance. We track 25 to 30 major companies representative of the types of businesses we're in. We compare our performance and their performance against factors such as sales growth, gross profit, SG&A—selling general and administrative expenses—and return on investment, as well as tax rates and so on, so we can see how we are moving. We then target areas to improve and invest the savings from those improvements into R&D.

We also seek out companies that are "best in their class" outside of our main competitors and incorporate that information in what we do. We're trying as a corporation to continuously improve and use best practices.

> We've found ourselves talking to competitors about sharing things we would have never shared before, if the information is nonproprietary and nonconflicting. The market now is so driven by costs that it becomes much more of an advantage for all of us if we can share more.

We've even found ourselves talking to our competitors about potentially sharing things that we would have never shared before, if the information is nonproprietary and nonconflicting. But because the market now is so driven by costs, especially in the professional area, it becomes much more of an advantage for all of us if we can share more.

HOW DID YOUR COMPANY GET STARTED IN COMPETITIVE INTELLIGENCE?

Mr. Hathaway: About a year-and-a-half ago, we decided that Best Foods was too internally focused. We didn't have enough of an external perspective about consumers, customers, and certainly competitors. We hadn't been spending nearly enough time trying to put those aspects of the external environment into our strategic planning. So we decided we needed to set up a program of competitive intelligence.

This doesn't mean we didn't have competitive data around. We had a fair amount of bits and pieces of information that were interesting but isolated. They certainly weren't cohesive and they were coming in from various areas of the company. Nobody was pulling these data together, integrating them and trying to understand the "why." Why are competitors doing things, how does this relate to their strategy, and more importantly how does it relate to us?

We had tended, when we had competitive information, to react to it. But the key is to be proactive and do something before the fact, instead of reacting to someone else's actions.

> We found out that we knew more than we thought. We just hadn't been listening to each other, and we hadn't been corralling the information.

We used outside consultants to climb the learning curve. We established a director of competitive assessment—one person reporting directly to me—and began to develop the program. In addition, we started internal networking, meaning we were reaching out to our own organization, which we really hadn't done before, asking for those bits and pieces of information to be sent to us.

We found out, low and behold, that we knew a whole lot more than we thought. We just hadn't been listening to each other, and we hadn't been corralling the information. We then hired an additional consulting firm to come in and do some very important focus projects, because while it's important to get a lot of bits and pieces, you need focus to understand what it is you're doing, and to develop that capability. We picked out two competitors, in directly competitive situations, to evaluate in a comprehensive manner.

This effort included putting together comprehensive profit and loss statements on a comparative basis for the competitors. We developed competitor P&Ls, updated periodically, which are every bit as comprehensive as they have in their own companies, and they're just about as accurate.

The reason for doing that, again, goes back to not just knowing what they're doing, but why they're doing it, as well as how well their plans fit in with their financial capabilities. And all of us who have worked for large companies know that we have financial constraints. You have to get at your competitors' overall portfolio to see what kind of constraints they have managing all their businesses. You can pick out fairly easily where they are if you understand what kind of pressure they're under in terms of the job they have to do in a particular year.

Mr. Thomas: At IBM, we felt it had to start with ownership at the executive level, where the line executives had the role to lead the competitive intelligence efforts. We also knew we had to have a team of individuals who were dedicated to this effort. You often have most of this intelligence already if you can just put it together.

The key for us was executive leadership, getting dedicated teams focused on the companies we felt were going to be our strategic competitors for the long term. Because of our size, our challenge has been to create a cross-functional team because to have an intelligence environment that works, along with sales and marketing we have to include R&D, we have to include our services organizations, and, to avoid being just theoretical, we have to make sure the field operations are brought in.

We have immediate feedback from our field organizations as to what the competition is actual doing in the marketplace versus what we might read in the newspapers that they're going to do.

We have immediate feedback from our field organizations as to what the competition is actually doing in the marketplace versus what we might read in the newspapers that they're going to do.

How Does Competitive Intelligence Add Value to an Organization?

Mr. Flynn: Competitive intelligence information gleaned from different sources around the world is based on what you're committed to doing. Because if you don't know where you're going, any road will get you there. Competitive intelligence allows you to focus on the things that are critical to your success. It's a third or a fourth leg to a very important stool.

> The big payoff for competitive intelligence is that it will point out weaknesses that you have internally because you find the strengths of your competitors. Companies that don't do this will fail.

Mr. Costley: You can't get to strategy if you don't have a vision of where you want to go. Competitive intelligence is a mechanism for looking at the future, so a strategy can be put in place that will give the company an opportunity to adapt to a changing world. At Kellogg, we didn't know enough about ourselves or about our competitors. The big payoff for competitive intelligence is that it will point out weaknesses that you have internally because you find the strengths of your competitors. **Companies that don't do this will fail.**

But competitive intelligence has to be as high up in an organization as it can possibly go, so the information won't be filtered.

HOW HAS COMPETITIVE INTELLIGENCE CHANGED THE COURSE OF YOUR COMPANY?

Mr. Allen: Duracell started marketing our Copper Top batteries in Europe in the late 1970s, becoming the only pan-European competitor using a single brand name, which is our policy worldwide. In the late 1980s, we started picking up competitive intelligence from a number of sources on Eveready's European strategy. They started to go after several of the small regional competitors and purchased three of them outright. That occurred over a period of about two or three years. We picked up competitive intelligence on reorganizations where a U.S. vice president of marketing was transferred to Europe.

In addition, we started to hear rumblings through the trade and in meetings throughout Europe that there was a strong possibility Eveready might decide to continue this acquisition route and then to make its Energizer a pan-European brand, switching all of its acquired local brands to the Energizer name—in effect, to clone what we had done over the prior 15 years.

As a result of that intelligence, we reordered the allocation of our marketing expenditures, creating a war chest for Europe. We increased our trade marketing and focused our advertising copy and our claims work. In general, we went to a heavy marketing defensive posture.

As a result of that intelligence, during planning sessions in 1990 and 1991 we reordered the allocation of our marketing expenditures, creating a war chest for Europe. We increased our trade marketing and focused our advertising copy and our claims work. In general, we went to a heavy marketing defensive posture in Europe that started about 1991, 1992.

In fact, Eveready did do what we thought, and what made sense for them to do—they moved to convert all their acquired brands in Europe to the Energizer.

When we look at market shares in Europe today, Duracell remains the European leader with a 45 percent share. Eveready's share has not grown above the combined shares of the companies it acquired; today, it's around 17 percent. So obviously we feel good about that and it was a direct result of picking up the right intelligence from a number of sources.

Mr. Hathaway: We've been introducing a major new product that is high-risk, high-reward. We developed plans, went through a war game exercise and tried to anticipate, based on our introduction, what the competitors would do so we could change our plans before the fact to protect ourselves.

We brought about 25 of our top people from a variety of categories together for two days. We had three or four different groups representing our company and competitor companies and put together information that we suspected that the competitor would observe. Once we put that together, we formed teams to look at this information and decide what the competitors would do in response to our new product introduction.

The second day was even more interesting, asking, in light of what we anticipated they knew and would do, what should we do initially? So we weren't reacting, we were pro-acting.

We looked at our strengths and weaknesses. Some of the weaknesses are potential vulnerabilities you might be able to do something about, but you can't necessarily correct because every company has its own strengths, whether it's brand image, pricing strategy, geographic strength, advertising spending, product quality, and so on. We found we could do some things that would minimize our competitors' strengths, we thought. More importantly, we could enhance our strengths so that we could use them as a leveraging device to increase our chances to be successful.

As I mentioned, it was significant that we changed our plans as a result of the war games exercise. Something is going to happen differently in the marketplace as a result of investing a lot of people's time for two days and trying to think through how we might increase the probability of our success on something that is very high risk/high reward.

Now, of course, we want to continue to update that intelligence, and we're doing that.

Mr. Wood: Using competitive intelligence, we've already analyzed our competitors to understand what they're doing and how they're doing it. We concluded that they aren't doing that well, they are getting returns that we wouldn't be satisfied with, and they're not taking any earnings away from us. We've been able to use that information internally to give people more confidence and externally with our pricing structures.

Mr. Flynn: There are a number of acquisitions that I made because of competitive intelligence, and there are a couple of what would have been tragic errors that I *didn't* make because of a competitive intelligence.

WHAT DO YOU DO TO ENCOURAGE TOP EMPLOYEES TO SHARE INFORMATION?

Mr. Thomas: My job is to make sure that we do a very candid assessment in front of the other executives, to tell them that you may think your business is here and your competitor is doing this, but here's what we think. Involve their teams, provide them with the tools to input information—we use a worldwide portion of Lotus

Notes to enable us to get day-to-day information. You may see something pop up in Japan, in Asia, or in Europe first and to tie that all together.

It's getting that whole community involved, keeping a cross-functional team on target, creating the periodic follow ups, monthly follow ups, that provide an opportunity to report whether we've done anything to really affect the competition and their ability to hurt us in the marketplace.

Mr. Mauch: The overall importance of getting a "buy-in" on the part of your key executive officers and others throughout the organization. You really have to create a sense of urgency and that's much easier if you're in a situation where employees can see the impact of competitive activity—on the bottom line, and on their future livelihoods, future job prospects, and so on.

Once you do that, you need to carefully select a competitive intelligence officer. They clearly need to have freedom to interact at all levels of the organization, but in our company they report directly to the CEO—directly to me. They participate in all executive committee meetings, all strategic planning meetings, they are a distinct group yet they're part of the mainstream and, as such, they are accepted in the organization.

> You need to create an environment where the competitive intelligence officer can share competitive information with different managers at varying levels of the organization in a way that causes the manager to use the information to solve a problem or to achieve an objective.

One final point: You need to create an environment where the competitive intelligence officer can share competitive information with different managers at varying levels of the organization in a way that causes the manager to use the information to solve a problem or to achieve an objective.

Once a manager anywhere in the company receives help from the competitive intelligence officer that helps to achieve an objective, they will strongly support intelligence activities and, through the "word-of-mouth" network, other employees recognize the potential value to them of having an organized competitive intelligence effort.

WHEN DEVELOPING AN INTELLIGENCE CAPABILITY, WHAT ARE THE FUNDAMENTALS?

Mr. Costley: It has to be at the top because it is basic. It's a strategic function, not a tactical function. It should be more important than marketing because if your strategy is wrong, you'll be spending an awful lot of marketing money on the wrong ideas.

The way we finally got it in place was to convince ourselves and the company that it was an absolutely critical strategic function.

And having done this first, we avoided a big debate over where it would go, whether it would go at the top, and a big debate as to whether you could have a travel budget or not. Because if it's a critical strategic function, it will get what it takes.

> It's very easy for competitive intelligence to get sucked into business plans and stop being a strategic function.

But we kept it completely out of the strategy group so it wouldn't get caught up in business plans. It's very easy for it to get sucked into business plans and stop being a strategic function.

HOW DO YOU BUILD AN ANTICIPATORY MANAGEMENT CAPABILITY?

Mr. Herring: Let's start with whose responsibility is it to anticipate, to be sure that we're not surprised by either opportunities or failures; it's clearly the leadership. They get all of the credit for any success, they're going to take the blame for any failures.

When I joined Motorola as director of analytical research, I was taken aside by Bob Galvin, the chairman. He told me several failures that that company had experienced from not understanding the competition. He didn't want the company to be surprised again. As the senior executive, his responsibility was to prepare the company for the future competition. He believed that companies, like governments, should have their own intelligence capability for that purpose.

Today, you'll find that Motorola's intelligence program is a world-class benchmark. But this early warning or anticipatory capability must be seen as a management priority. The key is the process, not the organization; processes are very powerful, organizations are rather restricted.

So how do you do that? By establishing an early warning process and being prepared to act on the intelligence that it provides. Simply, the early warning process is identifying the most likely threats to your business and the possible opportunities that you could profit from should they occur. Then use your intelligence operations to continuously search for indications that these threats might be developing. Then be prepared to act on them at the earliest possible time. Even if they don't happen, at least you're ready should they occur and you will not be surprised.

What are the key elements in an early warning or participatory capability? The direct involvement of the management team. Senior managers and executives know where their business vulnerabilities are. They also know where and how they would act so that new opportunities surface. They just don't know when.

Identifying these hunches is the trick. Psychologists call this "declarative memory." Most executives have a lot of data in their heads, they just can't put it all together. They don't have time to sit down and figure it out. But usually there's a basis for the actions that they anticipate.

Being prepared to act requires contingency planning. One way of anticipating how you would act is war gaming. You can do the same thing with scenario planning. By understanding what the situation will be like, you're prepared to act effectively.

Being prepared to act requires contingency planning. One way of anticipating how you would act is war gaming. You can do the same thing with scenario planning. By understanding what the situation will be like, you're prepared to act effectively.

WHY DO SOME COMPANIES NOT
HAVE AN INTELLIGENCE CAPABILITY?

Mr. Thomas: Companies don't realize that they are losing customers and become too internally focused or too plan driven versus how are they performing in the marketplace. Unfortunately, the sense of urgency that has to happen sometimes comes at the pain of bad performance in the marketplace.

One way to get people mobilized is by forcing the line management to be the champions, getting the leadership team to ask questions about competitors differently than they asked before.

Why does it go away? Companies get comfortable and they start paying more attention to themselves than they do to what their competitor is doing. We're always looking for this balance of how much do you watch the competitor versus how much do you watch your customer.

> You develop as a result of your success a corporate arrogance. Life is wonderful, and what can you possibly learn from the competition?

Mr. Mauch: You develop or create, as a result of your success, a corporate arrogance. You view your competitors as, and I don't like the word, "inferior" to your company and your company's culture, primarily because you're successful, you're performing well, life is wonderful, and what can you possibly learn from the competition? That's a principle reason why many companies don't become involved in competitive intelligence.

Insofar as the way to cause employees to buy-in, again, in our situation we were performing very well and then we reached a period where there were a number of new small entrants that had nontraditional approaches to the business. Quite frankly, early on they were ignored.

We got into a situation where we began to see some erosion in market share. We responded by communicating this performance to employees at all levels and explaining the consequences of the negative trends that we were seeing, which caused them to rally around the need to do something, to incorporate the competitive intelligence activity as a way to learn and bring about change that would reverse those trends. We, by the way, have reversed those trends.

> Many companies have deluded themselves into thinking they have an intelligence program; they don't. Part-time intelligence is a recipe for failure.

Mr. Herring: Many companies have kind of deluded themselves into thinking they have some intelligence activity, they have an intelligence program; they don't. Part-time intelligence is a recipe for failure, so be careful about that.

The flip answer, in a sense, why they don't have it is because they don't have leadership. People of vision, like Bob Galvin, Bob Flynn, Gary Costley, Dave Thomas. It takes that kind of leadership to create an intelligence organization. The basic problem, however, is ignorance. Some people might say arrogance. There's a fine line between the two.

Mr. Costley: If you look at Apple, if they had had an effective competitive intelligence system in place they could not have made the strategic decisions they made in the early 1990s, because it was obvious to almost everybody except them where that world was going.

That kind of blindspot inside companies will occur if this function isn't in place. It's incredible that so few companies have it and that, of those that do, so many put it in at too low a level.

Developing a World-Class CI Program in Telecoms

Stéphane Marceau and Kenneth Sawka

DELOITTE CONSULTING

EXECUTIVE SUMMARY

Given the liberalization of telecommunications (telecom) markets, the proliferation of new entrants, and the overall acceleration of the industry, telecom providers from around the world are taking a careful look at their competitive intelligence (CI) capabilities. Deloitte Consulting has interviewed several CI leaders from the largest telecom operators in North America, Western Europe, and Australia to identify current CI practices within the telecom industry. Results from these interviews and insights from experience in the field, coupled with internal and external research, allowed us to develop a framework to guide the development of a competitive intelligence program for telecom operators. This article summarizes our preliminary findings.

ompetitive intelligence is rapidly becoming a management priority for operators in deregulated markets. Deloitte Consulting has conducted in-depth interviews with competitive intelligence leaders of eight of the largest telecom operators from Canada, France, Spain, Portugal, England, Italy, and Australia to identify the drivers of CI and, more importantly, to identify current CI practices in telecommunications. The interviews were conducted during the second half of 1998. More than half of the participating operators are incumbents in

Competitive Intelligence Review, Vol. 10(4) 30–40 (1999). © 1999 John Wiley & Sons, Inc.

their respective markets, while the others represent a cross-section of challengers in the wireless, international, and national long distance markets. Results from these interviews and from other expert interviews, coupled with internal and external research in the fields of CI and of knowledge management, allowed us to develop a framework to guide the development of a competitive intelligence program for telecom operators.

THE TELECOMMUNICATIONS COMPETITIVE LANDSCAPE IS CHANGING RAPIDLY

The telecom sector continues to make headlines all over the world. From the *Financial Times* to *Le Monde* to *USA Today,* the press is extensively covering the sector with batteries of experts trying to make sense of the transformation it is undergoing. The fast pace, the competitive intensity of the sector, coupled with the massive investments committed to its growth make it a rather sexy, yet complex topic.

While some countries like the U.K. initiated the liberalization and deregulation process many years ago, most industrialized countries are just opening or opened their markets for local voice telephony to competition several years ago. Clients now have the option to leave, and new entrants are vying for the most lucrative segments of the historical operators. The battle for the client's telecom budget has just begun!

The technological evolution is also driving radical changes in the industry; the Internet is changing its economics as new entrants build networks optimized to carry Internet traffic and as IP (Internet Protocol) networks are used to carry both voice and data. The impact of IP is only one of the facets of convergence, this ill-defined discontinuity in the telecom and Information Technology (IT) environments that has also been a source of speculation for many yeas. Convergence generally refers to the idea that communications are becoming more and more seamless; that you will be able to access the Internet and to send/receive messages from your PC, TV, Mobile handset, Personal Digital Assistant (PDA), and from any other IP-compatible terminal. From a competitive standpoint, convergence also means the ability of a provider to offer more services, in a seamless fashion, to the customer. The race for convergence is now seriously underway. Microsoft's investments in several cable operators are the latest sign that the boundaries between the traditionally separate IT and telecom markets are falling.

OPERATORS ARE INVESTING IN THEIR COMPETITIVE INTELLIGENCE PROGRAMS

The mutation of the competitive landscape is now evident to everyone. There are approximately 140 new fixed operators (New entrants, 1998) that have recently entered or are about to enter the fixed telecom market in Western Europe alone. There are now between four and seven wireless carriers (Cellular, E-SMR, and PCS are examples) in large U.S. urban centers compared to two prior to 1995. The current (but ephemeral) fragmentation of the Internet Service Provider (ISP) markets in developed countries makes it virtually impossible to track the number of ISP players. Just the sheer proliferation of competitors in all sectors of the communications market warrants a renewed effort on competitive intelligence.

Beyond the imperative of building intelligence on direct competitors, the blurring of boundaries between the converging markets requires that providers keep an eye on ancillary players as well. Fixed incumbents are increasingly concerned about the strategies of their wireless competitors, due to the increasing substitution of fixed service by mobile. Just to anticipate attacks on their core fixed-voice business, they also need to include, within the scope of their radar screens, a wide array of competitor types: cable companies (cablecos), satellite providers, ISPs, wholesalers, international providers, public utility companies (gas and electricity provision), resellers, and other key players of the software industry at the edges of the currently defined telecom service market. Incumbents or dominant operators within the most competitive markets are concentrating their CI efforts on their more direct competitors and are monitoring underlying fundamental competitive, technologic, and regulatory trends to palliate for the lack of resources to track even a fraction of the potential competitor base. Regardless of the approach to building competitive intelligence, a study by Deloitte Consulting/The Futures Group revealed that 76 percent of companies recognize that they need better competitive intelligence. Based on our interviews, this figure would be higher for a pure telecom sample. All of the operators we spoke with had, during the summer of 1998, ongoing initiatives to implement a CI program or to improve current ones.

> Beyond the imperative of building intelligence on direct competitors, the blurring of boundaries between converging markets requires keeping an eye on ancillary players as well.

The Competitive Intelligence Program

While there is consensus on the necessity of having a strong CI program as discussed earlier, approaches and intensity levels with respect to CI vary widely between telecommunications operators. Nonetheless, we feel our preliminary research allowed us to develop a model of a world-class CI activity. We found that a prerequisite to achieving world-class CI is a corporate culture that is conducive to information sharing. Another critical success factor is a clear interface between the core CI function with the rest of the organization; both the interface with key processes and the "location" of the CI function will affect the results from the CI effort. A more intuitive and evident quality of a world-class CI function is the relevance and extent of the CI portfolio of services, and how these CI services are used to support decision-making throughout the company. Finally, the technical infrastructure that supports the aggregation, organization, and diffusion of the CI information is found to have a growing impact on the ability of companies to leverage CI as a competitive weapon. Figure 1 illustrates the principal development planes to consider in the design of your competitive intelligence program.

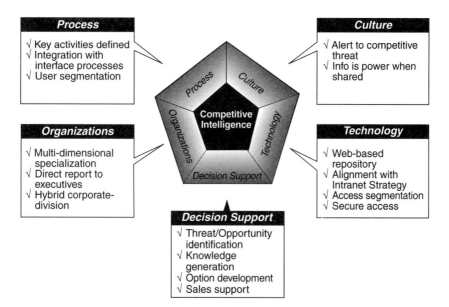

Figure 1   Qualities of a world-class competitive intelligence function in telecoms.

CULTURE: THE "INFORMATION IS POWER" SYNDROME MUST BE NEUTRALIZED

Why do decision makers at some companies consistently receive intelligence that makes a difference, while others receive little more than data summaries? Without question, the one thing that all effective intelligence operations—private sector or government—have in common is direct involvement of senior-level decision-makers. Professor Ben Gilad of Rutgers University, a noted expert on effective competitive intelligence systems, has said "Any intelligence program that is not initiated, or at least strongly backed and used by top management, is doomed to obscurity and lack of real influence on decisions."

Successful programs involve working closely with executives to clearly define their intelligence needs right from the start, to focus the effort, and then keep them involved, not only with timely updates, but also as participants in the process. Executive managers often have excellent sources, and their broad experience enables them to participate effectively in the interpretation of information.

Invariably, there is a wealth of latent competitive intelligence within the organization. Generally, this dormant information is untapped for two main reasons: People perceive that holding onto information gives them additional power; or there is a perception that it would take too much effort to effectively share it. The former cause is sometimes a cultural legacy of the public utility background of the incumbent operator or is derived from the Chinese Wall approach enforced by the regulator. The latter cause is a question of awareness and of having the right communication channels in place.

The "knowledge is power" syndrome was cited as the second greatest barrier to effective knowledge management in a recent study of the dynamics of knowledge creation and exchange (Good practices in knowledge creation, 1998) within large companies. We found it particularly present in newly liberalized operators as the fear of downsizing caused people to hold onto information as an element of job security. The same study found, however, that almost half of the surveyed companies rewarded knowledge sharing to some extent. While we found no operator systematically rewarding information sharing, the emphasis on team and corporate values and the recognition of contribution to the CI process were quite effective tactics in our experience.

We also found that different divisions perceive themselves as competing against each other given the aforementioned overlap of businesses. Once again, there is no silver bullet to alleviate this information-sharing hurdle but to stress the one-ness of shareholder value; that the ultimate goal is not to maximize the profit of a division, but to maximize company profit and cash flow. Another imperfect cure to this problem consists of restricting access to information by division, only keeping part of the CI information accessible by all. At least one of the study participants was considering this configuration, if only on an interim basis. This, of course, is suboptimal as the goal is to increase information flow and channels. One of the lesser known laws of Metcalfe's states that the value of a network is the exponential of the number of terminals (people) using it. Hence, constraining access is constraining the value of the CI exercise.

> The "knowledge is power" syndrome was particularly present in newly liberalized operators, as the fear of downsizing caused people to hold onto information as an element of job security.

A more important, yet simpler way to augment the sharing of CI knowledge is to lower the information-sharing effort hurdle. All but one of the operators we interviewed had a CI hotline. One of the first actions of a CI program should be to implement effective CI collection channels: an 800-number, a CI e-mailbox, and systematic sales and marketing briefings are examples of methods used by operators to tap the company's CI knowledge. Another important consideration is the perceived value that contributors get out of the CI effort. Implementing a systematic and ongoing communication plan, tailored to different user segments, is a way of generating value.

PROCESS: KEY ACTIVITIES AND INTERFACING WITH CORE PROCESSES

One way to both guarantee greater information sharing within an organization and to whittle away at information silos is through a well-thought-out intelligence process. Many telecom companies new to the concept of competitive intelligence typically attempt to identify and produce intelligence on a variety of environmental issues without thinking through the process, program, and organizational requirements of institutionalizing a lasting competitive intelligence process. The result—false starts and an inability to provide decision-makers with actionable information that specifically addresses implications for the company's strategy. Experiences like that are quick to sour senior management on competitive intelligence and is largely responsible for the poor showing of most telecom competitive intelligence programs.

For companies to realize lasting benefit from competitive intelligence that pays dividends to strategy development and execution, it is critical that the competitive intelligence be a systematic, ongoing activity that resides within the organization. The process cycle depicted in Figure 2 demonstrates the key components of that process. Too often, companies believe they can short-circuit the intelligence process and fail to develop one or more of the components. Typically, the analysis and production function is given short shrift, resulting in a poorly conceived program that provides little more than data summaries to management under the guise of intelligence.

No one process can stand alone; all are necessary and add value to each other.

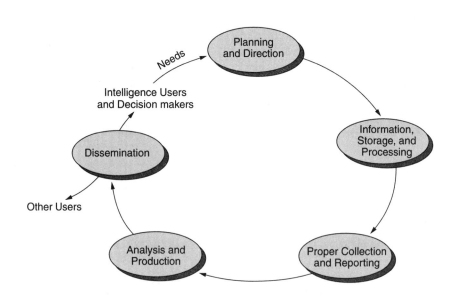

The CI Cycle: 5 Basic Operations Each is necessary and adds value.

Figure 2   The competitive intelligence cycle.

Needs Identification

Successful intelligence systems are, by definition, needs driven and must generate intelligence that meets the explicitly stated requirements of decision makers. We have witnessed several U.S. telecom companies that have established intelligence programs that failed to take into account management's intelligence requirements. In all cases, these programs ultimately devolved into mere generators of information and brought no identifiable strategic value to their organizations.

Planning and Direction

To avoid collecting and analyzing information that is not directly relevant to management's intelligence requirements, careful planning procedures must be part of any intelligence system. The planning component seeks to define specific and focused intelligence collection targets and to identify the most likely sources for that intelligence. It also points out relevant analytic resources within the company that may be tapped to provide expertise and assistance. Careful planning also ensures that scarce intelligence resources are used wisely.

Information Storage and Processing

Efficient intelligence systems make use of information storage, retrieval and searching applications to facilitate the collection retrieval, archiving, and analysis of information. In most cases, these are electronic in nature and typically reside within company intranets or in groupware applications like Lotus Notes. Intelligence systems also leverage information services to acquire and exploit relevant secondary information.

Proper Collection and Reporting

To provide competitive intelligence that is decision-specific and exclusive, intelligence systems must harness both published and nonpublished sources. Harnessing a network of internal and external human sources of intelligence can infuse an intelligence system with unique, new, and competitively relevant information that can provide management with insights and decision options that secondary information alone simply cannot match. Of course, strict legal and ethical guidelines must be in place to dictate how and under what circumstances human-sourced intelligence is collected and utilized.

Analysis and Production

For intelligence to be truly decision-relevant and for it to address future competitive situations, intelligence systems must apply robust analytic techniques and methodologies. Doing so moves the program from providing mere data summaries that talk about what competitors did yesterday to providing analyzed intelligence that anticipates future competitor behavior and discusses implications for company strategy. A U.S. regional Bell operating company relied on specialized analytic techniques—such as alternative outcomes analysis—to anticipate the strategy of several Inter-exchange carriers to compete for local dial-tone service in their operating region. Without analysis, the company would have been left nothing more than a description of how IXCs competed for local services in the past in selected markets—information that is of little value in crafting forward-looking competitive strategies.

> A U.S. regional bell operating company relied on specialized analytic techniques—such as alternative outcome analysis—to anticipate the strategy of several Inter-exchange carriers to compete for local dial-tone service in its operating region.

What's interesting to note about the intelligence cycle's components is that much of the "best" intelligence is sourced for humans, rather than text. And much of that is available from company employees. Further, many companies, despite having huge research budgets and rigorous financial and cost analyses, often don't perform effective intelligence analysis. Good intelligence programs include the use of specific methodologies designed to deal with "soft" or qualitative data, which doesn't fit neatly into the more quantitative tools standard in many companies.

One European operator, for example, possesses an elaborate system that leverages text-mining and topical clustering techniques to exploit secondary data. Their system offers partial mirroring for relevant high-traffic Internet sites, and they claim to have access to 350,000 validated secondary sources, and are adding 5,000 per day. It is clear that from an informational standpoint this company is among the strongest we have seen. However, their overall intelligence process is comparatively weak—it fails to include a rigorous human-source network as well as strong analytic capabilities that can transform the wealth of data into direct, strategically relevant, and actionable intelligence.

In addition, the intelligence unit must ensure its products reach decision-makers in a timely manner. Unless intelligence is delivered to those with both the authority and responsibility to act, *no intelligence has been created*. Key findings must be delivered in formats that not only encourage management to pay attention, but to do something about it. Despite the proliferation of information technology advances that would seem to make timely and effective delivery easy, the intelligence unit must make sure that users are not inundated with e-mails or databases that obscure the intelligence message.

It is not hard to notice how many of the components of the intelligence cycle fit well with existing corporate structures. Leveraging current information technology platforms and information services capabilities can typically satisfy information and storage processing needs. Likewise, companies can properly collect human-sourced intelligence by developing communication procedures around functions such as sales force field-reporting, customer needs'-tracking initiatives, supply chain-management techniques, and other existing business processes. And, sound intelligence dissemination is typically a natural component of executive information systems.

STRUCTURE: THE "OWNERS" OF COMPETITIVE INTELLIGENCE WITHIN THE ORGANIZATION

For most operators, competitive intelligence is generated and managed locally with limited central coordination. The market research group is often already gathering comparative attitudinal information from clients. The network engineers are reading a variety of technical magazines to acquire a perspective on the capital investment- and technology-adoption patterns of their international and domestic counterparts. Of course, senior managers and planners are deploying their individual contact networks, albeit informally, to get hints on what the next move of their competitors might be.

However, these efforts are almost invariably the result of personal initiatives. No one owns the responsibility nor possesses the authority to acquire, process, and disseminate competitive intelligence where it is needed. Although, we found at least one competitive intelligence person (or FTE) within each of the operators we contacted, only half of them had a formal competitive intelligence group. On the other hand, more mature operators had more than 20 people dedicated to the CI effort, not counting the multiple part-time collaborators and liaisons with the CI group. In most cases, it is advisable to assign corporate management of the competitive intelligence and to have cross-divisional processes to feed and disseminate intelligence.

> While half of the operators we contacted had a formal CI group, more mature operators had more than 20 people dedicated to the CI effort, not counting the multiple part-time collaborators and liaisons with the CI group.

Motorola, a pioneer in the area of CI has adopted this type of organization. In the words of the company's CEO: "We have a core intelligence department that numbers circa 10 people. But the divisions have discovered they benefit by having one, two, or three of their own people who are responsible for interfacing with the intelligence department, so the intelligence activity of the corporation numbers between 25 and 30 people. We are a hybrid, with a centralized yet widely disbursed intelligence program. . . . " (Galvin, 1997). A recent study on different aspects of competitive intelligence (Pine Ridge Group, Fairfax, VA) revealed that it was most common to find the CI function within the corporate unit. Another recently published survey sponsored by the Society of Competitive Intelligence Professionals found that most CI operations are under the roof of the strategic planning group. While both findings are somewhat consistent with what we observed in our telecom sample, half of the contacted CI leaders reported directly to the company's board or to a top-executive steering committee. We feel that either configuration is viable but that competitive intelligence should at least be coordinated from the corporate division, given the benefits of information sharing.

In another case, a European telecom company claims that is saved roughly $20 million last year by centralizing the purchase of third-party studies and research. Moreover, to avoid different parts of the organization duplicating research efforts, the competitive intelligence group will finance 20 percent of any study two or more divisions want to do together. Clearly, some element of coordination of competitive research can result in direct and measurable cost savings.

While we recognize that the organization of the CI activity in telecommunications companies is a function of many factors, some of which relate to historic and political considerations, and that each operator will have idiosyncratic needs, we have outlined in Table 1 a generic sample of the desired role split between the corporate and business units.

The rationale for implementing such a *modus operandi,* not only lies in the avoidance of redundancies built into the overall CI effort but, more importantly, in the ability to achieve greater specialization in a holistic context. This latter benefit is particularly important given the increasing complexity of telecom issues and the overlap between the target market of different types of competitors. Today, carriers already competing with mobile offerings are also a threat to the incumbent's fixed revenues due to the increasing mobile-fixed substitution effect. Other nontraditional contenders for the voice (long distance and international) markets are the ISPs and ITSPs that offer IP telephony services. While these are only two generic examples, the holistic perspective will become more and more a *sine qua non* condition for operators as the voice and data, wireless and fixed worlds collide, coalesce, integrate, and merge. The implication is that a parochial and decentralized approach to CI for a full-service provider equates to exposing the organization to a significant competitive blind spot. While limitations apply to the proposed model due to regulatory constraints, the non-transactional nature of the CI operation makes it easier, from a legal standpoint, to build interdivisional bridges within the company. The incumbent will obviously have greater difficulty in getting the corporate CI effort approved if it implies the integration of customer databases of different divisions.

**Table 1   The Split in Competitive Intelligence
Roles between Corporate and Business Units**

Corporate Role with Respect to CI	*Business Unit Role with Respect to CI*
• Info brokerage between business units	• Info brokerage within business units
• Convergence-related analyses	• Sector specific analyses
• Development and maintenance of CI repository	• Definition of CI requirements
• Regulatory-related analyses	• Collection of info through channels
• Library and documentation management	• Performance feedback to CI

DECISION-SUPPORT: THE TOOLS AND TECHNIQUES TO GENERATE INTELLIGENCE

In the end, however, it is the transformation of information into intelligence that provides decision support. Sadly, traditional forms of business analysis—financial forecasting, budget analyses, cost-benefit studies—are necessary metrics to evaluate company performance, but they are not adequate to guide companies strategically, especially in the fast-moving telecom world. They fail to enable them to capitalize on unforeseen opportunities or avoid sudden threats, and to head-off aggressive competitors. The reason we still rely on them? Traditional measures and estimates such as these have for decades represented the ingredients of most forms of typical business analysis. However, they customarily cannot capture external factors that influence corporate performance, the very factors that cause corporate leaders to lose sleep at night.

> Especially in the fast moving telecom world, traditional measures and estimates cannot capture external factors that influence corporate performance—the very factors that cause corporate leaders to lose sleep at night.

Specially designed intelligence analytical techniques can allow for sound interpretation of the external environment and thus support strategic decision-making. This new business analysis must collect and interpret non-numerical data that measures a company's own financial, sales, or market performance. However, it must target information that captures the behavior of competitors, regulators, technologies, and other external influencers in ways that allow for rigorous, disciplined analysis by trained professionals. The end result of this analytic activity is an assessment of what is occurring externally and what it means for the company.

The variety of intelligence-analysis methodologies is too great to cover in one article, and the selection of which methodology to use in which circumstances inevitably falls to the analyst. However, there are about a half-dozen techniques that tend to frequently offer the beleaguered analyst the ability to make sense of confusing data and information that have demonstrated their versatility:

Alternative Outcomes provide multiple explanations for a particular intelligence problem. They are useful when the analyst is facing contradictory or confusing reporting, or when the user demands a discussion of a range of scenarios or wants to build view on the long-term future. We recently conducted a long-term (7-year) scenario analysis with the executive group of a European incumbent operator. The scenarios described to the group were designed to vividly evoke radically different domestic and international telecommunications environments. The scenarios were articulated around drivers pertaining to regulation, technology, markets, competitive intensity, and aggregation level. Surprisingly enough, a show of hands revealed that there was an almost even split between the believers of each of the scenarios. The sheer exercise of sharing mental models can be instrumental in aligning decision-making around one or several corporate goals. Clearly, the business strategies implied by each scenario were quite different. One or two strategic pillars only were appropriate in all cases. The scenario analysis can also surface deficiencies in the overall strategy, holes in the portfolio of assets, or even suggest the imperative of tracking the evolution of given environment indicators as part of the CI process.

Opportunity Analysis allows the business intelligence analyst to think like a decision-maker and identify occasions for corporate action. It highlights the risks and opportunities facing the company as it seeks to influence a particular competitive situation by seeking to answer the question "how?" not "whether?" The first step in using opportunity analysis is to redefine the intelligence problem in the decision-maker's terms. For example, suppose you are concerned that the development of a new technology can significantly lower the entry barriers in segments of the telecommunications industry and make it easier for new competitors to enter the business. Traditional intelligence analysis would examine the technology and likely ways competitors might adopt that technology to enter the selected marketplace. Opportunity analysis, on the other hand, would address the potential effectiveness of measures your company might take to make it harder for competitors to take advantage of the technology proliferation, such as striking technology licensing deals with select partners or re-examining your own research and development strategy to develop and own obsolescing technologies.

Linchpin Analysis forces analysts to change or abandon their basic assumptions about a competitor and re-think their lines of analysis. Linchpin analysis is valuable in challenging conventional wisdom, avoiding stereotypes, and mitigating against groupthink and other bureaucratic analysis derailers. It is a technique that constantly challenges the analyst to carefully consider all the competitive possibilities and explanations for competitor or other-actor behavior, and prevents analysts—and their intelligence consumers—from being locked into a single, narrow view of an industry actor.

To illustrate, telecommunications companies frequently worry about their competitors' pricing structures, and make assumptions that a competitor's costs are either higher or lower than their company's. Analysts are inevitably clouded by those assumptions when making judgments about the competitor's behavior in the marketplace. Linchpin analysis asks the analyst to evaluate the competitor's behavior, temporarily, under the assumption that their cost structure is the opposite of what the analyst believes it to be. Then, alternative explanations become clear to the analyst that may have otherwise been missed if the analyst remained locked in his or her paradigm of the competitor.

Event Analysis isolates external events and highlights trends, commonalties, and aberrations in competitor or other-actor behavior. It is a technique that most analysts probably already employ automatically, though not with the rigor and discipline that it demands. When done systematically, it is a technique that can uncover important trends about a company's competitive environment and serve a strong early-warning function by highlighting when a competitor or other player is straying from its normal course of behavior. Simple chronologies of competitive activity, an isolated look at patterns evident from recent acquisitions, or a geographical representation of competitor activity all make for excellent event analysis applications.

Analysis of Competing Hypotheses allows different analytic judgments or explanations of competitor behavior to vie for each other's attention. It also enables the analyst to perform consistency checks on the gathered intelligence to look for questionable or non-diagnostic reporting.

Human nature forces us into a pattern of analysis that fails to perform the consistency checks mentioned above. Typically, analysts pore through a body of intelligence reporting and try to develop in their mind explanations—hypotheses—of what is happening and why. An analyst will select a hypothesis that appears sound and keep hold of it until a sufficient quantity or evidence refutes the hypothesis. The analyst will then pick another possible hypothesis and perform the same exercise until he has selected the "right" one.

The problem with this approach is that by evaluating each hypothesis in isolation, the analyst fails to assess the entire body of collected intelligence against the hypotheses. A better way is to evaluate several hypotheses at once, evaluating collected evidence against each one simultaneously. This not only makes it clear which hypothesis is supported by the greatest quantity of (hopefully) credible evidence, it enables you to check the validity of your sources at the same time by eliminating that evidence which fails to support any hypothesis or supports most or all of them and therefore, is not diagnostic.

TECHNOLOGY: GETTING THE INFRASTRUCTURE IN PLACE

The wealth of various information flows to manage as part of a CI program requires appropriate support from the IT function. Most operators have a CI web site on their Intranet, or are in the process of developing one. Interestingly, all of the interviewees with a CI web site reported having developed it in-house.

The main considerations in the design of a CI web site revolve around security of access and relevance of content. Beyond a secure technical environment, the strategic nature of competitive intelligence calls for a stratification of user access. As an example, the board of directors will have "unrestricted read" access to all CI information, including the operators' competitive Achilles' heels versus its competitors; the sales person or product manager on the other hand, will not have access to this area of the web site. Our experience with CI projects has taught us that people will be more inclined to volunteer information if they are confident that it won't fall into the wrong hands. As an interim measure for the dominant full-service providers, sections of the CI web site could be maintained and viewed by only one division (e.g., wholesale) to avoid regulatory related problems. Although we have not seen this configuration, some interviewees were considering it.

The relevance of content speaks to several aspects of the web-site information and navigation. A multi-dimensional organization is desirable. As an example, information about the latest webphone offering should be accessible through queries by sector, competitor, or by competitive trends. The deletion of obsolete information is also imperative. As for any web site, frequent content updates are required to build a regular audience. Several operators claim to be investigating push technology (e.g., Pointcast) to customize the information flows to users. On a given day, the product manager for the prepaid fixed voice services would be downloaded a different set of information than the R&D manager. Clearly, the administration of this level of customization is rather resource intensive but the benefits could be substantial.

In line with our view that integration of the CI activity to core process is fundamental, we also believe that the CI support tools should gradually align with the users' workflow. As an example, we implemented a software tool supporting a newly designed strategic planning process for an RBOC. The software supports various brainstorming and decision-making sessions involving different stakeholders at different times; one of its module allows the capture of CI information.

Do's and Don'ts

Telecom companies in the early stages of creating a business intelligence capability, should be cognizant of likely start-up problems faced by most newcomers to effective intelligence systems.

1. Intelligence needs are poorly defined.

Unless intelligence activities are demand-driven, intelligence units risk spending scarce resources answering questions that will not result in helping make a better decision or action. Without face-to-face interaction with intelligence users, intelligence producers rarely are able to deliver intelligence that can be acted on—somewhat like launching a new product without input from the consumer; while it may succeed, the risks are certainly higher.

2. Intelligence efforts are not organized.

Effective intelligence units find that between 50 percent and 80 percent of the information they need is available from their own employees; the trick is to develop procedures to make the extended network of employees aware of how they can contribute.

3. Creating databases and calling them intelligence.

One consumer products company attempted several times to let a Lotus Notes discussion database serve as the basis of its intelligence program. Employees were expected to populate the database with information about competitors, markets, and technologies. Yet, the efforts failed because employees were not educated on what specific information was needed by management nor were they empowered to make any effort to ask their contacts for specific information.

4. All or nothing: Gun-shy versus overkill.

Inexperienced intelligence units are often reluctant to report valid intelligence when they mistakenly believe they do not have enough proof, often causing their organizations to miss opportunities; conversely, when they do report it, the message often gets lost as they attempt to overwhelm management with details. Most often, personnel untrained in using or reporting qualitative information, particularly in highly quantitative cultures cause this.

Some of the lessons we have learned over the years are summarized in Table 2.

Decision-makers at organizations that have overcome these problems receive concise answers to specific questions rather than thick binders of outdated information. Another significant benefit is that employees share more relevant information across traditional boundaries. Effective intelligence units bring personnel from all departments directly affected by a specific analysis or event. Because they are actively engaged in the gathering and interpretation of information, actions and decisions are made much more quickly and effectively.

It remains a puzzle why many companies in the telecommunications industry continue to squander millions of dollars without even the most rudimentary looks at the environment and then ask why a new initiative failed. While this may have been acceptable during times of heavy regulation,

Table 2   Competitive Intelligence Do's and Don'ts

Do's	*Don'ts*
• Involve the decision-maker from the beginning	• Don't start the effort unless there is a senior management champion
• Focus on only a few intelligence topics	• Don't try to serve everyone
• Focus the effort on key decision-makers and issues that will make a difference	• Don't become just another corporate staff; ensure that each intelligence activity clearly supports a decision or action
• Establish an integrated analysis and collection unit	• Don't focus only on published information
• Establish legal and ethical guidelines early	• Don't create databases until the process and procedures are proven

there is no excuse in a deregulated competitive environment to fail to take a judicious look at how competitive factors affect strategy. Intelligent companies have figured out a better way.

In summary, the success of the competitive intelligence program relies on a deliberate and holistic approach that is explicitly supported by senior management. Centralization may increase the implementation challenge, but a high degree of coordination at the corporate level has become a requirement in a converging communications environment.

A holistic approach to competitive intelligence also requires that all components of the intelligence cycle be represented in the intelligence program. Companies that rely on published, secondary information over human intelligence collection, or fail to develop strong intelligence analysis capabilities, will not recognize the strategic benefits competitive intelligence can deliver. Integrating all elements of the intelligence cycle, and striking the right balance among them, is the key to moving your competitive intelligence program from an information-based, research library function to a program that is delivering forward-looking, strategic analysis in ways that support both the development and execution of corporate- or business-unit strategies.

As competitive intelligence continues to become a vital part of telecom company operations, we believe that there are more and more opportunities to explore linking competitive intelligence programs and processes to other information-generating assets. Competitive intelligence systems can be complimentary to a customer relationship-management process, for instance, adding to the body of actionable information that is available to a sales team by summarizing and analyzing recent competitor overtures to high-value customers. Ultimately, competitive intelligence managed under a holistic and coordinated approach should be a critical information input into telecom managers' efforts to plan and run their business.

In the end, an unfavorable asymmetry of competitive information between yourself and your competitors has the potential to be disastrous in the increasingly volatile and merciless telecommunications market.

ABOUT THE AUTHORS

Stéphane Marceau is a manager, specializing in competitive strategy, in the European Telecom & Media Group of Deloitte Consulting. He is based in Paris, France.

Kenneth Sawka was a senior manager in Deloitte Consulting's U.S. Telecommunications and Media Practice and the practice leader of The Futures Group's Competitive Intelligence practice. He is now vice president and director of the intelligence systems consulting practice at Fuld & Company, Inc.

REFERENCES

New Entrants. (1998, Third Quarter). *FT Telecoms World,* 13–18.

Galvin, R.W. (1997, Spring). Competitive intelligence at Motorola. *Competitive Intelligence Review,* 8(1), 3–6.

Good practices in knowledge creation and exchange. (1998). *Focus Central,* London.

Small but Powerful: Six Steps for Conducting Competitive Intelligence Successfully at a Medium-Sized Firm

Amy Berger

LARSCOM INCORPORATED

Y ou've heard it before. It's not what you know, but rather *who* you know. As a competitive intelligence professional in a medium-sized firm, I can attest that this adage still holds true.

When I began work at Larscom I wasn't quite sure what the terms "competitive intelligence" actually meant. I had never worked for a manufacturing firm before. My lack of understanding caused me great concern because one of my charters as market research manager is to monitor the competition. As a 1.25-person, brand new department (my boss helps me as time permits) with a limited budget, nonexistent mission statement, and no personal contacts in my industry, I had to get creative—*and FAST!* After a year and a half I have learned that personal contacts, both inside and outside the organization, are invaluable.

Here are my six keys to success for conducting competitive intelligence in a small- or medium-sized company:

Competitive Intelligence Review, Vol. 8(4) 75–77 (1997). © 1997 John Wiley & Sons, Inc.

STEP 1: CREATE AND USE AN INTAKE FORM

My department's most prized customers are our sales representatives and product managers. I was hired, mostly, to keep these hard-working professionals well informed about competitors, industry trends, and events. In order to institutionalize our department's data collection and dissemination services, we created Larscom's *Competitive Intelligence Hotline*—my office telephone number at present! Because our Market Research/CI department was new when I first arrived, I decided it wouldn't hurt to keep track of these customer requests. Therefore, at the end of the year if necessary I could use the record to justify the department's existence.

After making it through my first year with flying colors, I continue to use my *Customer Request Intake Form* to monitor the quantity and nature of my colleagues' queries. I include this information in my monthly status report to my boss. It also enables me to determine patterns in customer needs. Occasionally, I will use this helpful record to determine how, and when, I answered a specific question. I then save time in my search when a similar question arises. I highly recommend you implement this intake process in your CI department.

> I use our *Customer Request Intake Form* to monitor the quantity and nature of my colleagues' queries. I include this information in my monthly status report.

Our form has room for four basic information categories:

1. Name of Requester.
2. Date of Request.
3. Department of Requester.
4. Description of Information Request.

By means of this simple spreadsheet, you can keep track of every request you receive—whether it's a price for a competing product, or an in-depth analysis of an industry trend. This record will help you see where your time is spent. It will also provide a nice list of accomplishments when it's time for your performance evaluation at year's end.

Feature	Larscom Product	Competitor 1 Product	Competitor 2 Product	Competitor 3 Product
Shelf				
Multiple DS3s				
Multiple DS1s				
Supports Imuxing				
V.35/RS449				
HSSI				
Channelized DS3				
Clear Channel DS3				
Ethernet mgmt. access				
SNMP				
Telnet				
Software Download				
BERT				
ATM Migration Path				
System List Price				

Figure 1   Sample competitive product spreadsheet.

STEP 2: ASK FOR COMPANYWIDE HELP—AND BE SPECIFIC

The first thing I did when I arrived here at Larscom was to compile a list of our competitors. The second thing I did was send it around asking for help. I was anxious to hear about things like competitor product announcements, prices, mergers, and new strategies, but I neglected to ask for these things. I simply sent out the list to the 20 people in my department (marketing) and asked for "any information" about our competition.

Our Product: *Product Name Here*
    Strengths/Advantages:
-
-
-

Competitor 1 Product: *Product Name Here*
    Strengths and/or Weaknesses:
-
-
-

Competitor 2 Product: *Product Name Here*
    Strengths and/or Weaknesses:
-
-
-

Competitor 3 Product: *Product Name Here*
    Strengths and/or Weaknesses:
-
-
-

What This Means to You:
-
-
-

How to Respond to Your Customer
-
-
-

THANKS FOR YOUR GREAT WORK!

Figure 2   Sample sales guide sheet.

The response was slim for many months. I was often asked for details on a competitor that I just could not track down. After feeling much aggravation, I hired a few, affordably priced outside consultants to make up for the personal industry contacts I lacked. After several long months, my fellow marketers began to give me articles, price lists, e-mail with information nuggets, and so on.

After even *more* months, companywide colleagues started to contribute to my files as well. Today, I am well known enough to receive priceless tidbits of information about our competitors from folks who stop me in the hall. But it has been a long, arduous process.

I strongly suggest that you send out your list and call for help to *everyone* at the company—not just members of your department. Explain in detail the type of information you need to make it easy for your fellow workers. I have never offered an incentive in the form of a gift or cash—again due to budget limitations. If you have the money, however, it might speed up your collection success. I'm told this methodology has worked for some fortunate CI managers with deep pockets. If you have a lean budget, however, your personal courtesy, eagerness to help in the future, and simple thank you notes will keep your in-house data channels open.

> I am now well known enough to receive priceless tidbits of information about our competitors from folks who stop me in the hall.

STEP 3: START A CI NETWORKING CLUB

As a new Market Research Manager, one of my self-imposed charters was to quickly learn some creative, effective competitive intelligence techniques. I decided to create a safe environment in which I could do just that. I remembered that a few former colleagues had also taken competitive intelligence positions with manufacturing companies in the area. I called four people I knew and asked if they would be interested in forming a market research analysts' supper club. I explained the purpose of the group as I saw it: for research professionals in similar positions to share ideas about business online services, market research databases, analytical tools, CI consultants, conferences, and so on.

Proprietary information about our individual company's activities would not be shared. The point was to learn systems and processes from each other and to offer general moral support. The group has grown to 13 members and is now in its second year of meetings at local, fun restaurants, where we gather once every two months. The information and support I have gleaned from my affiliation with this club has been invaluable. I highly recommend bringing together fellow professionals that you trust and enjoy on a regular basis. The CI rewards are tremendous!

> Composed of colleagues from different firms, our networking supper club allows us to learn systems and processes from one another and to offer moral support.

STEP 4: GET TO KNOW YOUR SALES FORCE

One of the most enjoyable and well-received projects I completed during my first year as Market Research Manager was a summary sheet/matrix of our top accounts and how our equipment was being used there. This spreadsheet was designed for in-house use only, and was based solely on input from the sales force. Having to rely on people I barely knew—and they didn't know me from Adam—was challenging, to say the least. First, I had to get a buy-in from the VP of Sales so he wouldn't feel I was invading his people's time. Second, I had to ingratiate myself to a sales force of 30 or so reps that were scattered around the country. Because I had never met many of these individuals, I had only my telephone skills and prayers to rely on!

Via e-mail, assorted phone calls, and help from our regional sales managers, I was able to put together the major accounts matrix. It took me longer than I wanted, due to my learning curve (technology and people), but the accounts matrix received a very positive response when it was finally distributed. With the extra time I spent getting to know our sales executives, and inviting them to know me, I developed strong business relationships with many of them.

If your customers include your sales representatives, be sure to interview your vice president of sales. Gather information about each sales representative: his/her territory, family background, years with the company, and major accounts. If I had done this prior to implementing the accounts matrix project, I could have completed it faster. Our sales reps are hardworking people who are constantly in the "trenches"; they are an excellent source of news about competitors, new products, pricing, and the industry in general. Now, these individuals often "gift" me with excellent pieces of data that help me do my job. Larscom's direct sales force are my office angels!

STEP 5: SEND THANK-YOU NOTES AS OFTEN AS POSSIBLE

After being in the corporate world for almost two decades, I have learned one very important thing: *People like to be acknowledged.* While this is true for life in general, it is extremely significant in the working world. As

CI professionals, we often must rely on sources other than ourselves for data. Whether you're hiring a consultant or depending on your colleagues to help fill in the blanks, it is important to recognize people for their contributions. After I completed the accounts matrix I cited above, I sent a handwritten Thank-You note to each and every salesperson who participated. I stayed late at the office one evening to write out the notes. That one simple and inexpensive gesture on my part has gleaned an enormous amount of actionable information from the sales executives. I have also created (thanks to the student intern hired earlier this year) a standard department Thank-You note to give to donators to our company library. Recipients of such correspondence now eagerly donate publications of all kinds, rather than just throwing them away.

> Handwritten Thank-You notes to the salespeople who participated in compiling an accounts summary matrix helped to cement ongoing relationships.

One you become well known as the company "information guru," people will inadvertently drop articles on your chair, stop you in the hall to divulge an industry tidbit, and/or e-mail you with some gold nugget of competitor information. Acknowledge these folks as much as possible with a Thank-You note.

STEP 6: KEEP YOUR EYES OPEN, STAY FOCUSED, AND EXPECT MIRACLES

As a CI professional, you know that you cannot do it all. Tracking hard to get information can be frustrating and tiresome. I remember desperately needing to get a retail price on a competitor's unit. After sending out e-mails to the sales force, calling third-party distributors, and even trying the 800-number at the competitor's office, I had no luck. I decided to let it go and told my client that the information was not to be had. The very next day, however, an article with that precious price arrived on my terminal via our company's online news service. What a nice surprise!

Working for a medium-sized company is like living in a small village. Association with fellow employees is easy. I have received obscure bits of information from colleagues based in many different departments. Colleagues that hear significant news items commuting to work in the morning often keep me informed. I find that where I least expect it, I receive important information that enables me to better assist a customer.

> Working for a medium-sized company is like living in a small village.

A medium-sized company of 250 persons often has the same desire for global leadership as a corporate giant with thousands of employees. With some corporate creativity, a willingness to listen, and a smile, you and your CI department can help *your* firm realize its strategic vision.

ABOUT THE AUTHOR

Amy Berger was the market research manager at Larscom Incorporated, a leading provider of high-speed wide area network (WAN) access equipment. She completed her undergraduate work at the University of California, Berkeley and received a master's degree at the Massachusetts Institute of Technology. Ms. Berger was the first market research manager hired at Larscom, and laid the groundwork for the company's growing market research department. She is the author of *The Twenty Year Itch: Confessions of a Corporate Warrior* (1999). Ms. Berger is currently the president of Berger Technology Research in Fremont, California.

Leveraging Information for Action: A Look into the Competitive and Business Intelligence Consortium Benchmarking Study

John E. Prescott
UNIVERSITY OF PITTSBURGH

Jan P. Herring
HERRING & ASSOCIATES

Pegi Panfely
ENRON ENERGY SERVICES

EXECUTIVE SUMMARY

In 1996, the American Productivity and Quality Center (APQC) initiated a benchmarking study of competitive intelligence practices. John E. Prescott and Jan P. Herring were the subject matter experts for the study, which focused on identifying the processes that leading-edge companies use to implement their competitive intelligence programs. Pegi Panfely was the project manager for the six-month Competitive and Business Intelligence Consortium Benchmarking Study. *The following is adapted from a presentation about the study findings, given last May at the Society of Competitive Intelligence Professionals 12th Annual International Conference & Exhibit in San Diego.*

Competitive Intelligence Review, Vol. 9(1) 4–12 (1998). © 1998 John Wiley & Sons, Inc.

Mr. Prescott: This study began with the fundamental question "How do we create actionable intelligence in our organizations?" This is what most managers want from their CI operations.

In this regard, the study tried to uncover the mechanisms and processes that several of the best companies use to create actionable intelligence. Seven key findings were the output of the study. Each of these findings re-enforce and support one another. The best-practice companies did pieces of each of these. Not all of the best companies did all seven in an excellent way, but they all did parts of these seven, and many of those parts in a very excellent way.

Mr. Herring: We tried to look at how world-class companies were operating differently from others—the activities and processes that separated them from everybody else. The significance of this study was that it focused on issues other than dollars, people, and types of organization. The premise was, "It's what they do that makes them different." We looked at the seven findings and asked, "What is the pattern? What is there about these intelligence activities that reveals something important about world-class operations?"

FINDING 1: EVOLVING, YET STABLE, CI INFRASTRUCTURES

Mr. Prescott: The first finding was that CI systems that effectively create actionable intelligence evolve over time, while creating stable mechanisms to allow this evolution to happen in a systematic way.

Table 1   Seven Key Findings of the APQC Study

1. Evolving, Yet Stable, CI Infrastructures
2. Decentralized—Coordinated Networks
3. Responsive IT System Operating as a Learning System
4. Linkages
5. Customer-Feedback-Implementation Linkage
6. Hypothesis-Driven Recommendations
7. Institutionalizing Intelligence Cultures

We discovered some of the stabilizers of these CI systems, and some of the indicators of why CI programs evolve over time.

We identified four key stabilizers in our benchmark companies:

1. Personnel

The personnel in the best CI operations had a good deal of experience in their companies, and had a good deal of experience in their industries. For example, individuals at Merck had an average of 25 years of experience in the pharmaceutical industry.

We also often saw that CI personnel in these companies moved from CI operations into line positions. In fact, one of the curses that some of the companies mentioned to us was that if you were good in CI and you came up with some good business opportunities, you might have to go over and manage those operations that you created.

We also saw certain traits in the personnel. Fidelity has about 18 different business units. And while they have CI groups in many of those, one of the ways that they leveraged their personnel was to say, "Okay. You have created a CI operation very well in this division. Why don't you go over and help start the CI operation in another division?" With 18 different business units with different types of competitive intelligence needs, it became a way for Fidelity to use its personnel in very creative ways.

> CI personnel at Merck had an average of 25 years of experience in the pharmaceutical industry.

2. The Development of Networks

One of the consistent findings among the best companies was that they developed their networks slowly over time. The CI networks were not put in place all at once. Different parts of the network were selected at different times for development. The companies asked, "How do we systematically expand that network over time?"

3. Dispersed Champions

Often when we talk about champions, we talk about that top manager or CEO, and the need for him or her to be the champion. However, we found that there were at least three levels of champions in most of the best companies. First, there were the top corporate-level management champions. Second, there were the champions who ran the CI department. Third, most of the companies had developed local champions throughout many parts of the organization.

For example, Pacific Enterprises has many champions dispersed throughout its organization, in varied parts of the company. When an issue arises that the CI department needs to work on, these dispersed champions can be called on for their advice, and the champions can bring issues to the CI department as well.

At Bell Atlantic, one of their managers, who was a champion, was also involved with cross-business relationships. So, while she was a champion in one of the divisions, she also oversaw common issues facing Bell Atlantic across all of its different divisions. This role enabled her to say, "Since these different businesses are all facing similar issues, how can we coordinate the CI operations in a similar manner?" And so, we see champions playing a very significant stabilizing role.

> At Pacific Enterprises, the CI department can ask CI champions dispersed throughout the company for advice, and the champions can bring issues to the CI department as well.

4. Substitutes for Champions

In many operations, you don't always have a champion. What do you do if you don't have a champion? One of the ways to compensate is to develop substitutes for champions. Examples that we saw included mission statements, codes of conduct, and business processes. Each of these were very important ways to substitute for the missing champions.

At Kodak, part of the mission statement for its CI operations is to avoid surprises. Taking this notion of avoiding surprises, and diffusing it through the various organizational members, serves as another way of stabilizing the operations.

At Xerox, we saw an example of business processes as a substitute champion. Xerox integrated its CI operation with its Total Quality Management process. So, when you think about TQM, you think about CI and vice versa. That was significant in helping to stabilize the whole process.

Next, we found indicators of how these organizations evolved their processes over time. Pacific Enterprise is a good example. It has gone through three phases of evolution. The first phase was to get the organization to take an external focus. Its management felt that they weren't looking outside of the company as much as they should. In the second phase, management asked, "Okay. We have gotten people to look outside. Now, how can we influence the actions and the thinking of top management?" Now in the third phase, they are asking "How do we get individuals further down in the organization to engage in a two-way conversation with those at the top in order to see how CI can be dispersed throughout the whole organization?"

And so, we see that these benchmark companies were very good at evolving themselves, yet creating stable mechanisms so they didn't fall apart.

> Xerox integrated its CI operation with its Total Quality Management process.

Mr. Herring: I was able to compare the APQC "best practices" companies with another world-class group identified in an Industrial Research Institute (IRI) study and found some strong similarities. For example, we found that the IRI group consisted of companies that had been in existence seven or eight years. They had average staffs of 14 people. Clearly, there is a benefit to longevity in this field. But you have to perform well to last that long.

The second level of IRI companies were almost at the world-class level. They had been operating for about four years. They had staffs that averaged six people. As they went about producing CI, they got better at it over time, and they learned how to adapt to changes in management. They provided management with what it wanted and needed.

The companies that are just getting started, the CI operations that have been around for about a year, have maybe one or two CI professionals, and some only a part-time CI employee. This is not a critical mass. They are not going to have a truly effective operation with this kind of very limited capability. They are not going to have the core institutional knowledge John talks about. This is the challenge to companies starting up a CI operation.

FINDING 2: DECENTRALIZED-COORDINATED NETWORKS

Mr. Prescott: The second key finding is that benchmark organizations create decentralized, yet centralized, networks. What I mean by that is if you look at many of our operations, we are in companies that are diversified. Whether we are diversified because we have many different business units, or because we just do different things within our organizations, we see that this diversification creates a need for a network that is decentralized.

As CI professionals, we can't be experts in everything that we are doing. So, how do we leverage this limited set of resources in our organization to create actionable intelligence? This is why networks are required to be decentralized, yet coordinated.

At Kodak, they have a "managed matrix." At the corporate level, there is a group of individuals that specifically examine key competitors. They have another group that monitors technologies. They have yet other groups doing CI within functional areas such as manufacturing.

> Kodak has a "managed matrix" that allows management to draw on individuals at different levels, or different geographical locations, to help them address an issue.

Now, when you start to think about problems that Kodak might have or issues that the company wants to look at from a competitive intelligence perspective, management can draw on individuals at each of these different levels, or different geographical locations, to help them address an issue.

That is a very creative way of using resources and leveraging them over time. The decentralized network is its very strength. The network was developed over a considerable period of time and CI personnel continue to nurture this network.

In virtually all benchmark companies, networks were developing. A different type of example is provided by Xerox, which has a decentralized organization. One of the activities that they created was a CI supplier network—CI individuals from different parts of the organization, who would get together on a periodic basis—monthly, or every six weeks, to discuss key questions such as, "What are we doing in CI in our units? What are some of the issues that we are running into? How are we solving some of our problems?" A key purpose of the supplier network is to share knowledge and best practices with each other. That was one way in which they created their network.

Bell Atlantic created a network in a slightly different way, but very effectively. They had a similar CI forum, where the individuals in CI would get together and discuss some of their issues. But they would also bring in an executive. At every one of these meetings, they would have an executive raise such issues as, "What are some of management's intelligence needs? What are some of their intelligence challenges?" And then the CI people would be able to interact with this executive to see how they could jointly address these problems. This was a creative way of addressing these issues.

Another company approached networks in a different way. Let's say that you are going out on a plant tour, or that you are going to another country for some type of business. You, as an individual, regardless of your position in the company, could contact the CI department. The CI department then would find out who else in the organization, or what studies they had that could help you to prepare for the plant tour, trade show, or geographical tour.

In addition to helping you to prepare your intelligence questions, they would also bring your competitive knowledge up to a high level by drawing on the resources that currently existed. And so, we see these decentralized-coordinated networks as a very important way of creating actionable intelligence.

Mr. Herring: The networks may be there, but it takes leadership to maintain them and to get everyone to work together. This is what takes place at the world-class companies. At the same time, by using networks, by involving different people over time, you are creating a broader acceptance of CI within the organization. Networks have a very important role to play in this.

Networks are important not only for information collection and analysis, but for changing the way that people interact. Getting a group of diverse managers together to work on a CI project is a good way of transferring knowledge and getting them to act on the intelligence that is produced.

FINDING 3: RESPONSIVE IT SYSTEMS OPERATING AS LEARNING SYSTEMS

Mr. Prescott: The third finding that we have is what we called, "responsive information technology (IT) systems" that operate as learning systems. One of the issues that always concerns me is that some people think that information technology is CI. I am uncomfortable with that type of notion. Intranets are being created within all of our companies. So, we all have an intranet now, and we think it is going to solve a lot of our competitive intelligence problems. And, indeed, it does address many of those problems.

We found two key traits within this finding: One was that the best companies are fostering cooperation between different functions. Let me give you an example from what is happening at Merck. The IT specialists, the vendors, and the corporate librarians—Merck is having those groups work together and coordinate their activities to create greater efficiencies, rather than having everybody going out and looking for their own vendors and creating their own information products. The three groups are working together, creating real efficiencies, and leveraging the IT needs.

Next, they incorporate managers' needs, and thus address an effectiveness issue. The cooperation established between suppliers and users is creating very powerful information technology platforms.

The second issue is the information technology platform itself. If you could have what you wanted in an IT system, you would want it at a very low cost. You would want it to be very adaptable. You would want it easy to use. You would want it to be self-maintaining.

Well, Pacific Enterprises created such a platform as a discussion forum which does all of those things. They created it in-house and it requires hardly any maintenance because it self-cleans itself. It establishes a way to discuss key issues and allows people throughout the organization to share their knowledge. It is very adaptable because you can bring new topics in and take other topics out as needed. Their discussion forum is a very powerful tool.

As another example, Xerox uses intellectual capital databases. They have a database that catalogs all of the intellectual assets that they have throughout the organization. And so, if you are working on a project, you can get into that database to see who in the organization may be able to assist you.

One other characteristic we found with the best companies' information technology was the ability to catalogue information that could be shared and coordinated. The companies found that different individuals would go out and commission the same type of study, generating excess charges. They decided to catalogue all the studies that they had to see what they already know before anyone commissioned another study. That's another way in which their information technology systems have been working as good learning systems.

> Pacific Enterprises created an in-house IT platform that allows people throughout the company to share their knowledge, bringing new topics in and taking old topics out as needed.

Mr. Herring: John says that an information system is not *the* intelligence system. He is very right about that. World-class companies—the Mercks and the Pacific Enterprises—actually created their information systems to support their intelligence operations. They may have purchased systems, but they adapted them to fit their CI needs and their company cultures.

Each company has a different set of needs. You will need basic platforms and databases, but eventually you also will have to create your own information system to support the types of CI operations and user needs of your company.

As John has said, the information system is not the first thing you do. It should be the last thing you do after you have put in place the right people and the right processes. Then you institutionalize the intelligence operations and make them more effective by bringing in the advanced technology.

FINDING 4: LINKAGES

Mr. Prescott: The fourth finding involved linking up the strategic planning process of organizations with the tactical part of the organization. We found that the best organizations did this as a circular process.

Bell Atlantic, for example, started by defining its key intelligence questions. From the key intelligence questions, they were able to ask, "What are the strategic issues that we have to focus on?" Those strategic issues then were filtered down to the tactical units. From the tactical units, intelligence and other issues were filtered back up to the strategic level, which then set this whole process off again. And so, we saw this very circular process of linking strategy to tactics simultaneously and interactively, in a very positive way.

We also saw symbiotic relationships being developed. Local champions dispersed throughout the organization would identify key issues they had to deal with. They then filtered those up through the organization and noted their impact on the strategic part of the organization. Then, the strategic group filtered down the appropriate tactics to the local champions. And so, we saw a whole set of symbiotic relationships that allowed the organizations to link up their strategies with their tactics.

Mr. Herring: Regarding the strategic-tactical linkage, this is fairly complex. It involves taking strategic intelligence and, at some point, transferring it into the operational end of the business, and maybe into sales. This finding says you've got to have intelligence woven through the whole business cycle. That is different from the way we usually think, where we provide both—but separately—strategic intelligence and tactical support. To create a process that provides the intelligence throughout, from strategic planning to operations and sales implementation, is a difficult task.

The challenge for us as CI professionals is that we are of two different mindsets. Often, the person who does strategic intelligence analysis thinks in longer terms, maybe years. The person who is working day-to-day and supporting sales and operations has a different mindset, thinking short-term, quick turnarounds, and being there when they need you in the sales effort. Our challenge is to find the ways we can bring those two intelligence mindsets together, so we are working the complete business cycle.

FINDING 5: CUSTOMER FEEDBACK-IMPLEMENTATION LINKAGE

Mr. Prescott: The fifth finding identified was the relationship between receiving a request, obtaining feedback, and implementation/follow-through. Initially, we thought each was a separate activity relatively independent of the others. What we found in these companies was that the customer identification, need identification, feedback, and implementation is one process. One of the best examples is what Merck is doing.

Merck has a very nice process of saying, "Okay. If you have a request as a manager, here is a form." Now the CI people would say, "As I understand this request, here is what you want, and here are the deliverables, the findings." They will go through this process to make sure that everything was on schedule. Then, when they delivered their products, they would also get feedback related to the same form of how well they did. Now, I am simplifying this, but it was a very nice process that linked the customer request to actual implementation. And then, they could even tie it to performance evaluation for the CI personnel, a very nice-type interactive process.

As another example, Bell Atlantic does not consider a project done until there is implementation. The CI people make sure they are in constant contact with the managers to say, "Okay. What has happened with this project? We have spent a lot of money. We have spent a lot of time. This was an important intelligence topic for you. Now, how is implementation occurring?" They would also ask if they could assist in any other ways to achieve high levels of implementation.

Bell Atlantic doesn't consider a CI project completed until the findings are implemented by management.

Mr. Herring: In the evaluation process you must find a way to identify and measure the intelligence being produced, but you must also define the actual need itself, and define the successful application of the intelligence.

This is a complex process, but it is something that these world-class companies have found ways to do. It makes them more effective. By working the evaluation process into the intelligence production process, they are creating something that adds value to the whole competitive intelligence effort.

FINDING 6: HYPOTHESIS-DRIVEN RECOMMENDATIONS

Mr. Prescott: The sixth finding involved the question, What role should CI personnel be adopting? We found that at the best companies the CI personnel considered themselves, in my words, hypothesis testers. They were analysts. They would not say, "Here is a key question that can't be answered by going into a database." But, rather, "Here is a key question for which we have developed a hypothesis." Then, the next question was, "How do we go out and try to address this hypothesis?"

When we examined some of the activities that they were doing, they were centered around creating value-added products.

One of the key aspects of this approach used by analysts was an appreciation for the importance of formatting the deliverables. Many of the analysts figured out the important format in which to deliver findings to management. They tried to deliver their products in a context that was appropriate for the organization. Here's an example of how one company learned from their experiences. There was a merger in Europe. At this company, the CI people put together a report on the merger. Because the organization was geographically dispersed, they gave this report to the European managers, the North American managers, and the "rest of the world" managers.

With the merger set in Europe, they adopted a European context. One of the things that they learned from this, in terms of putting the report into a proper context for managers, was that the

European loved the report; the Americans found it to be a good, interesting report; and the rest of the world said, so what? And so, the CI people learned very quickly how to put a report in context and format it in ways that the managers could use to create actionable intelligence.

Mr. Herring: This was probably the least satisfying result for me. We all believe that we have got to produce intelligence that has implications, and foresight, and contains recommendations. But we didn't get any closer to how they do it. We have some excellent analysts in these companies. When we would ask, "Now, tell us again. How do you do this?" they would scratch their heads and say, "Well, you know, it is just the way we do it." Therein, lies the challenge to use in the field.

In my government experience, we always said there were three essential elements in any analytical effort. The first is knowledge about the subject that you are analyzing. The second is clarity of thought—that is, how you organize and relate the data, and then communicate the information so that the user understands how you came to your conclusions. In drawing your conclusion, there is a very important third element called judgement. The first two elements we can teach. Judgement is something we cannot. It's a part of you. Analysts must have good judgement, or they can't draw the right conclusions.

As a profession we need to do more to teach intelligence analysis. In my own experience, there are two very important attributes to effective intelligence analysis: credibility and anticipation.

Nobody is going to believe you unless you have credibility. That was one of the strong suits at Merck. These people, with an average of 25 years in the business, had an enormous amount of credibility. And so, when they offered their conclusions—while they couldn't always articulate how they got there—they were believed.

The second attribute is anticipation. This is the ability to assess a current situation with an intelligent mind and be able to put that situation into a future context. Anticipating how that current situation is likely to change and its implications for your company and/or business is a learned attribute.

FINDING 7: INSTITUTIONALIZING INTELLIGENCE CULTURES

Mr. Prescott: Our last finding is critical to the future of CI. How do we get our organizational members to do CI when many times it is not part of their jobs? What we saw was that the best practice organizations were doing three broad sets of things. They were (1) sensitizing the firm to CI; (2) demonstrating their CI capabilities; and in some cases, (3) providing CI training.

At Bell Atlantic and in many of the best companies, they would go on the road to say to their people, "These are the capabilities that we have in-house." Bell Atlantic actually has what they call "tailgate meetings," similar to tailgate parties you'd see at football games. For instance, in their telephone operation, they have a lot of warehouses with individuals who are in the field installing and repairing telephone systems. They would go into those facilities to work with these individuals and teach them what CI is all about: "These are the things to look for." Moreover, they would try to identify some of the issues the field personnel were dealing with so that the CI group could lend some assistance.

Pacific Enterprise created war games for the managers in the company, to sensitize them to CI issues. It was a very successful process.

Some organizations actually gave tangible rewards. Bell Atlantic, for example. Not a lot of money, but little gifts here and there, to say thank you for giving us this intelligence, working with us in this process.

One of my favorite incentives was at Fidelity. To help their sales force with CI, they created a "Jeopardy" game. They gave the sales force a lot of information prior to the sales meeting. Then, at the sales meeting, they played "Jeopardy" to allow the sales force to see how much of this they actually absorbed. They have a lot of fun with this game at the sales meeting. The sales people like the process and its helps institutionalize CI issues.

To help their sales force understand CI, Fidelity created a "Jeopardy" game played at sales meetings.

Another aspect of institutionalization involves CEOs or top managers. One of the roles that we see CEOs playing is that of CI champions. At Pacific Enterprises, the CEO was the champion of the operation. Structurally, in the executive offices, there was the CEO's office, a boardroom, and the CI professionals. And so they had very close contact with top management, which is usually not the case. At this company, it worked well.

Another way to institutionalize CI was to require it in their strategic and operational plans. So, when managers developed their business plans, their strategies, and their tactics, they had to justify the CI implications.

We also saw that in many of these organizations, including Xerox, Bell Atlantic, Fidelity, and Merck, CI was becoming an increasing part of everyone's job.

Let me briefly summarize. These seven findings re-enforced CI's role in the organization and helped to thread each part together. And the best companies worked on each of these seven areas in a highly interactive way. I would view each of the findings as an objective. Then, I would measure my CI operations relative to how well we were achieving each of the findings. Finally, I would establish a process for achieving improvement relative to the level achieved in each finding domain.

> In many of these organizations, including Xerox, Bell Atlantic, Fidelity, and Merck, CI has become a growing part of *everyone's* job.

Mr. Herring: At Motorola, my old boss, Chairman Bob Galvin, talked in what I call "modern parables." He called me in one day and said, "I want to tell you about a situation I have faced." He went on to say, "Well, I recently made a bad decision. I had to make this tough decision and I thought I had all of the information I needed to make it. I made the decision with all of the information I had at the time." And he concluded, "It was wrong. I found out subsequently that there were one or two people in the organization who had some vital information about that issue, and had I had that piece of information I would have made a different decision."

Now he asked, "Did I make the wrong decision?" And, of course, I thought it was a test. I responded, "No. Those folks should have shared the information with you so you could have made the right decision." He said, "That is what I want you to do. I want you to get out among our employees and be sure that everybody knows that their job is to share competitive information with us. We need to be sure that that competitive intelligence, market intelligence, and technical intelligence gets to us. I don't want to make the wrong decision. I want people to share it with me."

That was one of our goals at Motorola, to create a sharing culture in that company. So, the employees knew he needed their information. If they didn't, they couldn't share it with us. I think that is the secret of the Japanese intelligence programs. It is a sharing culture. The President of a Japanese company visits with a government official. He comes back. He has learned something about a competitor's technology. He gives it to the planning department and it shows up on the salesman's or the R&D manager's desk the next day.

Everybody in the company has to have that sharing culture. The competitive intelligence process helps us to accomplish that.

For more information about *The 1996 Competitive and Business Intelligence Consortium Benchmarking Study,* or to order a copy of the study's *Competitive and Business Intelligence Report,* call the American Productivity and Quality Center at 800-776-9676 or 713-681-4020, or visit the APQC Web site at http://www.apqc.org.

APPENDIX: STUDY OVERVIEW

Methodology

The study used the American Productivity and Quality Center's four-step benchmarking methodology:

- Plan
- Collect

- Analyze
- Adapt

Plan

The study team, comprised of John E. Prescott (Professor, University of Pittsburgh), Jan P. Herring (Herring & Associates), and the APQC team, formed a consortium with 28 companies that sponsored the study (Table 2). The sponsor companies are representative of a broad range of industries including pharmaceutical, insurance, telecommunications, energy, and others. In June 1996, the consortium met to cooperatively design and develop the contents and structure of the study, including the study scope and data gathering instruments.

The sources used to select innovative companies included secondary research supplemented by the first-hand experience and knowledge of Dr. Prescott and Mr. Herring. Roughly 94 companies were identified and asked to participate in a screening process. Respondents were thoroughly screened by using a two-phase approach. First, an intensive detailed screening questionnaire was administered. The field narrowed to 16 respondents, who were asked to participate in a phone interview. During the phone interview, the respondents were given the opportunity to clarify responses and elaborate with more detailed information about their competitive and business intelligence operations. The quantitative and qualitative results of this

Table 2   Sponsor Companies

• Allied Signal Aerospace	• Nationwide Insurance
• Arthur Andersen	• Northern Telecom
• Astra Merck	• Pacific Bell
• Boehringer Ingleheim	• Pfizer, Inc.
• Bristol-Myers-Squibb	• Public Service Electric & Gas
• British Telecom	• Rockwell International
• Chevron Corporation	• Shell
• Novartis	• Stentor Canadian
• Educational Testing Service (ETS)	• Texas Instruments
• Embraco	• United Parcel Service (UPS)
• Ford Motor Company	• USAA
• Kaiser Permanente	• Warner-Lambert
• Lanier Worldwide	• Wisconsin Electric
• MAPCO (Mid America Pipeline Co.)	• Wisconsin Public Service & Gas

process were analyzed by the consortium and discussed in detail during a second group meeting. From the data and knowledge gathered during this process, the consortium selected seven companies to participate as partners in the study (Table 3).

Collect

The best practice partner group, seven stellar companies representing industries such as the pharmaceutical, telecommunications, energy, consumer products, and others, participated throughout the remainder of the study by providing detailed information and insight into their competitive and business intelligence operations. Partner companies were investigated for further insight through a four-hour site visit and a self-administered questionnaire. During the site visits, a subset of consortium members traveled to the partner companies in order to participate in discussion and to experience the intelligence operation first hand.

Analyze

The results of the screening process, the detailed data collection and the site visits were fully analyzed by subject matter experts and APQC. The knowledge created through the study was organized into seven compelling ideas, which we have termed the key findings. The study team prepared a detailed final report around these seven ideas.

Adapt

In order to facilitate a transfer of the knowledge across all participating companies, a final meeting of the consortium and the best practice partners was held in January 1997. Best practice partners and the subject matter experts gave insightful presentations on the knowledge created by the study process. The workshop was enhanced through implementation planning and other group activities.

Table 3   Partner Companies

• Bell Atlantic	• Merck & Company
• Eastman Kodak	• Pacific Enterprises
• Fidelity Investments	• Xerox Corporation
• Ford Motor Company	

About the Authors

John E. Prescott is a professor of business administration at the Katz Graduate School of Business at the University of Pittsburgh. His research focuses on CI and the network of relationships among a firm's industry, strategy, organizational processes, and performance. Dr. Prescott has extensive experience in the design and management of CI operations, has published numerous articles in academic journals, and is the editor of two books, *Advances in Competitive Intelligence* and *Global Perspectives on Competitive Intelligence*. He also is the executive editor of *Competitive Intelligence Review*, a founder and past president of the Society of Competitive Intelligence Professionals and a recipient of the Society's Meritorious Award. Dr. Prescott earned his doctorate in business administration at Pennsylvania State University.

Jan Herring is a founding member of the Society of Competitive Intelligence Professionals and a recipient of the Society's Meritorious Award. He is currently the principal partner of Herring & Associates. Mr. Herring was director of intelligence at Motorola, where he designed, developed, and managed that company's highly acclaimed CI system. Before that, Mr. Herring served 20 years with the U.S. Central Intelligence Agency as an intelligence officer. His last government assignment was National Intelligence Officer for Science & Technology. Upon leaving the government, he received the Medal of Distinction, the Agency's highest award. Mr. Herring is the author of the book *Measuring the Effectiveness of Competitive Intelligence: Assessing & Communicating CI's Value to Your Organization.*

Pegi Panfely is a manager of Competitive and Business Intelligence at Enron. Working closely with product development and sales, she is initiating processes for centralizing and communicating this vital information across the company. Ms. Panfely was formerly a senior benchmarking specialist for the International Benchmarking Clearinghouse, a service of the American Productivity and Quality Center (APQC), and was project manager for the six-month *Competitive and Business Intelligence Consortium Benchmarking Study* in 1996. Prior to joining Enron and APQC, she managed research projects for the marketing research department at ComEd in Chicago.

Organizing the Competitive Intelligence Function: A Benchmarking Study

Conway L. Lackman, Kenneth Saban, and John M. Lanasa

DUQUESNE UNIVERSITY

EXECUTIVE SUMMARY

This article provides information on the current state of industry practice in the areas of competitive intelligence and market intelligence, and—building on a process model the authors previously developed—discusses how to take a closed-loop intelligence process model and evolve it into a living, breathing organization. A benchmarking study of 16 companies was conducted to determine how the market-intelligence function is structured in these enterprises. The study's purpose was to obtain information that can be used as input for organizing and staffing of a market-intelligence function. Implications of how to take a process model and change it into a workable, effective organization are discussed.

INTRODUCTION

Competitive intelligence (CI) is a strategic tool that enables senior management to improve its competitiveness by identifying key driving forces and anticipate future market directions (Kahaner, 1996). It is the process through which information from multiple sources is gathered, interpreted, and communicated. Competitive intelligence can provide support for

Competitive Intelligence Review, Vol. 11(1) 17–27 (2000). © 2000 John Wiley & Sons, Inc.

strategic decision-making, early warnings of opportunities and threats, competitor assessment and tracking, and advice on effective implementation. It is proactive, opportunistic, and forward thinking (Montgomery & Weinberg, 1998). Today, more companies are attempting to incorporate some form of CI into their organization (Tresko, 1999). With the competitive nature of the marketplace, companies are finding they have less room for mistakes. The consequences of executing a business strategy without having actionable competitive intelligence are serious (Bernhardt, 1994). Despite the recognized significance of CI in an organization, little research has been done to demonstrate the process for effectively organizing the intelligence process (Rose, 1999). This article briefly describes a closed-loop model previously developed by the authors. It then presents a review of previous research and the results of a benchmarking study to answer questions regarding resources and organizational commitment in the development of a competitive intelligence function. Combining previous research studies and the benchmarking report, this study represents information about the organizational strategies of 569 companies.

CLOSED-LOOP MODEL OF COMPETITIVE INTELLIGENCE

The authors have developed a closed-loop model that incorporates various functions into a market intelligence system. The functions include: *identify users, assess their intelligence needs, identify sources of information, gather information, interpret information,* and *communicate intelligence.* The closed-loop model is shown in Figure 1. Central limitations of these models include lack of benchmarks to analyze trends and reveal problems versus symptoms, that is, low product-line margins (Bartholomew, 1999).

Identify Users

The market-intelligence process should begin and end with the users. There are two categories of users: strategic and tactical. Strategic users employ information to set and deploy long-range business strategy, while tactical users deploy information to enhance immediate decision making and programming. Although the initial emphasis should be on strategic users, tactical users should become involved as the process becomes institutionalized.

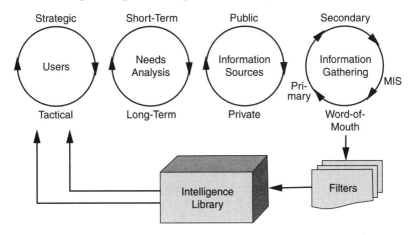

Figure 1   The closed-loop model.

Assess Intelligence Needs

This is a critical component that is sometimes overlooked and yet is the key to the success or failure of the intelligence function (Montgomery & Weinberg, 1998). There are certain guidelines a company should follow to assess the immediate and long-term intelligence needs of users. A company should establish a mechanism to continuously assess their needs. For example, a management process could be applied before and after the strategic planning process. Then, the needs must be prioritized and a future plan generated.

Identify Sources of Information

There are many diverse sources of information such as customers, competitors, associations, employees, and company records. From some of these sources, information is actively sought and for others it is accidentally found. Another critical stop is to properly align user needs with the information constantly flowing into the system from numerous sources. Many sources are housed within the organization itself. Sales reps, customer service agents, employees with relatives working for competitors, are all rich sources of information. Although CI is often thought of as corporate espionage, much of the competitive intelligence is readily available in untapped public sources.

Gather Information

Companies gather information from four basic areas: secondary data, primary research, word-of-mouth communication, and management information systems (MIS) or information within the databases of an organization.

Interpret Information

The next phase includes the compilation of information from these various sources. Zaltman and Barabba (1993) compare it to a knowledge loom that weaves together various types of marketplace information.

- *Filter:* A filtering process must sift through the large volumes of data and selectively choose which information is significant and to whom. In that sense, one can minimize information overload and information anxiety. This process can be benefited by technology.

- *Intelligence Library:* This model proposes a departmentalized library as a repository for intelligence and a focal point of the entire intelligence process. The library should also be at the heart of the secondary data collection. A retrieval system should be user-friendly to encourage utilization.

Communicate Intelligence

The key to success of any CI system is the infusion of market intelligence into the institution's strategic business process. Communication can take many forms, such as competitive profiles, executive summaries, electronic mail, briefings, and executive meetings. The form (personal or systematic) presented should be consistent with the desires of users.

In the next sections, literature is reviewed and we discuss the results of a benchmarking study conducted to determine how to take this process model and develop it into a living, breathing organization that is an effective, integral part of the company.

PREVIOUS RESEARCH ON ORGANIZING THE INTELLIGENCE FUNCTION

While there is overriding consensus supporting the value of CI, business executives are generally dissatisfied with the performance of their "intelligence systems" in place. After studying 104 corporations, Swaka, Francis, and Herring (1995) found that on a scale of 1–10, the average effectiveness rating was 5.9. To understand where this "ineffectiveness" originated, three studies were identified that provide a rich description of current practices by U.S. firms on organizing the CI function (Prescott & Bhardwaj, 1995; Jaworski & Wee, 1993; Prescott & Smith, 1989). These studies looked at various organizational issues regarding the placement of the CI function and the commitment of resources to the intelligence function. The Prescott and Bhardwaj study examined 390 different companies; the Jaworski and Wee study examined 138 companies including 22 telecommunication companies, 11 packaged food companies, and 95 pharmaceutical companies; and the Prescott and Smith study looked at 95 different companies.

Organizational Location of CI Programs

The location of CI programs is important because it often influences reporting relationships, budgets, and the type of projects undertaken. It is clear from the studies that there is no single organizational structure used by the majority of firms. Table 1 shows that the most common organizational location of this function is either in the marketing or planning departments.

Human Resources Allocated to the Intelligence Function

Table 2 shows the human resources allocated to the intelligence function as reported in the three studies. The data includes 593 observations, and

Table 1 Organizational Location of the CI Function

Study	Marketing	Planning	Stand Alone	R&D	Other
Prescott & Bhardwaj, 1995	40%	32%	9%	8%	11%
Prescott & Smith, 1989	40%	50%	0	0	10%

Table 2   Staff Allocated to the CI Function

Study	Average No. Employees	Average No. Full-Time Professionals	Average No. Part-Time Professionals	Average No. Clerical Staff
Prescott & Bhardwaj (390 companies)	4.5	3	.5	1
Jaworski & Wee (22 telecomm.)	3.15			
Jaworski & Wee (11 pack. food)	12.65			
Jaworski & Wee (95 phar.)	2.58			
Prescott & Smith (95 cos.)	5	3	1	1

indicates there is wide variance in the employees allocated to this function. The data shows the average number intelligence staff to be 5.6—which lowers to 3.8 after adjusting for the potentially skewed results from the packaged-food industry. As shown, CI staffs normally constitute professional-level employees.

Financial Resources Allocated to the Intelligence Analysis Function

The average budget reported for the CI function also shows significant variance—from a high of $651,000 to a low of $350,000—creating a variance of some $301,000 per study. While difficult to explain, the authors suggest that the variance may stem from a variety of factors such as industry type, goals assigned CI, location of CI function, and so on. Table 3 shows the financial resources allocated to the intelligence analysis function.

Table 3   Budget Allocated to CI Function

Study	Size of Budget
Prescott & Bhardwaj (390 cos.)	$350,000
Jaworski & Wee (22 telecomm. cos.)	$363,000
Jaworski & Wee (11 packaged food cos.)	$651,000
Jaworski & Wee (95 pharmaceutical cos.)	$391,000
Prescott & Smith (95 cos.)	$550,000

BENCHMARKING

Benchmarking activities can generally be divided into two types. The first is the formal *partnership-based* approach that is presented in most books, journal articles, and conferences. In a partnership-based benchmarking study, the best-practice information is developed through a formal sharing relationship with a single best-practice organization.

A second approach to benchmarking can be used when the formal partnership-based approach is not appropriate. This second approach, sometimes referred to as *preliminary or fast-track* benchmarking, is used to obtain information about industry practices when costs or time constraints prevent partnership benchmarking, or when the goal is to obtain a broader set of best-practice information than can be obtained from a single or small number of partners.

In this study, the fast-track benchmarking approach was used to obtain information on various practices involved in the organization of the market intelligence function.

DESCRIPTION OF THE BENCHMARKING STUDY

A benchmarking study was conducted to determine the organizational structure of the competitive intelligence function in various companies. Telephone interviews were conducted with market intelligence directors from 16 companies considered leading organizations in market intelligence, as recommended by experts in the field. These leaders were:

- Minnesota Mining and Manufacturing (3M)
- Arizona Public Service Company
- AT&T
- Eastman Kodak
- US West
- Aluminum Company of America (Alcoa)
- Bayer
- Pittsburgh Plate Glass (PPG)
- Allina Health Systems (Minneapolis)
- Astra Merck

- Blue Cross of Illinois, Iowa, Minnesota
- Health Net (CA)
- Health Partners (Minneapolis)

The purpose of the telephone survey was to address the following questions:

- How is the competitive intelligence function structured within organizations?
- What are the personnel requirements of CI?
- How does the library fit organizationally into the intelligence process?
- How is intelligence stored and communicated?
- How is the CI function evaluated?
- What is the philosophical approach to CI within the organizations?

Details of the responses to these queries are presented in the Appendix. A general summary of the responses follows each key to the Appendix as denoted by Q.1–Q.17.

SUMMARY OF RESULTS

Organization of Marketing Intelligence Function

- There is no single organizational structure which is used by the majority of firms. (Q.1) Flat organizations were the modal case—25 percent.
- The CI function is usually housed in the marketing/marketing research (46%) or sales (14%) departments. (Q.2)
- At most companies, the CI function relies on internal sources. (Q.3) Two-thirds source outside, less than 6 times per year.
- When CI personnel had both market intelligence and marketing research responsibilities, the marketing research responsibilities took precedence (90%) and the intelligence shifted to a secondary function. (Q.4)
- Those organizations with a more established CI function had senior management playing a critical role (67%) in the assessment of intelligence needs. (Q.5)

- When a company emphasized active participation among all company personnel to gather intelligence, the CI function seemed to be more effective (40%). Many used some form of multidivisional teams (70%) to gather the intelligence. Training programs, motivational programs, and other incentives were used to capture word of mouth. (Q.6, 6A)

- The number of employees staffed in the intelligence function varied depending on the size of the organization (the larger the organization, the larger the CI staff) and the length of time the intelligence function has been in place (the newer the CI function, the larger the CI staff). (Q.7)

3M

At 3M, the corporate position of CI is part of the marketing department. The CI department does most of the analysis, while everyone within the company does data gathering and assists with the analysis. 3M believes internal people should do CI gathering to get more buy-in and to get better use of the intelligence. 3M uses the multi-division team approach. In these multi-division intelligence teams, people from manufacturing, the lab, R&D, marketing, sales, and a variety of functions are included.

> 3M uses a multi-division team approach, in which people from manufacturing, the lab, R&D, marketing, sales, and a variety of other functions take part in data gathering and assist with analysis.

Competitive intelligence is critical at 3M and the company undertakes numerous activities to nurture this culture. 3M trains its personnel through formal training seminars to gather information. They bring in outside experts to conduct the seminars. A recent two-day conference (which included 95 VPs) devoted half a day to CI. 3M has its own CI group, started 12 years ago, which has 1,200 members. They invite nationally recognized experts to address CI issues.

PPG

Competitive intelligence at Pittsburgh Plate Glass (PPG) is positioned in the marketing research function. It was originally placed in the controller's department, but that didn't work due to the lack of commitment and support from the chief decision-maker. It was recommended that the chief intelligence officer (CIO) should report to the CEO. With unneeded channels in the communication process, there is the likelihood of distorted or lost information.

PPG formed six CI cells that were organized within business units and serve as information-gathering groups. This is a cross-section of disciplines headed by marketing which includes engineering, manufacturing, sales, etc. The CI cells meet quarterly at a minimum. The CIO is a part of each group and provides the big picture. The members of the CI cells contribute what is going on in each of their divisions. Part of the meeting is devoted to the CIO asking what are the needs of the group. Everyone at PPG is involved in intelligence. An example given was of a shipping supervisor calling with information.

At the introduction of the CI function to PPG, the CIO did a great deal of "selling" throughout the glass group. The CIO's role was to present CI as interesting, sexy, and fun. The CI group provided AWARENESS presentations. These were to educate and to sell the value of the function at the start. In the first year, 20 to 30 seminars were held. (To get the group's attention and spark a level of interest, the CIO wore a trench coat and hat and played the theme from Pink Panther as he walked in.) Counter intelligence training was also provided.

Personnel / Staffing

- Education levels were high for CI personnel; a master's degree was required by most firms (80%). (Q.9)
- Seasoned veterans were best suited for the director position. (Q.10)
- Those surveyed suggested individual characteristics needed for success in CI (in rank order of importance) included: being well-connected in the industry, having integrity, being creative, having imagination, expressing curiosity, having good networking skills, and possessing good communication skills. (Q.11)

3M

The director of CI at 3M believes that the stage of development should determine the number of people in the marketing intelligence function. He believes that the earlier development stages needed more individuals to get the MI function running. In CI at 3M, they claim that there is no game plan, no blueprint. Intuition and good people skills are needed.

Kodak

Those individuals who do competitive intelligence need different mindsets than those who do traditional marketing research. Although Kodak hasn't quite pinned down what it takes to be good at CI, they look for experience in the company, including a strong sense of curiosity and a lively interest in things that are not internal. "We look externally in the future rather than internally backwards." They want courageous people who will stand up for things. And they require imagination, tenacity, and networking skills.

> Although Kodak hasn't quite pinned down what it takes to be good at CI, they look for experience in the company, including a strong sense of curiosity and a lively interest in things that are not internal.

PPG

According to PPG, the CIO should be a seasoned veteran who knows people throughout all facets of the industry. The CIO should be well-connected. Those who work in the CI function must have a reputation for integrity. The CIO needs excellent communication skills, clever interrogation skills, and to know how to get more than is given.

Role of the Library

- Although the placement of the library varies from company to company, 70 percent had it housed within the marketing function. (Q.12)
- 90 percent of directors believed the library should be within the marketing function. (Q.12A)
- Much of the CI literature (90%) suggests that the library would be a strategic asset for the CI function. (Q.13)
- 96 percent of leading intelligence companies such as Kodak are looking to add the library to the CI function. (Q.14)

Storage and Communication of Intelligence

- Electronic storage was frequently used (80% often used) and allowed for easy access by many within the firm. (Q.15)
- 80 percent of health care organizations provided monthly newsletters with competitive information. (Q.16)

- 94 percent considered technology as a critical component in the success of CI. The results suggest technology drives CI. (Q.17)

Kodak

Kodak stores its information in the form of business reports. They have a standard format, in which reports are numbered and entered into the business report INFO system. Anyone in the Business Research organization can access these reports. Kodak has been storing reports in this manner for 20 years. In the competitive area, Kodak has COINS, which stands for Competitive Information Systems. This is a collection of news clippings and published information about competitors that any employee can access.

HealthNet

Competitive intelligence comes from three sources at HealthNet: public information, regulatory files, and tracking of individual rates and benefits. A total of 127 data elements are tracked to determine what's happening with management, ratings, and financials of competitors. Demographic components will soon be added. They want to be able to cross-reference price with demographics and with D&B information to determine what's happening in a segment of a market, what they're buying, and what's growing.

US West

US West's CI practitioners keep intelligence they have created in a variety of formats but primarily in document form. They publish a regular newsletter and are developing a dissemination approach that will rely on visual and textual information. One example of the visual approach is that they are establishing a "war room." In this highly visual environment they are planning displays to show competitor alliances, mergers and acquisitions, and the progress being made by various customers and competitors in their marketplaces.

US West's CI staffers have also developed report templates that enable them to boil down their communications into a two-page format. They have developed several processes that they use to involve people at all levels of the organization in the intelligence process:

- *War Games:* Using simulation software senior executives play the roles of competitors in various marketplace scenarios. This enables senior executives to more accurately recognize competitor information that they require.

- *Quarterbacking:* US West turns conference attendants into an information-gathering activity. Under the direction of a "quarterback," conference attendees are given specific intelligence-gathering targets. They are debriefed upon return by the quarterback and other CI staff.

- *800 Number:* An 800 number has been established so that people throughout the organization can call in with information whenever they hear it.

- *Senior Management Briefing:* They are trying to initiate a monthly 45-minute briefing of the executive staff to disseminate recent competitor intelligence. They hope that discussions following these briefings will better elicit the intelligence needs of the executive staff.

Corporate Approach to Competitive Intelligence

3M
In assessing senior management needs at 3M, CI does *not* ask senior management "What intelligence do you need?" but asks, "What are you worried about?" "What decisions are you going to be making in the next few years?" According to 3M, the focus is on SUPPLY, not demand. The emphasis is on how management will use the intelligence. Intelligence must be focused on the executive decision. They believe that CI is still a relatively new field. 3M views the 1990s as the Decade of Knowledge. Companies must do everything to bring in knowledge. Companies must be learning organizations. "You must out-learn your competition to survive."

Alcoa
At Alcoa, there is an evaluation plan that determines what information is working and what is useful. This occurs on a continuous basis. Competitive intelligence interacts with senior management in many ways. There are "scoping meetings" and "kick-off meetings." At these meetings, senior management is kept abreast of what's going on.

Allina Health Systems
The implementation of the CI function has started out rather slowly at Allina Health Systems. Other projects deemed more important have delayed the implementation. To many at Allina, being a non-profit organization which serves the community does not allow for competitive analysis to be a top priority.

AT&T

There is enormous awareness of CI by everyone at AT&T. It is part of the corporate culture designed into the organization top-down. It has been in place for a number of years. This mentality is reinforced over and over through their reward system. Intelligence is a big part of the vision statement. What drives the intelligence focus is the customer focus. Making the customer the critical component of everything they do is what drives everyone at AT&T to know as much as they can about that consumer.

US West

The intelligence group at US West is undergoing a transition from a project-orientation to one based on more systematic ongoing assessment. They are also shifting their focus to become more oriented toward the senior executive team, while they would previously take on intelligence needs of anyone throughout the organization they now regard senior management as their primary client. They are trying to better understand what intelligence-gathering projects are most actionable. They are making a formal effort to strengthen the link between the creation of intelligence and corporate decision and action.

> The intelligence group at US West is undergoing a transition from a project-orientation to one based on more systematic ongoing assessment. They are also shifting their focus to become more oriented toward the senior executive team.

PRACTICAL CI IMPLICATIONS

Based on the research presented, herein, three recommendations are appropriate to any organization preparing to build a CI function:

Recommendation 1: CI Development

To insure that your CI function has the staying power to weather pending and longterm challenges, it is important to:

1. Select a reporting relationship where leadership embraces the core values of CI and will support it during its formative years.

2. Attract and hire top-flight professionals who are highly motivated and committed to CI.

3. Obtain the required capital and operating budgets to support the CI function over the long haul.

Recommendation 2: CI Structure

The process of CI requires three basic building blocks. They can be combined in a couple of ways. The three building blocks are:

1. *Research*—This group will have responsibility for gathering the four major classes of information described in the closed-loop model (Figure 1). This group will also perform a significant amount of data filtering. Functions performed by this group will be task- and project-oriented. Members will be presented with prescribed information objectives and will carry out the activities necessary to bring appropriate data streams to the intelligence process.

2. *Intelligence Library*—This unit will have the responsibility for building and maintaining the corporate intelligence repository. This database will integrate both paper and digital media. The library will also be responsible for exploring new information management technologies, which may be useful in gathering and disseminating information throughout the organization.

3. *Strategic Marketing Intelligence*—This unit will be responsible for planning and analytical aspects of the intelligence process. It will filter, synthesize, and interpret information that is developed by the research unit. This group will provide the expertise in content areas that will permit the translation of external data into market intelligence.

Recommendation 3: CI System Selection

The third recommendation involves the selection of a closed-loop intelligence system such as described in Figure 1. It is important for practitioners not to equate popular CI tools—for example, data-mining, data warehousing, and information software products—as functional "intelligence systems."

SUMMARY AND CONCLUSION

This article examines the functions of the competitive intelligence process within 16 leading intelligence companies. The building blocks proposed are the foundation of constructing an effective closed-loop intelligence system within an organization. A company committed to CI needs to lay the foundation, build the infrastructure, and leverage market intelligence on an ongoing basis. A user orientation, total corporate commitment beginning with the CEO, and effective distribution channels are key elements to the success of any CI function.

REFERENCES

Bartholomew. (1999). Elusive Goal: Useful Information. *Industry Week,* 248(3), 26.

Bernhardt, D. (1994). I Want It Fast, Factual, Actionable. Tailoring Competitive Intelligence to Executives' Needs. *Long Range Planning,* 27(1), 311.

Caudran, S. (1994, October 3). I Spy, You Spy. *Industry Week,* p. 3540.

Gilad, B. (1991, May/June). Intelligence System: Model for Corporate Chiefs. *Journal of Business Strategy,* 2025.

Jaworski, B., & Wee, L.C. (1993). Competitive Intelligence and Bottomline Performance. *Competitive Intelligence Review,* 3(4), 2327.

Kahaner, L. (1996). *Competitive Intelligence.* New York: Touchstone Books.

Montgomery, D., & Weinberg, C. (1998). Toward Strategic Intelligence Systems. *Marketing Management,* 6(4), 44–52.

Prescott, J., & Bhardwaj, B. (1995). Competitive Intelligence Practices: A Survey. *Competitive Intelligence Review,* 6(2), 414.

Prescott, J., & Smith, D.C. (1989). The Largest Survey of Leading Edge Competitor Intelligence Managers. *The Planning Review,* 17(3), 613.

Rose, R. (1999). CI Effect: Not Luxury, Its Survival. *Computing Canada,* 25(5), 21.

Sawaka, K.A., Francis, D.B., & Herring, J.P. (1995). Evaluating Competitive Intelligence Systems: How Does Your Company Rate. *Competitive Intelligence Review,* 6(4), 22–25.

Tresko, J. (1999). Leveraging the ERP Backbone. *Industry Week,* 248(3), 25.

RELATED READING

Competitive/Market Intelligence Takes Varied Forms; Offers Key Lessons (January–March, 2000). *Competitive Intelligence Magazine,* 3(1), 7–8.

ABOUT THE AUTHORS

Conway L. Lackman, associate professor of marketing at Duquesne University, specializes in marketing research, industrial marketing, and new product development. He has over 25 years experience in marketing management. He holds a Ph.D. from the University of Cincinnati.

Kenneth Saban, assistant professor of marketing at Duquesne University, specializes in new product development and marketing strategy. He has over 15 years experience in marketing management. He holds a Ph.D. from the University of Pittsburgh.

John M. Lanasa, associate professor of marketing at Duquesne University, specializes in sales management. He has over 15 years experience in sales management. He holds a Ph.D. from the University of Pittsburgh.

APPENDIX

Summary of Survey

Q.1. Please indicate which organizational structure below best fits your company.

	N	%
a. Structural functional	7	15
b. Matrix organization	5	10
c. Flat organization	25	50
d. Other	13	25

Q.2. What department is "primarily responsible" for monitoring the flow of information, evaluating its relevance, and analyzing the data. Check one.

46%	23	Marketing	6%	3	Finance	4%	2	R&D
24%	12	Sales	6%	3	Planning	14%	7	Other

Q.3. Over the last 5 years, how often has your business employed the services of an outside market research firm to conduct tailored customer or competitive research. Check one.

67%	31	0–5 times	24%	11	6–10 times	?%	5	11–15 times
	0	16–20 times	7%	3	> 21 times			

Q.4. When do you have dual accountability between CI and marketing research? Indicate which takes precedence.

	N	%
Marketing research	45	90
CI	5	10

Q.5. Indicate:
(A) How well-established is your CI function and; (B) What level of management plays a critical role in same?

Number:	SR	Middle	Lower	%	SR	Middle	%
Well-established		25	5	0	67	25	0
Somewhat		10	10	0	28	50	0
Not		2	5	3	5	25	100

Q.6. How (A) broad and (B) effective is CI participation among employers?

	Broad		Effective	
	N	%	N	%
Very	20	40	15	30
Somewhat	25	50	30	60
Not very	5	10	5	10

Q.6A. If your answer to Q.6. was very, indicate what organizational approach you used with what incentives are used to capture word-of-mouth information?

CF Teams		Departments		Other	
N	%	N	%	N	%
35	70	5	10	10	20

Q.7. Indicate if (yes, no) and how many staff members are allocated to CI and indicate full-time and part-time?

	Total		Full-Time		Part-Time	
	N	*%*	*N*	*%*	*N*	*%*
Yes	35	70	28	85	7	15
No	15	30	—	—	—	—

Q.8. Indicate your company size by sales (M)—number of CI employees and vintage of your CI organization.

Sales	Average CI Employees	Average Vintage (yrs.)
1,000M >	22	18
800–999	18	16
600–799	15	14
400–599	13	8
< 400	10	6

Q.9. Indicate your minimum educational requirement for your CI employees.

	Masters	Bachelors	High School Diploma
N	40	10	0
%	80	20	0

Q.10. Please rank the factors below that you use in selecting a CI director.

Factor	Rank	Average Score
Experience > 5 years	1	1–2
Experience < 5 years	2	1–8
Education	3	2–7
Experience in your industry	4	3–8

Q.11.   Please rank the factor below you use in predicting success in CI.

Factor	Rank	Average Score
Industry Connections	1	1–4
Integrity	2	2–1
Continuity & Imagination	3	3–3
Networking Skill	4	4–2
Communication Skill	5	4–7

Q.12.   In which department does CI reside in your company?

	N	%
Marketing	35	70
Corp. Planning	5	10
MIS	5	10
Finance	3	6
Other	2	4

Q.12A.   If you are a CI director, please indicate where should CI reside?

	Marketing	CP	MIS	Finance	Other
N	45	4	1	0	0
%	90	8	2	0	0

Q.13.   How strategically important is a library to CI?

	N	%
Very	45	90
Somewhat	5	10
Not at all	0	0

Q.14.   What priority do you give to adding a library to the CI function?

	N	%
High	48	96
Medium	2	4
Low	0	0

Q.15. How frequently do you use electronic storage for company personnel access?

	N	%
Often	44	88
Sometime	6	12
Rarely	0	0

Q.16. Do you utilize monthly newsletters to disseminate B competitive information?

	N	%
Yes	41	80
No	90	18

Q.17. How important is technology to the success of your CI function?

	N	%
Critical	27	54
Very	20	40
Somewhat	3	6
Not	0	0

"TAP-IN" to Strategic and Tactical Intelligence in the Sales and Marketing Functions

Cynthia E. Miree, Ph.D.
OAKLAND UNIVERSITY

John E. Prescott, Ph.D.
UNIVERSITY OF PITTSBURGH

EXECUTIVE SUMMARY

This article describes the results of a benchmarking study of mechanisms used in corporate CI operations to coordinate strategic and tactical intelligence for sales and marketing. The American Productivity and Quality Center (APQC) sponsored the study, for which the authors served as subject-matter experts. The objective was to identify a set of mechanisms that establish a conceptual and operational integration of strategic and tactical intelligence. In-depth case studies of five best-practice companies (Amoco, Boehringer Ingelheim, Dow Chemical, MetLife, and SBC), supplemented with quantitative surveys from an additional nine firms, provided the study data. The findings show that best-practice firms use a set of five coordinating mechanisms that the authors label TAP-IN™: (1) Teams, (2) CI human-resource job design and Allocation, (3) the Planning process, (4) Interaction (dialogue), and (5) human intelligence Networks. The use of these five mechanisms in tandem provides a sophisticated means of coordinating strategic and tactical intelligence in the sales and marketing functions and throughout the firm. All of the companies in the sample used the TAP-IN mechanisms to some degree. The data reveal a relationship between the number of mechanisms used by a company and the overall effectiveness of the coordination process. For

Competitive Intelligence Review, Vol. 11(1) 4–16 (2000). © 2000 John Wiley & Sons, Inc.

instance, Dow Chemical and Amoco used all five mechanisms. These two companies also reported they were able to achieve coordination between strategic and tactical intelligence to a very high degree.

INTRODUCTION

How do firms coordinate strategic and tactical intelligence? The field of competitive intelligence has conceptually and operationally separated strategic from tactical intelligence. This separation has resulted in competitive intelligence (CI) practitioners focusing either on one to the detriment of the other or establishing independent methodologies to handle their strategic and tactical CI. This is unfortunate because strategic and tactical intelligence interact in many synergistic ways. We sought to better understand this synergistic relationship by exploring the mechanisms by which firms' coordinate strategic and tactical intelligence.

This article presents the results of a consortium benchmarking study that examined the types of mechanisms used by organizations in their CI processes to facilitate the coordination of strategic and tactical intelligence in the sales and marketing functions. The American Productivity and Quality Center (APQC) sponsored the study, and we served as subject-matter experts.* In-depth case studies of five best-practice companies, supplemented with quantitative surveys from an additional nine firms, provided the data for our study. Our findings reveal that best-practice firms use a set of five coordinating mechanisms that we have labeled TAP-IN™. Firms deploy TAP-IN in sophisticated ways to ensure the coordination of strategic and tactical intelligence. The implications of our findings are summarized in Table 1. We use representative examples throughout the article to illustrate our main findings.

CI: Strategic and Tactical

Competitive intelligence as a discipline has been primarily concerned with the processes and tools of gathering, analyzing, and disseminating intelligence

*Seventeen companies sponsoring the study worked with the APQC. These companies included: AAA Michigan, Arthur Andersen, Bank of America, Carolina Power & Light, DuPont, Imperial Chemical Industries Technology PLC, Lifeway Christian Resources, Ontario Hydro, Perstop Flooring, Pharmacia Upjohn, Prudential, Renault North America, Telcordia, The Timken Co., TRW Linkage and Suspension Division (Canada), United Illuminating, and the United States Postal Service.

Table 1   Key Findings and Their Implications for
Coordinating Strategic and Tactical Intelligence

Key Findings	CI Implications
1. Coordination of strategic and tactical intelligence is made a priority.	**Design:** What is the current orientation of the CI function (strategic or tactical) and how can that orientation be expanded to include the other? What types of information technologies will be most appropriate given this priority? How does the location of the CI process within the organization's hierarchy affect the coordination of strategic and tactical intelligence.

Operational Effectiveness: Articulate the coordination process. Companies who were able to articulate the process of coordination were more likely to achieve coordination than those who couldn't articulate the process were. What role(s) does the CI unit play in coordinating strategy formulation and strategy implementation? Does the CI unit primarily assist in coordination within a particular functional area or the business unit or the entire company?

Measurement: Does the CI function measure the degree to which coordination is achieved? Is the coordination of strategic and tactical intelligence linked to any other outcomes? |
| 2. Effective communications between the sales and marketing departments enhances the coordination of strategic and tactical intelligence. | **Determine the CI unit's role in the communication process. Are you a:** *Equal Partner:* Intelligence flows freely between the three functions. The CI unit has balanced intereaction with both the sales and marketing functions and the sales and marketing functions have frequent interaction with each other. *Willing Liaison:* The CI unit has frequent contact with both the sales and marketing functions but the sales and marketing functions do not interact with each other. Thus, the CI unit is the primary means through which intelligence is communicated between the sales and marketing functions. *Referee:* The sales and marketing functions often have turf battles and/or conflicts over resources. Therefore, on strategic or tactical decision making teams, the CI unit represents the interests of marketing to the sales function and vice versa. In essence, the CI unit is a necessary conduit of intelligence between sales and marketing. |
| 3. TAP-IN mechanisms ensure coordination of strategic and tactical intelligence. | **Important Questions to Ask:** *Teams:* What teams have direct or indirect CI representation? What teams does the CI function need to be on? Does the CI function have any influence on strategic or tactical team agendas? *Allocation:* Do you specifically designate CI personnel to strategic and tactical intelligence? How much time is devoted to strategic CI issues? Tactical CI issues? Does the CI function have products and services that meet the unique needs of their strategic and tactical |

Table 1   (Continued)

Key Findings	CI Implications
	internal customers? *Planning:* What aspect of the planning process does the CI function participate in? Does the CI unit support planning at the functional, business unit and/or corporate level? How can the CI function better inform the planning process? What planning parameters can CI directly or indirectly inform? *Interaction:* How often do members of the CI function engage in face-to-face discussions with various strategic internal customers? Tactical customers? Is the CI function able to facilitate face-to-face dialogue between various parts of the organization? In what areas does a common mental model need to be built? *Networks:* How developed are the current internal and external human intelligence networks? Where are members of the CI function positioned within these networks? What networks does the CI function want to be positioned within?
4. Industry contingencies affect the coordination of strategic and tactical intelligence.	Understand the structural characteristics of the industry and the accompanying constraints. How do industry regulations affect the CI job? The level of information available in the industry facilitates coordination especially through the human intelligence network. Information richness in terms of quality and accuracy facilitates the coordination of strategic and tactical intelligence. High levels of competition among industry players serves as a barrier to the coordination of intelligence. Utilize TAP-IN mechanisms to overcome obstacles wherever possible.

products that allow employees to make quality, effective decisions (Bernhardt, 1994; Gilad & Gilad, 1989; Prescott, 1989). These decisions may be either strategic (future-oriented, long-term) or tactical (present-oriented, short-term) in nature, depending in large part on the employee's place within the organization's hierarchy. Thus, the processes that company's adopt to coordinate intelligence across organizational levels and functions is central to an effective intelligence system. As the field of CI matures we need to devote more attention to managing CI processes to ensure that the intelligence products that are produced are integrated into decision-making processes.

THE CI PROCESS AND THE SALES AND MARKETING FUNCTIONS

Lately, there has been an increased interest in examining how a business's CI process can better capture and leverage the intelligence that exists in the sales and marketing functions (American Productivity and Quality Center, 1999; SCIP, 1999). Intelligence from the sales and marketing intelligence areas is highly desirable given its focus on products, competitors, and customers. Sales professionals continually interface with their firm's competitive market (e.g., customers, competitors, suppliers, and distributors). This interface allows for the continuous collection of "primary" (including human network-based) competitive information. Collecting competitive information from primary sources is critical to any intelligence operation (Sawka, 1996). Regularity in contact and engaging in meaningful conversations with customers and competitors adds depth to any competitive information obtained (Sawka, 1996; Tanzer, 1993). The continuous expansion of CI knowledge from primary sources provides an enterprise with cutting-edge dynamic competitive knowledge, as opposed to filtered, static, public and secondary sources. Thus, sales personnel are a particularly rich source of dynamic, "real-time" intelligence.

The marketing function develops and implements various marketing, positioning, advertising, pricing, and distribution strategies for the company's current and future products and/or services. Marketing professionals gather the decision-specific intelligence from a number of sources, including primary or secondary market and consumer research, and by interfacing with the other functional areas.

Both the sales and marketing functions provide a rich medium through which multilevel CI activities can be analyzed. Thus, we use the sales and marketing functions as a context to study the coordination of strategic and tactical intelligence.

The typical sales and marketing functions offers a rather clear demarcation in key activities across three levels of hierarchy. *Strategic* sales employees engage in forecasting, setting quotas, strategic control, market penetration, planning, and resource allocation. *Tactical* sales employees are focused on implementing strategic objectives, interacting with large accounts, sharing field intelligence with upper management, and managing the sales employees. *Operational* sales employees concentrate on developing proposals, bidding, interacting with customers, and managing assigned territories. *Strategic* marketing employees determine the scope of product offerings, develop budgets and marketing plans, and engage in product development and product positioning. *Tactical* marketing employees focus on product management, market development, pricing, promotion, and distribution. Finally, *operational* marketing employees engage in market and consumer research and gathering marketing intelligence. The most appropriate types of CI products and services will vary based on the hierarchical level of the decision-maker (Dugal, 1998). These differences need to be coordinated for strategic and tactical intelligence to interact in a symbiotic manner.

The Importance of Coordination in the CI Process

Ideally, the competitive intelligence process provides key insights into all levels of the organization. The necessity of tailoring CI products to meet a strategic or tactical decision-maker's specific needs is paramount. The production of tailored CI products, however, also creates a pressure within the CI process to ensure that the intelligence being produced and used in decision making is consistent and coordinated across the organization's hierarchy. Just as strategies need to be coordinated across the hierarchy to ensure success (Thompson, 1967), CI also needs to be coordinated. To maximize the potential benefit of the CI process in the sales and marketing functions, there must be coordination between the strategic and tactical levels. Coordination is difficult, however, in the face of different goals, activities, priorities, and performance appraisal measures (Knez & Camerer, 1994; St. John & Harrison, 1999). By designing a CI process that produces and coordinates strategic and tactical intelligence, an organization is able to not only meet the specific decision-making needs of managers and employees, but the organization is also able to achieve internal consistency in strategic and tactical actions. In the following sections of this article we will explore how these differences can be reconciled and what coordinating mechanisms are built into the CI process to facilitate this outcome.

Sample and Data Collection

The best-practice companies participating in this study were:

- Amoco Corporation
- Boehringer Ingelheim
- Dow Chemical Company

- Met Life
- SBC Corporation

Our data for this study was collected from two sources: recorded structured interviews with company officials during a half-day site visit and a quantitative survey. The questions for the data-collection tools were developed based on four key areas: (1) organizational background and industry context, (2) CI knowledge in the sales and marketing functions, (3) the emphasis of strategic versus tactical intelligence, and (4) measuring CI results. All of the interview data was collected using a standard study protocol. The interviews were conducted on site at the company and lasted about 4 hours. Approximately 2 to 4 key informants were interviewed from each firm. For every firm, at least one of the informants was the manager or director of the CI function. The other informants were employees in the CI function. In the case of SBC Operations and Boehringer, the CI managers were also former sales representatives and were able to offer insights from the perspective of a sales representative.

The interview data was supplemented by survey data. While the interview data was collected only from the companies in the study's sample, the survey data was collected from both the best-practice firms and nine of the firms that sponsored the study. The survey data provided a quantitative means of comparison between the sponsor and benchmark companies.

KEY FINDINGS

There are four major findings of our study. Table 1 summarizes each finding. Below, we describe each finding and provide examples from the best-practice companies.

- *Key Finding 1:* Companies that both (1) establish coordination of strategic and tactical intelligence as a priority, and (2) are able to articulate the formal and quasiformal (informal) processes that are used to achieve coordination, are more likely to achieve coordination than those who do not establish coordination as a priority and are not able to articulate their formal and quasi-formal (informal) coordination processes.

During the study, companies revealed that coordinating strategic and tactical intelligence in the sales and marketing functions was a deliberate as well as an emergent process. All of the companies in the sample stated that the coordination of strategic and tactical intelligence in the sales function was a high priority. The majority of the companies were also able to articulate how their CI process was designed to facilitate coordination. Consequently, those organizations created, continuously improved, and used CI systems, processes, and products that precipitated this outcome.

Each of the companies in the study was asked to provide a model of its CI processes. One of these models is described below. This example illustrates how establishing the coordination of strategic and tactical intelligence as an organizational priority affects the design and effectiveness of the CI processes. However, establishing coordination as a priority was not a sufficient condition to achieve coordination. In addition to prioritizing coordination, the company's ability to articulate the formal and informal processes that facilitated coordination was related to their ability to achieve coordination in practice.

Organizational Example: Articulated CI Processes for Coordination at SBC Operations

SBC Operations, Inc., a telecommunications company, noted that the symbiotic relationship between strategic and tactical intelligence in the sales function made the coordination of these two types of intelligence a high priority. In the past, the CI group was structured so that an internal customer would have one contact for strategic CI requests and another contact for tactical CI requests. The CI group found this formalized distinction too rigid. The artificial wall hindered the flow of information and confused internal clients. As a result, information would often fall between the cracks. While the CI group continues to have professionals that are dedicated to fulfilling either the strategic or tactical CI needs of their internal customers, these distinctions are salient only to those individuals working within the CI unit. Coordination is facilitated through the interaction of individuals within the CI group. Once the group minimized the formal distinction between the two types of intelligence when dealing with its customers, they were able to develop a synergy based on information sharing.

- *Key Finding 2:* Tightly coupled communication and other operational linkages between the sales and marketing functions can increase a firm's ability to coordinate strategic and tactical intelligence.

All firms perform a set of activities that constitute their value chain. Each firm's value chain is embedded in a larger stream of activities that compose the industry's value chain (Porter, 1980). This chain describes the metamorphosis of raw materials to a final product in the marketplace (Day, 1984). The companies in the study compete in different stages of their industry's value chain (e.g., Day, 1984; Porter, 1980). Amoco and Dow compete in the upstream part of the industry value chain (e.g., industrial product companies). The activities of SBC, Boehringer, and MetLife include a broader range of activities across the industry value chain.

All of the companies in the sample had operational linkages between the sales and marketing functions. However, the need to establish a tight communication link between sales and marketing was related to the scope of the company's activities in the industry's value chain. Firms that focused their activities in the upstream parts of the industry value chain coordinated sales and marketing to a higher extent than those competing in downstream activities. The tight linkage between sales and marketing facilitated the firm's ability to coordinate strategic and tactical intelligence. This relationship was not as pronounced for companies whose operations encompass a broader range of activities across the industry value chain.

> Firms that focused their activities in the "upstream" part of the industry value chain coordinated sales and marketing to a higher extent than firms competing on "downstream" activities. The tight linkage between sales and marketing also improved the firm's ability to coordinate strategic and tactical intelligence.

Organizational Example: Tightly Coupled Communication at Dow Chemical

Dow's scope of business operations exists upstream in the industry value chain for many of its customers and clients. Specifically, Dow's operations are primarily focused on the development and refinement of chemicals, plastics, performance chemicals, performance plastics, chemicals/metals, hydrocarbons, and energy. These products are then sold to other businesses in a variety of industries as key inputs into their final products. Dow has established and maintains a tight linkage between its sales function and marketing function. Linking sales and marketing structurally and operationally encourages and enables constant communication between these two functions. This linkage also allows Dow to quickly respond to conditions in the external environment and better coordinate the strategic and tactical levels of the organization's business units.

> Dow and Amoco used all five TAP-IN mechanisms. These two companies also reported they were able to coordinate strategic and tactical intelligence to a very high degree.

- *Key Finding 3:* The coordination of strategic and tactical intelligence in the sales function is facilitated through the sophisticated use of coordinating mechanisms such as: *T*eams, CI human resources *A*llocation, the *P*lanning process, *I*nteraction, and *N*etworks, hence the acronym "TAP IN."

The coordination of strategic and tactical intelligence in the sales function requires the sophisticated use of coordinating mechanisms, including:

1. *T*eams
2. CI human resource job design and *A*llocation
3. The *P*lanning process
4. *I*nteraction (dialogue), and
5. Human intelligence *N*etworks

The use of these five mechanisms in tandem—the TAP-IN process—provides organizations with a sophisticated means of coordinating strategic and tactical intelligence in the sales and marketing functions and throughout the firm. All of the companies in the sample used the TAP-IN mechanisms to some degree. The data indicated a relationship between the number of mechanisms used by a company and the overall effectiveness of the coordination process. For instance, Dow and Amoco used all five mechanisms. These two companies also reported that they were able to achieve coordination between strategic and tactical intelligence to a very high degree. The following subfindings describe the TAP-IN mechanisms.

- *Subfinding 3A:* Organizational processes are enabled and managed by teams and Information Technology (IT).

Teams are the first component of the coordinating mechanisms found in the TAP-IN process. Most of these permanent and semipermanent teams were task-oriented and involved focused activities with specific strategic or tactical agendas. Single-function teams were used to address functional issues and initiatives (e.g., CI teams, sales advisory teams, and product management teams). Multifunctional teams were used to address broader organizational issues and initiatives. In many cases, organizations effectively used both types of teams to enable organizational activity. Information technology was also important because of the role it played in supporting the team's ability to operate. The use of information technology allowed for high levels of consistency and continuity in team activities. The critical aspect of this mechanism is the degree to which CI participates on important teams. Best-practice companies have direct representation on important teams.

The following example highlights how teams and IT platforms are used by the best-practice organizations to enable and manage the organizational processes and coordinate strategic and tactical intelligence.

Organizational Example: Teams and Information Technology at Dow Chemical

Dow has a self-described team-oriented culture. A multi-functional business leadership team manages each of Dow's 14 business units. The leadership teams have representatives from the critical functional areas of the business unit including competitive intelligence. All of the leadership team members have global responsibility and are not necessarily located in the same country or even on the same continent. A strategically focused CI person representing the global CI unit helps to plan these meetings, attends the leadership team meetings, and has follow-up responsibilities. The business leadership team formulates strategy, and each of the team representatives is responsible for ensuring that the strategy is implemented in their functional areas. The marketing function is directly represented on the business leadership team. These individuals also represent the sales function's interests by synthesizing and reporting on the tactical sales-related issues that exist in the marketplace.

The most frequent technologies being used to collect and transmit intelligence to and from the sales force are the telephone, e-mail, voice mail, audio conferencing, video conferencing, and periodic meetings. The tactical competitive intelligence professionals (market research) also communicate with the sales force through Intranet publishing and Wincite (a database tool). A key challenge Dow faces is that most salespeople do not like to use the Intranet, thus reducing the effectiveness of this technology. Therefore, the primary forms of contact between sales and marketing are the telephone and e-mail.

- *Subfinding 3B:* CI human resources are explicitly designated to strategic and tactical activities through job design.

The deliberate allocation of CI human resources to either strategic or tactical activity is a key mechanism used to coordinate strategic and tactical intelligence within the sales function. All of the companies in the sample have explicitly designated CI personnel to strategic or tactical activities. Most importantly, these activities are often specified in individual job descriptions.

Organizational Example: CI Human Resource Allocation at SBC Operations

The CI group strives to spend equal effort on strategic and tactical issues. However, this mix can depend greatly on the stage of a products life-cycle and the conditions in the industry. Accordingly, the CI groups has the capacity to respond to both strategic and tactical CI issues, depending on the current business need. Individual CI practitioners are dedicated to tactical or strategic issues by job design. Approximately one-fourth of SBC's 25 individuals who conduct CI are dedicated to strategic CI activities.

The CI group also formally delineates between strategic and tactical intelligence based on the needs of the marketing function versus the sales function and the nature of the project or the request. For example, requests from upper-level management tend to be directed to strategic analysts due to the breadth of analysis required. The CI group also tends to physically deliver its output to this audience. This allows the group to present data and provide interpretation of complex issues. In contrast, tactically oriented internal customers typically want less volume in a CI response. For this audience, shorter formats with charts and graphs are becoming increasingly popular and if the internal customer desires more information, supporting data is available. The CI group orients delivery around the needs of its clients (i.e., large binders of data vs. one page). SBC emphasized that building customer relationships is important to achieving this outcome.

- *Subfinding 3C:* CI input is embedded in the strategic planning process.

Participation in the organization's strategic planning process is a key mechanism used to coordinate strategic and tactical intelligence within and between the sales and marketing functions. One of the key themes suggests that before strategic decisions are made and resources are allocated, CI input from the strategic and tactical levels is weighed, evaluated, and incorporated into the decision-making process. The outputs of the planning process are then used to further coordinate the collection and analysis of intelligence across organizational levels. Best-practice companies directly participate in the strategic planning process.

Organizational Examples: CI Participation in the Planning Process at Amoco Worldwide Exploration Business Group (WEBG)

CI input in linked directly to strategic planning. Competitive intelligence is shared with top management to assist in strategic planning. CI input is also linked to strategic planning indirectly through its incorporation into the following marketing Ps★ as outlined below:

- *Product:* How can CI help in formulating the structure of a deal?
- *Price:* What CI knowledge is needed to ensure a winning bid for a deal?
- *Promotion:*† What are the country teams doing with CI's information to create advantageous relationships with customers/countries?

CI influences all of the P's to some extent, but it particularly influences price and promotions.

★ There are four marketing Ps: price, place, promotion, and product. Product, price, and promotion were most influenced by CI at Amoco Exploration.
† Based on the nature of the business, promotion refers to the relationships created between external "customers" in the host country and the country teams, and the teams' ability to favorably position Amoco with the customer versus competitors.

The strategic planning and budgeting process requires both the sales and marketing functions of country teams to complete a structured report on the competitive environment. Completion of the report requires the input of specific competitive intelligence. The sales force engages in constant conversation with top managers who are responsible for dealing with tactical issues between the worldwide and country levels. When requesting funds, the sales force is also required to submit information regarding its tactical issues and how they "fit" in the competitor landscape in order to be funded. This requirement forces top management to be aware of the tactical issues the sales force faces on a daily basis. If management values what is included in the template, funding will be provided. CI is further used to provide price information on competitors' cost structures that may lend insight on how competitors bid for opportunities.

- *Subfinding 3D:* Interaction, in the form of dialogue, is the primary and preferred method of communication.

Interaction, in the form of dialogue between CI professionals and sales, marketing, and top management is the fourth important mechanism of the TAP-IN process. Interaction through ongoing dialogue is relationship-oriented and characterized by more implicit agendas than teams, where agendas are more explicit. All of the companies in the sample stressed the importance of regular interaction with their internal customers and other members of the CI team. Face-to-face and telephone conversations are also the preferred methods of communication. This type of interaction increases credibility and trust between the CI team and the sales and marketing functions as each better understands the goals, roles, and constraints of the other.

Organizational Example: Interaction at Boehringer Ingelheim

The Business Intelligence group interacts with the sales representatives on a monthly basis. Given the group's strong strategic focus, lower-level employees tend to be viewed mainly as sources of information. The sales employees are able to provide feedback to Business Intelligence by e-mail and via the sales advisory team, which is a team of approximately 10 senior sales representatives. The proximity to and close working relationship with the marketing function enables informal and frequent feedback. Boehringer's competitive intelligence team also engages in regular face-to-face conversations with its strategic internal customers in an effort to define and refine key intelligence topics and other intelligence needs.

- *Subfinding 3E:* The establishment and use of internal and external networks is expected and reinforced.

The final mechanism in the TAP-IN process is "net-works." The case studies revealed that internal and external human-intelligence networks are used as mechanisms to help coordinate strategic and tactical intelligence. These networks, whether formal or informal, provide structured patterns or linkages between individuals inside and outside the firm that can be leveraged to address a CI issue as needed. Most importantly, the use of these networks was expected and reinforced at the companies in the sample.

Organizational Example: Networks at Dow Chemical

Dow employees (CI and non-CI) develop and maintain internal and external human networks. These networks are valued within Dow culture and are viewed as one of its strong points. Participation in CI activities is implicit in job descriptions and viewed as a job responsibility in the sales and marketing functions. This duality in job design creates a high level of CI awareness, encourages CI collection, and strengthens internal networks. Identifying and leveraging appropriate members of Dow's external human-intelligence network is a strong part of the company's CI process. Dow also leverages external networks as part of its strategy development process. Relationships with members of the external network are used to strengthen Dow's CI process.

- *Key Finding 4:* The presence of various industry structural characteristics impacts the firm's ability to coordinate strategic and tactical intelligence in the sales function.

The external environment contains various conditions that act as either barriers to or facilitators of the coordination of strategic and tactical intelligence in the sales and marketing functions. These environmental conditions include information availability, information richness, inter-firm rivalry, and the presence of industry regulation. All of the companies in the study recognized the presence and impact of these conditions on their CI processes.

Companies in the sample were not faced with all external factors to the same degree. Naturally, depending on the industry, some faced more regulation and inter-firm rivalry and competition than others did. Likewise, while some companies may struggle to gather information, others are able to obtain information with ease. The following summarization provides one example of the constraints imposed by external conditions.

Organizational Example: External Condition Impacting Coordination: Industry Regulation at SBC Operations

The degree of industry regulation is an external factor that can impact firms' ability to gather strategic and tactical intelligence. SBC Operations, Inc., operates in a highly regulated industry. Industry regulations guide many of its activities in the area of competitive intelligence. During the site visit, SBC representatives reported that the highly regulated industry forces the CI group to be cautious when using external networks to gather intelligence. Under strict limitations, the CI group occasionally will network and leverage contacts with vendors' CI groups.

- *Minor Finding 1:* CI products and services are created and used to encourage a two-way flow between the CI team and the sales function. This two-way flow, in turn, facilitates the coordination of strategic and tactical intelligence.

The CI unit's ability to impact the company's bottom line defines its organizational value. Supplying actionable intelligence that meets the decision-making needs of strategic and tactical customers is one way to affect the firm's bottom line. The CI team must create and tailor its products and services to not only meet the intelligence needs of internal clients but also cross hierarchical, functional, and diagonal barriers. Hierarchical-based functional activities, priorities, and decision areas drive the types of CI products and services that are needed. By providing intelligence that is tailored to the specific needs of internal customers, the CI team is able to build trust and establish long-term credibility. Credibility and trust between the CI team and internal sales and marketing customers is key to the success of the CI unit. Therefore, to ensure that credibility and trust are built into the relationship with internal sales clients, each of the companies in the sample creates and uses appropriate CI products and services. When used, these value-adding CI products increase the two-way flow between the CI unit and the sales and marketing functions. The following organizational example provides an illustration of valuable CI products and services that create an important two-way flow.

Organizational Example: CI Products and Services at SBC Operations

The CI group provides different deliverables to target different audiences. To collect and transmit intelligence to/from the sales function, the CI group uses alerts and intelligence reports (both available electronically), a Web-based competitive database, and an internal information tracking database.

The CI group also attends sales staff meetings to distribute and gather information. According to CI practitioners at SBC, these meetings are excellent opportunities to internally market CI value and the CI group. To support these efforts further, the group includes contact information on every deliverable to build awareness and encourage further communication.

According to the CI group, the immediate needs of the sales force are a priority. Sales reps need intelligence that enables them to make immediate sales. Therefore, online databases, sales tools, and real-time bid support are all integrated into their "normal" repertoire of CI products and services. When dealing with ad hoc requests from the field, the CI group works directly with the representative to ensure that the deliverable created by the CI unit meets the needs of the sales representative.

- *Minor Finding 2:* Establishing effective coordination in the sales and marketing functions involves focusing on the key process improvement areas of outcome measurement and within-function intelligence flow.

The companies in the sample were committed to continuous improvement in the CI process. During the study, participants were asked what kinds of improvements they would like to see in their organizations. Each of the companies in the study was able to high-light and comment on the specific areas in the process that were targeted as key areas for improvement. Outcome measurement was an area of particular concern. The firms in the sample agreed that outcome measures must be designed to evaluate the quality and effectiveness of both CI content and CI processes. Key quantitative and qualitative measures should be well defined and used to foster continuous improvement of the CI process. However, within each company in the study, it was clear that measures remained a challenge. While some companies are better at measurement than others, there was room for improvement all around.

Organizational Example: Process Improvement Areas at Amoco Worldwide Exploration Business Group (WEBG)

The WEBG BIT (Business Intelligence Team) would like to continue to work on building relationships and having more frequent interaction with the sales/marketing functions of the country teams. As relationships between the BIT and its internal customers grow stronger, the mutual knowledge base and understanding also grows. This knowledge base will enable the group to do better work for the sales/marketing functions in the future. The BIT would also like to see more rigorous process-driven work and move further away from the current level of ad hoc work. This would require more planning and discussion with the internal customer base. In short, the WEBG BIT is continuously striving to improve its CI function.

Amoco has developed three types of quantitative and qualitative measures centered on the performance of the CI function. Data-quality measures, sales and marketing feedback, and vendor product measures are the three types of key measures that are used.

Data Quality Measures at Amoco
Operational data from external or public services is measured for accuracy by cross-referencing the information with the external (proprietary) network.★ Benchmarking and externally collected information on financial costs, etc. from other companies are also measured.

Sales and Marketing Feedback at Amoco
Feedback from the sales and marketing functions is collected and evaluated. However, this kind of information is informal and abstract. The BIT is currently trying to measure this feedback more formally.

★Amoco's Business Intelligence team formally participates in an external network comprised of intelligence professionals from other oil companies. These meetings are designed to share primary intelligence, confirm industry moves and initiatives, and form sales collaborations when appropriate.

Vendor Product Measurements at Amoco

A member of the BIT measures the quality of vendor products. By tracking user opinions of the product, networking, and informal analysis and research, the BIT assesses what kind of vendors may be valuable to the unit.

Senior management at Amoco does not measure the value of the CI function. However, the team does measure its processes internally to improve its value to the organization. Performance in these measures is openly discussed with management to demonstrate the function's value to the organization. The measures are obtained through a business assessment in the form of a "mini Baldrige" that examines processes and measurements. The assessment exercise also examines the possibility of creating improved internal measures. Because the measures are not as rigorous as Amoco would like, the BIT is working toward a more formal measurement process.

SURVEY DATA RESULTS

Survey data was collected from both the best-practice firms and the companies that sponsored the study. This data was used to support the qualitative findings and used as a means of comparison between the best-practice and sponsor companies. The responses from the two set of firms were quite different. In particular, best-practice companies displayed stronger evidence for the presence and use of coordinating mechanisms than the sponsor companies. Consequently, these companies also reported greater success in achieving strategic and tactical intelligence coordination and other positive outcomes. Table 2 compares the survey responses to the presence of the TAP-IN mechanisms.

As shown in Table 2, the best-practice companies utilized the TAP-IN mechanisms more heavily than did the sponsor companies. In general, best-practice companies more actively incorporated CI into their strategic planning processes, incorporated verbal and face-to-face communication more than the sponsor companies, and have and actively use established formal networks in the CI process.

Another key issue to address was whether the coordination of strategic and tactical intelligence affects organizational outcomes. Table 3 presents various potential outcomes of the coordination process.

Specifically, the sponsor and best-practice companies were asked to report on the outcomes of their coordination process. In general, best-practice companies reported that they were able to achieve a high level of coordination of

Table 2   Survey Comparisons of TAP-IN Mechanisms

Survey Responses	*Sponsor Companies [n = 9]*	*Best-Practice Companies [n = 5]*
Percent indicating the following technology is effective in disseminating and sharing actionable CI in the sales function:		
E-mail	60%	100%
Voice mail	13%	60%
Intranet	33%	60%
Databases	33%	20%
Web Pages	20%	20%
In-house developed software	— or 0	20%
CI and the strategic planning process (Percent of respondents that agree with the following statements):		
The strategic intelligence we gather directly impacts the formulation of our strategic plans.	53%	100%
The tactical intelligence we gather directly impacts the formulation of our strategic plans.	46%	80%
The strategic intelligence we gather directly impacts the implementation of our strategic plans.	60%	80%
The tactical intelligence we gather directly impacts the implementation of our strategic plans.	26%	60%
CI and interaction with internal customers (Percent of respondents stating that the following mode of contact is important):		
Verbal	86%	80%
Face-to-face	73%	80%
Written	33%	60%
Electronic	33%	60%
CI and the use of networks (Percent of respondents with the following statements):		
We have a formal network between the sales/marketing and the CI unit.	33%	100%
When addressing a CI request from our internal customers we rely on formal internal networks.	26%	60%

strategic and tactical intelligence in the sales function. The same was true for the marketing function. Best-practice companies also achieved coordination of business-level strategy and tactics in the sales and marketing functions. Best-practice companies reported that coordination was experienced to a great extent (4 out of 5 on a Likert scale). Finally, best-practice companies reported that based on the coordination of strategic

Table 3   Survey Comparisons of Coordination Outcomes

Survey Responses	Sponsor Companies [n = 9]	Best-Practice Companies [n = 5]
Coordination of strategic and tactical intelligence (Percent of respondents who agree with the following statements):		
The sales function has been able to achieve some level of coordination of sales-related strategic and tactical intelligence.	26%	80%
The marketing function has been able to achieve some level of coordination of marketing-related strategic and tactical intelligence.	60%	80%
Coordination of business-level strategy and tactics (Percent of respondents who agree with the following statements):		
The coordination of business-level strategy and tactics has been achieved in the sales function to a great extent.	6%	40%
The coordination of business-level strategy and tactics has been achieved in the marketing function to a great extent.	13%	60%
The coordination of sales-related strategic and tactical intelligence in the sales function has been achieved to a great extent.	0%	40%
The coordination of marketing-related strategic and tactical intelligence in the marketing function has been achieved to a great extent.	6%	60%
Percent of respondents who agree they have realized the following benefits as a result of the coordination of strategic and tactical CI:		
A strengthening in competitive position	77%	100%
Increases in customer satisfaction	44%	75%
Increases in repeat business	11%	75%
Increases in market share	33%	50%
Significant cost savings	0%	50%
More effective sales presentations	22%	50%

and tactical intelligence, they experienced greater increases in market share, greater cost savings, and a greater strengthening of competitive position than the sponsor companies.

> Best-practice companies reported that based on coordination of strategic and tactical intelligence, they experienced greater increases in market share, greater cost savings, and a greater strengthening of competitive position than the sponsor companies.

IMPLICATIONS FOR CI PROFESSIONALS

At the beginning of this article we noted that the CI field has conceptually separated strategic and tactical intelligence. We demonstrated that best-practice firms coordinate strategic and tactical intelligence and that there are positive organizational outcomes associated with this coordination. More importantly, we developed a process that we labeled TAP-IN that establishes a conceptual and operational process for the coordination of strategic and tactical intelligence. The influence that CI professionals have in the decision-making process within their organization is significantly enhanced when they actively use the TAP-IN mechanisms.

The use of coordinating mechanisms identified in this article establishes the CI professional as a key *bridge builder*. The CI professionals who assists in the coordination of strategic and tactical intelligence play a critical liaison role across levels in the organizational hierarchy. This liaison role is important for at least three reasons:

1. Strategic and tactical intelligence in difficult to coordinate due to the different languages, goals, and other orientations required at each level. Mark Lowenthal has coined the term "tribal tongues" to describe the difficulty in communications between managers and analysts. Tribal tongues also exist across levels in an organization's hierarchy. When the CI group is able to serve as a translator for the tribal tongues, their influence in the organization increases.

2. When the CI group is linked to both strategic and tactical activities, it is better equipped to activate networks within each level to address intelligence topics. The significant aspect of activating the two sets of networks is the diversity and richness of information sources that can be brought to bear on the topic.

3. Strategic intelligence that focuses on formulation and tactical intelligence that focuses on implementation are able to interact synergistically if the two are coordinated.

This study is the first in a series of studies that we are conducting that will focus on the relationship between the sales and marketing functions and the competitive intelligence process. As companies move into the 21st century, the leveraging of customer, competitive, and product-related intelligence will become increasingly important in strategy development and implementation. In addition, CI professionals will need to balance and integrate the often-competing demands of strategic and tactical customers.

There are several additional implications of our findings for the practicing CI professional:

1. Sales and marketing managers do value the contribution that the CI function makes to the decision-making process.
2. The coordination of strategic and tactical intelligence results from both a deliberate as well as an emergent process. Organizations that establish coordination as a priority are more likely to achieve coordination than those that do not. Therefore, CI professional should be able to articulate how their CI process achieves coordination.

In addition, we identified five coordinating mechanisms (TAP-IN) that best-practice companies have incorporated into the design of their CI process. Our findings clearly show that the effective management of the TAP-IN results in superior coordination of strategic and tactical intelligence. We also found that the use of these mechanisms was linked to other sales- and marketing-related performance outcomes. Thus, as a starting point, CI professionals need to assess the degree to which these mechanisms exist within their CI operations and how they are currently being used within the CI process. Table 1 identifies some of the key questions that must be answered by CI professionals. These questions are designed to assist the CI professional in assessing the current state of the company's practice and in identifying areas of improvement.

REFERENCES

American Productivity and Quality Center. (1999). *Effective Strategic and Tactical Intelligence for the Sales and Marketing Functions*. Houston: Author.

Bernhardt, D. (1994). I Want It Fast, Factual, Actionable—Tailoring Competitive Intelligence Needs to Executive Needs. *Long Range Planning, 27*(1), 12–24.

Day, G. (1984). *Strategic Market Planning*. New York: West Publishing.

Dugal, M. (1998). CI Product Line: A Tool for Enhancing User Acceptance of CI. *Competitive Intelligence Review, 9*(2), 17–5.

Gilad, B., & Gilad, T. (1988). *The Business Intelligence System*. New York: Amacon.

Knez, M., & Camerer, C. (1994). Creating Expectational Assets in the Laboratory. *Strategic Management Journal,* 15, 101–119.

Porter, M. (1980). *Competitive Strategy.* New York: Free Press.

Prescott, J. (Ed.). (1989). *Advances in Competitive Intelligence.* Alexandria, VA: Society of Competitive Intelligence Professionals.

Sawka, K. (1996). Demystifying Business Intelligence. *Management Review,* 47–51.

Society of Competitive Intelligence Professionals. (1999). Sales and Marketing Intelligence Symposium, June 10–11, Chicago, IL.

St. John, C., & Harrison, J. (1999). Manufacturing-Based Relatedness, Synergy and Coordination. *Strategic Management Journal,* 20(2), 129–145.

Tanzer, M. (1993). The Spying Game. *Sales and Marketing Management,* 45(6), 60–65.

Thompson, J. (1967). *Organizations in Action.* New York: McGraw Hill.

RELATED READING

Sales and Marketing CI: Study Draws Lessons from "Best Practice" Firms (1999, July–September). *Competitive Intelligence Magazine,* 2(3), 7–8.

ABOUT THE AUTHORS

Cynthia E. Miree is an assistant professor of management at Oakland University. Her research focuses on leveraging competitive intelligence within the sales and marketing areas.

John E. Prescott is professor of business administration at the Katz Graduate School of Business, University of Pittsburgh. He is an award-winning professor in the area of competitive intelligence, executive editor of *Competitive Intelligence Review,* and an international consultant in the design and management of competitive intelligence systems.

Key Intelligence Topics: A Process to Identify and Define Intelligence Needs

Jan P. Herring

HERRING & ASSOCIATES LLC

EXECUTIVE SUMMARY

Defining an organization's actual intelligence needs, and doing so in a way that results in the production of intelligence that management feels compelled to act on, is one of our profession's most elusive goals. The use of a systematized or formal "management-needs identification process" is a proven way to accomplish this task. The objective is to create a cooperative environment between intelligence users and CI professionals that supports the two-way communication necessary for identifying and defining the company's real intelligence needs. To accomplish this, the private sector can learn from government intelligence models, such as the National Intelligence Topics (NIT) process for identifying national-level intelligence requirements. As adapted for the corporate world, the Key Intelligence Topics (KIT) process has been used by many companies to identify and prioritize senior management's key intelligence needs. At the heart of the KIT process is an interactive dialog with key decision makers in the company. The outcome of KIT interviews provides the focus needed to conduct effective intelligence operations, while permitting CI program designers and managers to determine the resources required to address the company's actual intelligence needs. Sample KIT protocols are provided: (1) strategic decisions and actions; (2) early-warning topics; and (3) descriptions of key marketplace players. These KITs are not mutually exclusive, as a strategy-focused KIT might also require a competitor profile and some form of early-warning intelligence to alert the user to a change in competitor activities, which, in turn, would signal a need to modify the

Competitive Intelligence Review, Vol. 10(2) 4–14 (1999). © 1999 John Wiley & Sons, Inc.

new competitive strategy. The KIT process causes the CI unit to operate in a proactive mode, helping management to identify and define intelligence requirements. Competitive intelligence professionals' use of the KIT process should result not only in identifying the organization's key intelligence needs, but also in creating the critical communication channel's necessary to produce credible and actionable intelligence.

The critical success factor in any intelligence operation is meeting the user's real needs—and doing it in such a way that the organization acts on the resulting intelligence (and, as a consequence, succeeds in whatever business endeavor is involved). In the government, these intelligence needs are called "requirements." In the private sector, they are called by various names, including "management's needs" or their "intelligence topics." No matter what they are called, or by whatever process they are identified, they are the key to producing effective and actionable intelligence.

Surprisingly, there has been very little professionally written on this topic. In reality, the absence of management's stated intelligence needs is often cited as the basic reason for poor CI program performance and growing frustration among CI practitioners. However, in the more successful competitive intelligence programs, for example, Motorola, Merck, and NutraSweet—the use of a formal *management-needs identification process* is well known and viewed as one of their critical success factors.

So why don't more companies have such processes? The simple answer is it's not an easy task. For some intelligence managers it's a daunting task to get on their senior management's calendar and then having to interview them to identify their specific intelligence needs. More to the point, it requires a cooperative effort by both management (users) and CI professionals to create the environment necessary to support the two-way communications required to identify and define the organization's real intelligence needs. The remainder of this article describes the process, and how CI managers and professionals can go about accomplishing this all-important task.

BACKGROUND AND PURPOSE

I have been asking intelligence users for their intelligence requirements since the early 1970s, first as a new program manager at the Central Intelligence

Agency, working with White House staff and other Cabinet Departments. Later, as the National Intelligence Officer for Sciences & Technology, I became the "point person" for identifying the U.S. government's national-level needs for S&T intelligence. These rather important intelligence requirements were called National Intelligence Topics (NIT) and facilitated the Government Intelligence Community's task of organizing, prioritizing, and focusing its limited intelligence resources on those few critical needs of the national security community and its policy makers. This process worked well, once the users understood their role and how to properly articulate their needs.

One of the responsibilities of an NIO is to work with new government officials and policy makers to be sure they understand the Intelligence Community's capabilities and how to best use them. In many respects, it is similar to a senior account/client manager in the private sector. The NIO focuses on the task of identifying and defining those management needs that actually require intelligence and not information that could be acquired from their own departments or other government representatives overseas, such as commercial and scientific attachés. Both the NIO responsibilities and intelligence-requirements process are well developed, and usually result in well-directed intelligence collection and analysis operations that satisfied the "customers."

When I left the government in the mid-1980s to join Motorola, Inc. to set up their business intelligence program, I adapted the NIT-requirements process to the corporate world, and it became the "Key Intelligence Topics" (KIT) process—not *Business* Intelligence Topics," although I did consider calling the process "*Corporate* Intelligence Topics" before settling on *Key* in the title.

At Motorola, I used the KIT process to identify and prioritize both senior management's and the organization's key intelligence needs. Individual business managers and executives expressed their specific intelligence needs about topics such as strategic alliances and acquisitions, technology planning and decisions, and specific competitors. Some business groups would combine individual manager's intelligence needs and submit their organization's prioritized lists. And, whenever individual KITs overlapped or could be logically combined to the benefit of all, I did so, properly coordinating the intelligence operations and tailoring the delivery of the resulting finished intelligence to each user-group. The process worked as well in the private sector as it had in the government.

By the time I left Motorola to become a consultant in the late 1980s, the Key Intelligence Topics process for identifying management's specific intelligence needs had been both adapted to the private sector and used quite successfully. In my approach to assisting companies such as Nutra-Sweet, Southwestern Bell, Texas Instruments, Ford Motor Credit, and Rockwell Automotive Design in their set up of their business/competitive intelligence programs, the KIT process played a key role.

After educating the company's senior management about intelligence production and their role in using it, the first step in the design process was to conduct KIT interviews of the key decision makers and managers. This is also the first step in the traditional intelligence cycle (see Figure 1). More importantly, it made a lot of sense to the managers. They knew they needed intelligence, such as, business, competitive, technological, and once trained how to ask for it, they were more than willing to do so. Of equal importance, management soon became convinced that the better they could articulate their needs (KITs), the more likely they were to receive intelligence they could use.

> By the time I left Motorola in the late 1980s, the Key Intelligence Topics process for identifying management's specific intelligence needs had been adapted to the private sector and used quite successfully.

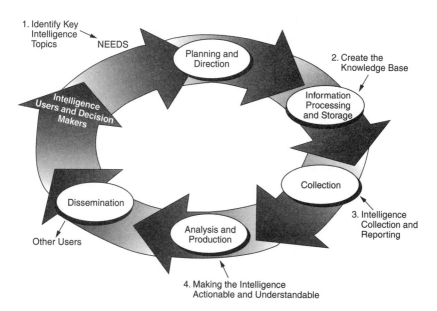

Figure 1   The traditional intelligence cycle.

Key Intelligence Topics' interviews at the beginning of a CI program provide the focus and prioritization needed to conduct effective intelligence operations and produce the appropriate intelligence. They also permit the program's designers and developers to determine the number of CI professionals, their skills, and the level of external resources needed to address the organization's actual intelligence needs. In effect, an analytical understanding of management's initial KIT (i.e., the nature and scope of the organizations' intelligence needs) permits the program resources to be optimally matched to the expected demand.

In a different vein, once management's KITs are identified and organized by business and/or functional category, the related intelligence operations can be better planned to maximize success and produce the required intelligence. Furthermore, I have found that a company's intelligence needs can generally be assigned to one of three functional categories:

- *Strategic Decisions and Actions,* including the development of strategic plans and strategies.
- *Early-Warning Topics,* including competitor initiatives, technological surprise, and governmental actions.
- *Descriptions of the Key Players* in the specific marketplace, including competitors, customers, suppliers, regulators, and potential partners.

This categorization can be very helpful to the CI manager, because different types of KITs require different types of intelligence operations. For example, intelligence to support decision making usually requires both business and intelligence analysis, supported by thorough secondary-source research with current human-source collection inputs. Early-warning intelligence is critically dependent on human-source collection and monitoring, with analysis serving as the detection mechanism that "signals" possible future developments that a company should be prepared to act on. Player-oriented intelligence usually takes the form of analytical profiles, sometimes tailored to specific user questions or planned actions.

Significantly, KITs are *not* mutually exclusive: A strategy-focused KIT might also require a competitor profile and some form of early-warning intelligence to alert the user to a change in competitor activities, which, in turn, would signal a need to modify the new competitive strategy.

Significantly, KITs are *not* mutually exclusive: A strategy-focused KIT might also require a competitor profile and some form of early-warning intelligence to alert the user to a change in competitor activities, which, in turn, would signal a need to modify the new competitive strategy. An insightful understanding of an organizations KITs usually creates a combination of intelligence operations that causes the CI program to become truly anticipatory and produces the timely and insightful intelligence necessary to cause management to act intelligently.

KIT EXAMPLES

Having interviewed over 1,000 executives and managers in almost every industrial sector, I found it somewhat surprising that their needs were rather similar, only the specifics were different. To illustrate these basic user needs I have listed a representative sample in Tables 1, 2, and 3. For the sake of brevity, I have left out some subtopics and shortened the original statement-of-need. Although there are only 12 sample KITs in each category, they represent a cross-section of over 20 varied industries. Let's take an analytical look at each category.

Strategic Decisions and Issues

In most respects this set is the most important for a successful CI program. Identifying and meeting the specific needs of management for planned decisions or pending actions provide the most visible and tangible measures of intelligence value. Producing useful and actionable intelligence in response to important business decisions and actions is what it's all about.

The intelligence topics (KITs) in this category will vary in form from specific questions and/or decision statements to the more typical "topic" subject, that must be better defined later through interactive dialogue with the user. Both forms are quite acceptable, particularly at the time they are identified, because both will eventually have to be refined when the KIT is turned into an intelligence action plan for management review and approval.

Decision/Issue KITs run the gamut from strategic investment decisions, to action plans for new product rollouts, to requests for intelligence inputs for the formulation of strategic plans and new competitor strategies. As long as management's stated need for intelligence involves business decisions or pending business actions, such requests are probably legitimate

KITs. The examples shown in Table 1, taken from actual KIT interviews, demonstrate the breadth and variety of management intelligence needs as well as the different forms they might take.

Early-Warning KITs

Early-warning topics typically stress activities and subjects by which management does not want to be surprised. They are usually heavily weighted toward threats, though they need not be because good intelligence operations

Table 1   Examples of Strategic Decisions and Issues

1. Provide intelligence inputs for the company's strategic plan to create "our" future competitive environment.

2. Formulating "our" global competitive strategy: Assess the role of competitors in achieving our business objective(s).

3. Globalization of (Our) Industry: How/with whom should we proceed? What are our competitors doing? With whom?

4. Asian/South American/etc. market development: Assess current competitive situation; describe the most likely future situations.

5. Strategic investment decisions: Identify and assess changes in the competitive environment, including:
   • Key/critical industry investments by others
   • Cash requirements of other industry companies
   • Involvement/role of investment community
   • Possible alternative sources for future investments, including alliances, acquisitions, etc.

6. Should we expand our present production capacity or build a new plant with a more cost-effective manufacturing process?

7. What plans and actions must we take to maintain (our) technological competitiveness vis-à-vis key competitors.

8. "Product" development program: Identify and assess the programs of our leading competitors and assess the status of other competing technologies.

9. New product development and roll-out: How and when will the competitors respond? How will they affect our plan?

10. How will our new distribution/sales/marketing strategy be viewed by the industry? Our competitors? Our distributors?

11. Protection of "our" proprietary information/technology
    • Competitors efforts to acquire it?
    • Others interested in it?

12. Human resource issues: Hiring and retaining key employees.

are also quite capable of searching for possible business opportunities. Again, topic subjects run the gamut, often reflecting the range and variety of the Strategic Decisions KITs. Table 2 shows a typical set of Early-Warning KITs (specific examples about competitors have been left out for the sake of brevity).

These KITs are often more cryptic than Decision and Player KITs, mainly because managers often are expressing hunches or "fears." This is natural, and your turning such KITs into intelligence monitoring activities will not only "quiet" a manager's fear but may, in fact, translate his or her unanalyzed concerns into potential business actions—even to the extent of contingency plans that can be initialed should intelligence discover early-warning signs of the realization of these fears and/or concerns.

Table 2   Examples of Early-Warning Topics

1. Areas of possible technological "breakthrough" that could dramatically affect our current and future competitiveness.

2. Technological developments, affecting either production capabilities or product development and their uses by competitors and others.

3. States and performance of Key Suppliers.
   - Their financial "health"
   - Cost & quality problems
   - Possible acquisition and/or alliances

4. Possible disruptions in supplies of crude-oil/components/and so on.

5. Change in (our) industry procurement policies and processes.

6. Change in customers/competitors perceptions of us/our services.

7. Companies and/or combinations of companies, considering possible entry into our business or markets.

8. Changes in international political, social, economic or regulatory situations that could effect our competitiveness.

9. Regulatory Issues: Near-term changes; deviations in long-term trends; other governmental changes that could impact current regulatory regimes, for example, people, policy.

10. Intelligence on Alliances, Acquisitions, and Divestitures among our competitors, customers, and suppliers:
    - Reasons and forces causing them
    - Objectives and purposes of completed deals

11. Financial Initiatives by major competitors:
    - Changes in current financial strategy(s)
    - Alliances, acquisitions, divestitures, and so on.

12. Interests and efforts by others to acquire our company.

Key Player KITs

Among the three KIT categories, Key Player KITs are the least actionable (see Table 3). They usually reflect a manager or management team's need to better understand the "player." Typically a group of managers each have a different mental model of the player and because of that they tend to think and act differently concerning that player. However, once the intelligence department provides a competitor profile or baseline assessment of the

Table 3   Examples of Key Players in the Marketplace

1. Provide profiles of our major competitors, including their strategic plans, competitive strategies, financial & market performance, organization & key personnel, R&D, operations, sales & marketing, and so on

2. Provide in-depth assessments of Key Competitors, including:
   - Their competitive intent vis-à-vis us and our major customers
   - Strategic plans and goals, including international objectives
   - Key strategies: Financial, technological, manufacturing, business development, distribution, and sales and marketing
   - Current operational and competitive capabilities

3. Identify new and emerging competitors, particularly those coming from entirely different industries and businesses.

4. Describe and assess our current and future competitive environment, including: customers and competitors; markets and suppliers; production and product technologies; political and environmental; and the industry's structure, including changes and trends.

5. New customers, their needs and future interests: What are they and how are our competitors trying to satisfy them?

6. Industry and customer views, attitudes and perceptions regarding "worth" of our branded products, services, and so on.

7. Identify and asses new industry/market players, including: Suppliers, major distributors, customers and/or competitors, that are considering entry into our business.

8. New technology/product developers: What are their plans and strategies for competing in our industry?

9. Need significant improvement in marketshare and growth data, including that of our competition.

10. Management and operations need better intelligence concerning regulatory and environmental activities for planning and decision making.

11. The investment/financial community: What are their views and perceptions of our business and industry?

12. What are the interest and purpose of various suppliers and industry observers in gathering information about our company?

player, all the managers at least have a common understanding—although they may still have different ideas about what to do about that player. Usually, the profile or assessment is developed at the beginning of an action or related decision-making process.

Player KITs can vary considerably depending on the management teams need and sophistication. The most important aspects of such KITs are the specific user questions regarding the players. For example, "Why did they change their manufacturing (or distribution) strategy?" The final intelligence report or profile should reflect all such user questions.

In one instance involving a large multinational corporation, I used the Player KIT questions posed by the heads of five different operating divisions about a common competitor to both define the competitor profile and to analytically frame the answers to their separate CI-requested questions. The resulting report was a comprehensive profile of the competitor that, in turn, supported the specific answers to their individual questions. Then, by analytically combining both, the competitor report provided the basis for developing a unified and coordinated response by several of the divisions to this common threat. In this case, addressing the users questions along with the requests for a competitor profile led to competitive action.

Using the KIT Process

Purpose is the essence of all successful intelligence operations. Therefore, that operation must begin with the identification of the intelligence requirement(s) of the company's key decision makers and/or senior management. There are two basic ways of doing this.

Responsive Mode

The first mode is entitled "Responsive." To perform in this mode, the CI organization must be prepared to address a broad range of user needs, that is, anticipate the "overall" needs of its clients. Essentially, the intelligence organization receives the user's intelligence requests and then must be prepared to deliver the necessary intelligence. This mode places a strong emphasis on taking the right orders. This, in turn, means that some intelligence requests have to be turned away.

There are two basic criteria for rejecting a user's request for intelligence. First, only true intelligence tasks should be taken: in other words, requests that are best satisfied by other departments such as market research should be redirected. The second acceptance criterion is whether the request is for intelligence or basic information. If it's for information, the request should be rejected, but with some advice on where and/or how the user can get the information from appropriate sources. But if the request is for "actionable information," i.e., intelligence focused on specific actions, decisions or issues related to the company's competitive situation, strategy or long-range planning, this task probably should be undertaken.

Proactive Mode

The second mode for identifying the users intelligence needs is entitled "Proactive." This requires the manager of the intelligence unit to take the initiative and interview the appropriate company managers and decision makers, to help them identify and define their intelligence requirements. An interview protocol can be very useful to ensure the consistency of results. Table 4 and Figure 2 are examples of such protocols. Table 4 would be used initially, possibly at the start of an intelligence program. Once the program is ongoing, the Figure 2 protocol would be more appropriate. In some cases, after a CI program has been well established, and there is good rapport between the intelligence manager and the various intelligence users, no formal protocol is needed.

The "proactive" mode, which I have called the Key Intelligence Topics (KIT) process, has several operational virtues. These stem mainly from the regular meetings with the principal intelligence users. Such meetings can be used to define and refine the users' needs as well as coordinate related intelligence requirements across the company for more effective and efficient intelligence operations. These meetings also provide a means for getting feedback from the users concerning past and ongoing work.

The operational benefits from the KIT process are also significant. First, it permits efficient planning and direction of the intelligence operations. Second, it actively involves management in the intelligence process. And finally, it, in effect, "guarantees" an interested user for the intelligence that is produced.

In my experience, some combination of these two user-selection processes is probably most appropriate. *However,* successful CI programs must also operate on their own initiative, identifying and addressing new and emerging intelligence topics that no manager has yet recognized. Intelligence programs that operate in all three modes are the most successful and produce the most valuable intelligence for their organizations.

Table 4 Competitive Intelligence Needs Survey

Purpose:

- To identify your needs for Competitive Intelligence (CI)
- To obtain your ideas and suggestions on how to best develop an intelligence capability for the company.

I. Intelligence Needs: Your Key Intelligence Topics (KITs)

A. *Decision making/Operational Responsibilities*
- Planned/future decisions or actions
- Strategic plans and related actions
- Strategic formulation and implementation

B. *Early-Warning Intelligence*
- Examples of "past" surprises
- Concerns about: Company; industry; government; etc.
- Competitors: Their actions and intent

C. *Players: Competitors, Customers, Suppliers, Others*
- Which players are you most concerned about?
- What types of information and intelligence do you need?
- What uses would you make of such intelligence?

II. Intelligence Capabilities and Uses

- What experience/familiarity do you have with intelligence?
- What types of intelligence do you currently receive?
- What intelligence capabilities does your organization have?
- Who in your organization do you expect to be regular users?
- Will your organization conduct intelligence operations to help other divisions?
- Any barriers to sharing?
- What types of intelligence products would you like to receive? (e.g., field reports, analytical alerts, competitor and competitor product assessments, intelligence briefings)
- How should the company's intelligence system be organized?
- How will you evaluate the intelligence that you receive?

GO AHEAD—TAKE THE INITIATIVE

When it comes to intelligence production, you have three basic choices:

1. Produce the CI *you believe* is needed by your management;
2. Wait until they ask you for it; or

1. Business Decisions and Strategic/Tactical Topics

What decisions and/or actions will you/your team be facing in the next ___ months, where CI could make a significant difference?

_____

_____

_____

_____

- How will you use that CI?
- When will it be needed?

2. Early-Warning Topics

(Begin by identifying/discussing a past "surprise" in your industry, business, or company.)

Identify several potential surprise topics that you do not want to be surprised by.

For example, new competitors, technology introductions, alliances & acquisitions, regulatory chances, etc.

_____

_____

_____

_____

_____

3. Key Players in Our Marketplace: Competitors, Customers, Suppliers, Regulators, etc.

Identify those players you believe the company needs to better understand.

- Who are they? _____

_____

- What specifically do we need to know?

_____

_____

Figure 2   KIT protocol.

3. Take the initiative and ask them what decisions and actions they are considering where good intelligence could help them make the right choices.

In reality you probably should be doing all three, but I would start with the third choice—the other two will evolve over time.

In taking the initiative and seeking management's Key Intelligence Topics, you should be prepared for what I call the *three classic problems*. These are situations that are likely to derail the efforts of most inexperienced CI professionals. But if you are prepared for them, you should be able to overcome them—at least on the second attempt.

The first classic problem is the reticent manager. Although most successful business managers I have interviewed are "naturals" when it comes to *using* intelligence, they are not good at *asking* for it—at least not in the beginning. They need a little coaching and/or some good examples to follow. The best way to do this is through some form of education. A management seminar on KITs and related action plans is one way. Another is having an experienced manager in the meeting with you and the executives during your first KIT interviews. Or, if you are a CI professional who is well respected in your company, you can conduct the KIT interviews by yourself, using past examples of successful intelligence operations to demonstrate how the KIT was initially described. Executive education about intelligence and how it's used is a critical success factor in the CI world.

The second classic problem is the manager who responds, "Tell me everything" about a particular competitor or competitive situation. He or she seems incapable of expressing intelligence needs in terms of a future decision or some plan or action they are contemplating. When asked what they are really looking for, they typically say, "I don't exactly know, but I will recognize it when I see it." This situation presents several dilemmas for the CI professional: The never-ending search for "the answer"; or possibly, they want an answer that fits their preconceived solution/decision. My best advice in this situation is to focus on helping managers define their need *before* beginning your intelligence collection and analysis. If this fails, try providing them with preliminary results quickly, and then using these findings to help the manager define the actual KIT.

This situation is likely to be a frustrating relationship for the CI manager. But when the intelligence operations are successful—and, they often are—the business manager is quite pleased, not only for the intelligence, but for your assistance in helping them understand the competitive situation they faced. (To understand management's decision-making styles better, I recommend you review the 1995 SCIP Annual Conference presentation on the "Dynamics of Decision Makers," by Hans Hedin and Katarina Svensson.)

A third classic problem concerning management's intelligence needs is the executive that responds with, "You tell me what intelligence I need." In my estimation this is the most frustrating situation. But you should be prepared to do just that. The KIT process is a proven and practical way of getting management's input and involvement in the intelligence process. It usually leads to a successful intelligence operation and the production of useful and actionable intelligence. But management cannot envision every possible need for intelligence, and most importantly they cannot anticipate those future competitive situations or competitor initiatives that are only beginning to evolve. These are the responsibility of the intelligence department.

So when asked, "What do I need to know?" be prepared to list several new and emerging competitors or an evolving competitive situation you have begun to study, or a new competitive strategy that others in your industry have recently begun using but your company has not . Raise any competitor-related topic that you know well, but stay away from issues and/or topics about your own company. You are the competitive intelligence expert and that is why they value your advice and input.

> The cogent identification and clear articulation of intelligence needs are the shared responsibility of intelligence users and intelligence professionals.

There are other difficulties and frustrations that you will likely face in the process of identifying and defining management's key intelligence needs. That's part of managing an intelligence department or operations. Hopefully, you will be able to cope with them based on your intelligence experience and managerial competence.

Not everyone in the organization program is "cut out" to interview management for their key intelligence needs. Not everyone wants to. But it's important that someone does it, and usually that person is the head of the unit. Managing an intelligence unit or department is a serious responsibility, including being responsible for legal and ethical practices as well as producing useful and actionable intelligence for some of the company's most important decisions and actions. Selecting the right person for the CI manager's job is tantamount to choosing the appropriate individual to identify and define the company's most important intelligence needs.

KITs ARE A SHARED RESPONSIBILITY

The identification of a company's most important intelligence needs is the *critical step in the intelligence cycle (Figure 1). Their cogent identification and clear articulation are the shared responsibility of the users and the intelligence professionals.* For management, *their stated needs for intelligence—*

by whatever process—provides them actionable access to CI resources throughout the company. For the intelligence professional, *well-defined intelligence needs are the prescription for planning and carrying out the right intelligence operations and producing the appropriate intelligence products. Both players have a critical stake in getting the "requirement" right. To accomplish this successfully requires a well-educated user and an experienced CI manager who together have created the professional environment necessary to identify and communicate real intelligence needs throughout the company. Mutual respect, trust, and confidential dialogue are the essential elements of such communications.*

REFERENCES AND RELATED READING

Barndt, W.D., Jr. (1994). *User-Directed Competitive Intelligence.* Westport, CT: Quorum Books.

Francis, D.B., & Herring, J.P. (1999). Key Intelligence Topics: A Window on the Corporate Psyche. *Competitive Intelligence Review,* 10(4), 10–19.

Hedin, H., & Svensson, K. (1995). Dynamics of Decision Makers, SCIP 1995 annual conference proceedings. [Cassette Recording]. Chicago: Teach 'em, Inc.

Herring, J.P. (1991). Senior Management Must Champion Business Intelligence Programs. *Journal of Business Strategy,* 12(5), 48–52.

Herring, J.P. (Speaker). (1993). Managing the Intelligence Operation, Vol. 1: Insight and Advice from Experienced Professionals, SCIP 1993 annual conference proceedings. [Cassette Recording]. Chicago: Teach 'em, Inc.

Herring, J.P. (1994). Managing the Intelligence Operation, Vol. 2: Producing Actionable and Effective Intelligence, SCIP 1994 annual conference proceedings. [Cassette Recording]. Chicago: Teach 'em, Inc.

Herring, J.P. (1996). *Measuring the Effectiveness of Competitive Intelligence: Assessing and Communications CI's Value to Your Organization.* Alexandria, VA: SCIP Publications.

Herring, J.P. (1997). Managing the Intelligence Operation, Vol. 3, Keys to Professional Management, SCIP 1997 annual conference proceedings. [Cassette Recording]. Chicago: Teach 'em, Inc.

ABOUT THE AUTHOR

Jan P. Herring has worked for over 35 years in the intelligence field, first as an intelligence officer at the CIA and later as the director of Motorola's intelligence program. At Motorola, his pioneering efforts resulted in the creation of the firm's business Intelligence system—based on national security principles—that is today recognized by many as the most advanced operation of its kind. Now the president of Herring & Associates, Mr. Herring helps companies design, develop, and operate their own competitive intelligence systems as well as improve their existing intelligence operations. Mr. Herring is a founding member of the Society of Competitive Intelligence Professionals, and in 1993 was awarded the Society's highest honor, the Meritorious Award for Excellence in Competitive Intelligence, in recognition of his contributions to the CI profession and to SCIP.

PART 2

COMPETITIVE TECHNICAL INTELLIGENCE

IDENTIFYING THREATS AND OPPORTUNITIES EMERGING FROM TECHNOLOGICAL CHANGE

In this second part, we delve into the subset of CI known as competitive technical intelligence (CTI). Being blindsided by a competitor's technological advances can have devastating consequences, which is why technology monitoring in its various guises is a crucial component of corporate competitive intelligence. Whether your firm operates globally or not, the ability to collect and analyze early signals indicating a competitor's future technological direction is key to maintaining competitive advantage. Yet, while the concepts of commercial competitive intelligence have been well documented, technology intelligence has not received the same level of attention. The case studies in this section go a long way toward remedying this situation.

Franz Tessun provides a look at how scenario analysis and early warning systems alert his firm, Daimler-Benz Aerospace, to technological threats. Derek L. Ransley describes Chevron's "external technology watching" program, as benchmarked against efforts at other companies. Next, Dr. Wayne A. Rosenkrans, Jr., a past SCIP president, provides an intriguing look at past, present, and future directions for technical intelligence, complete with models and case studies.

Rounding out this section, several leading authorities gathered at SCIP's first CTI symposium, where they shared views on starting a competitive technical intelligence function. The distinguished panelists share insights—and provide concrete examples—of CTI at work in major corporations.

All in all, these studies provide excellent models for monitoring—and exploiting—technology-based opportunities.

Scenario Analysis and Early Warning Systems at Daimler-Benz Aerospace

Franz Tessun

DAIMLER-BENZ AEROSPACE AG

EXECUTIVE SUMMARY

Among competitive intelligence professionals there is a perceived need to be more predictive of possible future events. By using scenario development designed to provide decision makers with insight into future possibilities, CI professionals can make significant contributions to corporate strategic planning. Based on scenarios, a strategic early warning system can be developed by constant monitoring of the company's vital statistics—financial situation, deliveries, orders received, and so on. These "signals" may not be able to be classified at the moment, but should be collected and analyzed for trends. Scenario planning points out the most important areas for monitoring. The author describes competitor analysis at Daimler-Benz Aerospace, where competitive monitoring is conducted through a strategic early warning system given its direction by scenario analysis, and how the analysis results are used to influence strategic decisions.

The complexity of the aerospace industry, with its multitude of interdependencies and interactions, calls for new ways of planning and researching into the future. Because conventional forecasting methods have proved insufficient, Damiler-Benz Aerospace adopted a scenario approach that describes how "the system" of future developments exists as a network, out of which are derived alternative future prospects for the next 20 years.

Competitive Intelligence Review, Vol. 8(4) 30–40 (1997). © 1997 John Wiley & Sons, Inc.

In a scenario, the main forces affecting future developments should be generated along with the relations between these forces. The focus is on how risk factors could change the future horizon. Scenarios describe the advent of completely different worlds, not simply different events in the same world.

Based on scenarios we create a strategic early warning system. In other words, we try constantly to keep an eye on the vital statistics, such as the financial situation, deliveries of aircraft, orders received, etc. Another indicator is the "weak signal." These are signals that cannot be classified at the moment; all you can do is collect them and try to find a trend after a few weeks of observation.

THE SCENARIO ANALYSIS TECHNIQUE

Why do we deal with the subject of scenarios within Daimler-Benz Aerospace, if we already have classical market forecasting tools for predicting the future, such as linear regression? It is not enough to use the classical and traditional methods of market forecasts because such methods deal only with historical data. Linear patterns are more or less quantitative (see Figure 1). The product cycles in our industry are more than 25 years, and it is nearly impossible to predict the need for airplanes over such a long-term period.

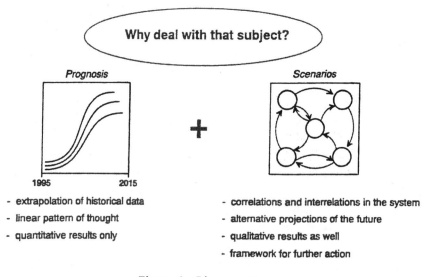

Figure 1   Linear patterns.

The scenario analysis technique is not a forecasting tool but a means of describing possible alternative futures. To repeat, a scenario describes different types of worlds altogether and not merely different events in more or less the same world as today's.

> Scenario analysis allows planning for the advent of alternative future worlds, not just for events that might occur in more or less the same world as today's.

EIGHT SCENARIO STEPS USED BY DAIMLER-BENZ AEROSPACE

The main steps in the dynamic scenario analysis process are shown in Figure 2. These consist of:

1. *Task Analysis*—Defining the problem and trying to achieve a common understanding of what you want to analyze in the future.

2. *Influence Analysis*—Analyzing all the relationships between the primary factors of the scenario. This provides the main knowledge about the dynamics of the whole system.

3. *Descriptor Determination*—Describing the contents and making definitions of all the influencing factors of the system, as determined in step two. The description most cover the current situation and give three alternative predictions of the future. This is a very creative step. Examples of a network of interrelationships and of a factor description are given in Figures 3 and 4.

4. *Building Alternatives*—Filling in a cross-impact matrix on which you evaluate the connections and interrelationships between all the predictions of the descriptor. This is not a very creative task, but nevertheless, an important one for the results of the scenario, and needs to be done carefully.

5. *Scenario Interpretation*—Entering this evaluation into the computer. The computer calculates all the possibilities and provides scenario frames, that are then formulated into standard language. Normally, two to five alternative scenarios are selected.

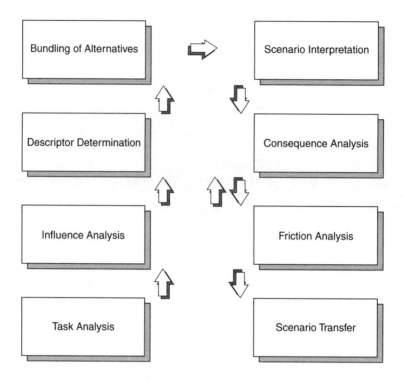

Figure 2 Steps of the dynamic scenario process.

The scenario methodology

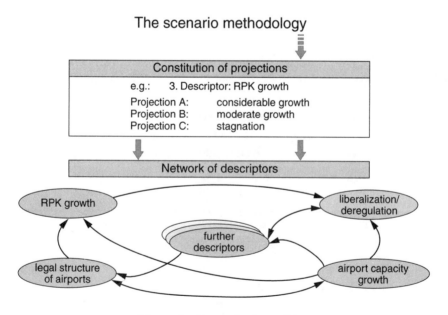

Figure 3 Example air traffic.

Descriptor: Volume of air transport

Alternative projections for the future (in percent)★

Projection A:	Strong growth (> 5 % p.a.)	30%
Projection B:	Moderate growth (1 to 5 % p.a.)	60%
Projection C:	Stagnation (medium-term reduction)	10%

★*The percentages reflect the degree of probability of the different projections.*

Description
Air transport consists of passengers (business, tourism) and cargo.
Focus is on intra-regional transport.

Premises:
• Demand for passenger and air cargo develop at different rates.
• Short- and long-haul air traffic do not develop at the same rate.

Current situation
• Currently, the annual growth in air traffic amounts 3–4 %.
• Cargo is increasingly transferred to other transportation means (typically road transport).
• Night flying is limited.

Remarks on the projections
A: The growth continues as hitherto. The main driving force is economic development and affordable ticket prices.
B: Less economic growth than expected. Transport growth is limited by capacity constraints and affordability of flying. Local crises/wars, terrorism, greater environmental consciousness and rising ticket prices dampen growth.
C: Several dampening factors coincide (projection B) and growing safety/security consciousness (accidents, terrorism, unsafe holiday regions) cause the growth to stagnate.

Figure 4   Example of a factor description.

6. *Consequence Analysis*—Establishing consequences based on the assumption that one particular scenario will take place in the future. For every chosen future world, both positive and risky consequences are suggested and interpreted.

7. *Friction Analysis*—Investigating factors that are highly unlikely, but which may have a great influence on the scenario if they do happen, for instance an atomic accident or military conflicts.

8. *Scenario Transfer*—Presenting management with various options for actions in the event of each scenario. There are normally many actions that can be undertaken regardless of how the various scenarios differ. These actions are an important starting point.

There are many examples of the scenario technique successfully applied in the past and the present. Royal Dutch/Shell, prior to the oil crisis of 1973, had developed a scenario outlining a course of action if oil prices were to rise dramatically. Shell was thus the only oil company that managed to survive the oil crisis satisfactorily. BASF, a member of the German chemical industry, currently carries out its strategic planning on the basis of scenarios. Boeing, our main competitor, also uses air traffic scenarios for strategic planning.

Daimler-Benz Aerospace has developed scenarios for the global revolution of air traffic up to the year 2015 as well as regional scenarios for the continents of Europe, North America, and Asia—investigating different regions and establishing the chances and risks in the various markets. In addition, our team recently developed a detailed scenario about the future possibilities of ground handling.

> Daimler-Benz Aerospace has developed global scenarios for air traffic up to the year 2015 as well as regional scenarios for Europe, North America and Asia.

THE EARLY WARNING SYSTEM

After having developed scenarios, you have possible pictures of the future and a better understanding of the interrelationships between the factors within the scenarios. But you know nothing about the realistic and short-term trends for these factors, or whether your future projections for these factors are really correct. In short, you need to develop and put into place a monitoring system to determine what will be going on in the future and whether, with the passing of time, the predictions you have made are still correct.

Figure 5 shows the qualitative information management system used by Daimler-Benz Aerospace. A key element of our information management system is scenario planning, which looks 10 to 20 years into the future. From that, we periodically evaluate a so-called "guide strategy."

We have also developed business plans for our operational business. So, the scenario planning is based on an environment monitoring system, into which we put in qualitative information. We have selected a number of individuals throughout the company to be monitors or "scanners," they are

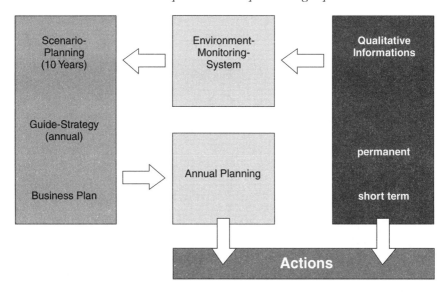

Figure 5   Qualitative information-management.

on the lookout for special areas of interest, new developments, and the latest research results from around the world.

If there is a trend that needs to be followed in the near future, we use it for our scenario planning, and for correcting and modifying our basic scenario. Business and scenario planning is made a part of the annual planning process. If necessary, we modify the strategies or business plans based on what the scenario analysis-based monitoring (the strategic early warning system) is telling us.

Strategies and business plans are modified based on the firm's scenario analysis-based competitive monitoring (the strategic early warning system).

Moreover, there are always some short-term developments that are observed by the scanners within the respective countries, and we try to dedicate some actions to these. We inform the management of such trends to give them the chance to decide whether the identified trends are important for our company.

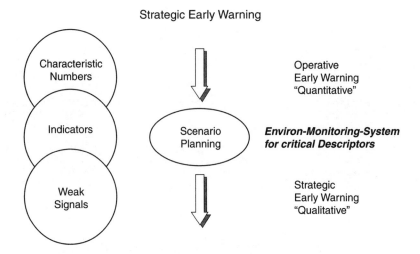

Figure 6   Strategic early warning system.

Figure 6 charts the strategic early warning system in our company. In other words, we constantly keep an eye on the vital statistics. These figures will, for instance, cover the financial situation, deliveries of aircraft, orders received, and so on.

Then, there are other important indicators, for example, the increase in the world population or the world economic growth. We consider the trends expressed by these indicators and look for those trends that could realistically influence our business at the moment.

"Weak signals" are also trend indicators. As noted earlier, these are signals that cannot be classified at the moment, so all you can do is collect them and try to find a trend after a few weeks.

It is clear that you can't monitor all the fields that are essential to your business. However, scenario planning provides hints as to what and where the most important developments are, and which ones are "driving" the system (and therefore need to be given priority monitoring).

THE INFORMATION BASE

What are the information sources for such a strategic early warning system? As shown in Figure 7, we need a great number of information sources. First, there is primary market research and benchmarking. Then, there is secondary market research, market studies, and branch studies.

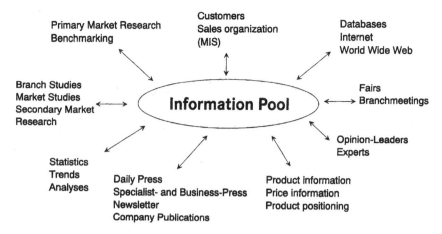

Primary Market Research
Benchmarking

Customers
Sales organization
(MIS)

Databases
Internet
World Wide Web

Branch Studies
Market Studies
Secondary Market
Research

Information Pool

Fairs
Branchmeetings

Opinion-Leaders
Experts

Statistics
Trends
Analyses

Daily Press
Specialist- and Business-Press
Newsletter
Company Publications

Product information
Price information
Product positioning

Figure 7 Information sources for a strategic early warning system.

We use statistics, plans, and analyses. We evaluate the daily press, specialist and business press, trend letters, company publications, product information, price information, product positioning, opinion leaders and experts, branch meetings, databases, the Internet and World Wide Web, and customers' sales organizations, including marketing information systems (MIS).

Nearly all available information sources are used in our company. This could only be accomplished through the cooperation of a number of people who have agreed to collect the needed information and pass it on to us.

THE COMMUNICATION PROCESS

We then evaluate and interpret this data, and summarize the information in a way that is readable and comprehensible to management. Within Daimler-Benz Aerospace, we have put the qualitative marketing information system into practice as described. We have marketing areas, the destination market, sales channels, competition, and the macro-area. All these elements are important for our strategic early warning system, for traditional market research, and for monitoring competitors.

We try to carry out enhanced management reporting, which takes place about every third month with the purpose of supporting management. We have specific reporting for our technical program leaders, which is intended

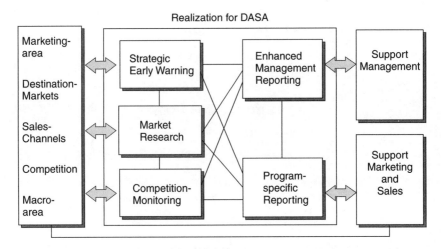

Figure 8   Marketing information system.

to support the marketing and sales functions in our company. Figure 8 shows the interrelationships between all these elements. As you would suppose, the main problem here is communicating and coordinating all these heterogeneous tasks.

CONVINCING MANAGEMENT

In today's competitive economy (see Figure 9), every company faces great turbulence, uncertainty, and complexity in its market environment. In the past, it often was good enough to have internal strategic development. We saw that we were dealing with structured markets that made future calculations, and thus stable forecasts, possible. Nowadays, we have a very uncertain environment, which is sure to become more uncertain as time goes on. We must learn to understand the complexity of this environment and incorporate it into our strategic development. We must react to the dynamics of the market and realize that the future is very difficult to foresee—things are changing faster than in the past. To cope with the surprises many trends present, we must try to incorporate new scenario techniques, to better deal with all the challenges of the future.

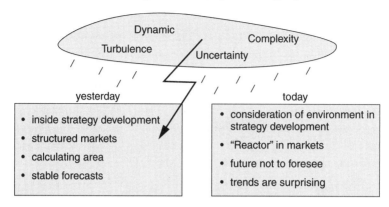

Figure 9   Market environment.

Unfortunately, management will often not accept the first weak signals and qualitative hints of a possible event. More than two years ago, we warned management about the possible merger between Boeing and McDonnell Douglas. Top management did not believe this intelligence because it was based only on weak signals, such as a rise in outsourcing at McDonnell Douglas, increased meetings held between Boeing and McDonnell Douglas as well as with the government, and so on.

> "Weak signals" such as an increase in meetings that McDonnell Douglas and Boeing were holding with one another and with the government warned of their possible merger.

IMPLEMENTATION OF THE TOTAL PROCESS

Let's turn to another area connected with competitive monitoring. What is to be done if there is a problem to be solved (see Figure 10)? The first step is to collect all the relevant ideas from key staff inside the company. For instance, we bring together the strategic staff, board of directors, product divisions, marketing experts, and relevant others. These people sit down together and view the problems, evaluate them, and then prioritize the problems to effectively deal with them. Our next step is the implementation of large-scale studies.

To help us, we have a "study board" that plans, monitors, and coordinates all the activities needed for such a large-scale study. We involve all the important and essential groups within our country, and all the external experts and databases we need. Then, we make a formal analysis, and the results are discussed with our experts within Daimler-Benz Aerospace.

We have learned from experience that it is important to involve all the product divisions in our study and decision-making processes to ensure acceptance of the results. Even the most painful decisions should be discussed with the departments involved at a very early stage.

Strategic studies help to formulate and evaluate strategies to achieve corporate objectives. They take into account environment, resources, and product interests. We involve people dealing with the technologies, R&D activities, manufacturing infrastructures, alliances, and with financial assets. We also have to keep politics, economics, industrial trends, markets, and all the relevant aspects of the global and regional environment in mind.

As I described earlier, we try to analyze all these factors within a large network of interrelationships to get a deeper understanding of the dynamics of the system. For instance, we have found that the anticipated pattern of the air transport system is more important strategically than the precise forecast of the numbers of aircraft required in the next century.

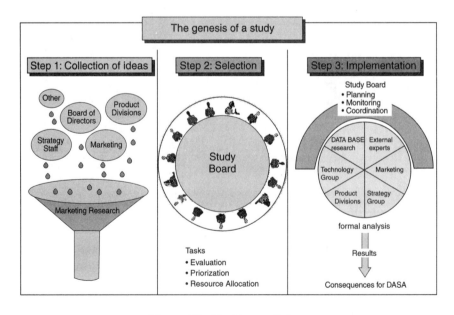

Figure 10   Problem solving.

Competitor Analysis

Finally, let me add a few words about competitor analysis. Competitor analysis in detail and with strategic conclusions is only carried out at Daimler-Benz Aerospace on demand. We have the current basic data for our main competitors in our database. On demand, we form small, competitor-specific expert groups to generate a new competitor analysis. We have developed a master document to guide the group through the analysis. If you can answer all the questions in this document, you will have achieved a competitor analysis by "150%."

All the analysis made by the team can be found in a special database called DAMIS, which stands for "Dasa Market Information System" ("DASA" is an acronym for Daimler-Benz Aerospace). Here, you can locate every single competitor analysis as well as all the people who know anything about this specific competitor. The experts from each division meet twice a year for the purpose of updating our DAMIS database.

Students do the basic work in the investigation of our competitors. They collect the basic data, put it into the database, and make basic interpretations. This is an important fact to note because many colleagues have doubted whether students could carry out this task. Our experience is that the students do a fantastic job, providing you take a little bit of care as to how they are working and what they are capable of doing.

We have many information sources that enable us to carry out good competitor analyses, including our own database, databases on commercial hosts, our company archive with annual reports, magazines, newspapers, etc. We are a large company, so we are fortunate to have some experts within our own Daimler-Benz Group. We also make use of people from our foreign representative offices. In addition, we have some good friends in other companies, some special contacts with banks and brokers, and so on, to whom we can turn to. This is a sensitive issue, but I'm sure every competitive analyst has such relationships.

In Figure 11, you can see the main competitors of our company together with aircraft sales for the year 1994. Boeing, McDonnell Douglas,

Competitor data and analysis can be retrieved from the company's own market information database, updated by experts from each division.

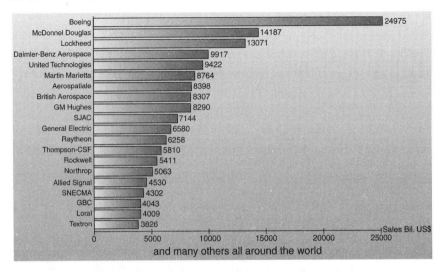

Figure 11   The main competitors of DASA.

and Lockheed are in front of us, a little behind us, there is United Technologies, Martin Marietta, Aerospatiale, British Aerospace, and GM. As you may well imagine, there is a tremendous amount of work to do in monitoring all these competitors to know at the earliest stage possible what their future strategies and technology planning will be. Boeing and McDonnell Douglas have merged recently, and therefore we must know as soon as possible what their strategic approach is to remain competitive in the market.

SUMMARY

Innovation is a driving factor in our future economy. Nonetheless, it is very important to have the right product at the right time. You don't want a product that no one will buy.

Unexpected delays in product development or market changes are the norm and not the exception. Such changes in the competitive landscape also lead to changes in the mental models in the heads of management decision makers, or at least lead to a systematic monitoring of the environment. For future-oriented knowledge management, it is not enough to buy some trend predictions or forecasts and to conveniently overlook possible trend frictions. We must understand at a fundamental level that the future is not just a continuation of the past.

ABOUT THE AUTHOR

Franz Tessun is vice president of Market Research for Daimler-Benz Aerospace AG, where he is responsible for the central market research department.

CTI at Applied Biosystems: Attracting, Monitoring, and Exploiting Technology-Based Opportunities

Tim Budd

APPLIED BIOSYSTEMS (FORMERLY PE BIOSYSTEMS)

EXECUTIVE SUMMARY

The following keynote address was delivered at SCIP's June 2000 Competitive Technical Intelligence Symposium, held in San Francisco, California. Mr. Budd is director of business development at Applied Biosystems, a unit of PE Corporation (formerly Perkin-Elmer) that is recognized worldwide as one of the leaders and innovators in the areas of biotechnology and advanced applications, and which is at the forefront of the momentous changes in the world of genomics. He describes how the firm's Science & Technology exploratory group acts as an idea incubator, reaching out to research labs in an effort to find and exploit new "quantum leaps." The role of partnerships, strategic alliances, and external collaborations in fostering exposure to new ideas is also discussed.

I'd like to share with you a little bit about Applied Biosystems—how we came into existence, how we continue to build upon our initial successes in the marketplace, and the kinds of systems we've put into place to ensure that we're continually focused on the outside world and future possibilities.

Competitive Intelligence Review, Vol. 11(4) 5–11 (2000).

Many companies are first set up based on a technology, and then look for problems to solve. Applied Biosystems was different. A number of venture capitalists in the San Francisco Bay Area, as they put together some of the large biotech companies centered here, noted that many of the processes that researchers at these companies wanted to do they could not do effectively. There was an unsatisfied need in the growing biotech industry for a "tool company" to generate advanced research instruments. So, in conjunction with a number of companies such as Amgen, the Salk Institute, Monsanto, Biogen, and the Genetics Institute, in May 1981, they funded a company to develop innovative tools to assist researchers in tapping into the genomic revolution, which was then just getting underway. Thus, Applied Biosystems was born.

An Outward Focus

Our firm started life with an outward focus on customer needs. We continue to look to our customers as a source of new ideas, giving us a broader perspective on the market, and to maintain close ties with universities to keep us focused on researchers' needs.

As researchers became more and more involved in the genomic race, they found that they had to cobble together systems. These systems were specific to their labs, often more art than science, and might involve grabbing a box from here and some chemistry from there and some software from somewhere else, and only one person was usually able to get those systems to work. The benefit we could provide our customers—the researchers who want to do research—was to develop and sell one-stop, complete solutions.

From the start, we established close ties with university laboratories, the public laboratories that have the problems that need solutions. These have been an excellent source of intellectual property and a key growth-driver for our business.

For example, in the early '80s, there was a significant need for greater protein sequence sensitivity—the ability to pull out specific proteins and study them (and to reduce the amount of material needed). For that reason, the first product out of Applied Biosystems was the 470A Protein Sequencer, allowing researchers to find the code that makes up a protein and determine what it does in the cell.

A prototype had been developed by Lee Hood at CalTech. This would become our typical pattern, to take a prototype from one of the labs (our customers) and add reliability and reproducibility such that it can be used on a much broader scale. We rely heavily on the researchers themselves to provide the germ of ideas, and this first product was founded on a technology customers wanted. From the standpoint of researchers working with prototype instruments and patching together solutions, we offered the ability to carry out their work with solutions from the same company (Applied Biosystems).

The Protein Sequencer used a gas-phase technology 100 times more sensitive than the competition. For the first time, researchers could rapidly decode a large number of proteins. In one year, we went from zero to 90% market share and doubled the market size.

Solutions always generate new questions. With more proteins decoded, researchers needed a way back to the related gene ("the golden trail"), so they could pursue possible targets for gene therapy, new drugs, an understanding of cellular control processes, and how gene mutation leads to disease. By being in close contact with these researchers, and focusing on ways that new instruments could save them time and money, we were there to help them. We were able to speed commercial development by combining engineering from the Protein Sequencer with innovative science, this time at the University of Colorado's chemistry department, and thus develop and sell an instrument that joined a protein sequence with a synthetic DNA probe to enable rapid gene identification. Thus, our second product, the 388 DNA synthesizer, was born.

In 1983, the firm went through its initial public offering (IPO), and was profitable the same year due to sales of these two research instruments. But if we were to continue growing, we knew we would have to maintain the ability to stay close to the market. For that reason, we established a European headquarters in Darmstadt, Germany, where many of the ideas were now coming from in the genomic race. We added manufacturing in Warrinton, U.K., where many of our customers were located. We acquired a Japanese distributor in 1986, and anyone who has worked in Japan knows that unless you're close to the customer, and selling directly to the customer, you're not going to know what's going on. We set up regional centers that were able to customize chemistries for individual researchers around the world, to stay current with customer needs, and thus became a global operation.

SCIENCE & TECHNOLOGY
EXPLORATORY GROUP

One question we faced as we continued to grow bigger and bigger was how could we maintain our innovative edge by staying closely attuned to the needs of our customers, and stay aware of emerging science that could help us to meet those needs?

Many of our business units are focused on the product they have today and on innovations that the customer wants tomorrow. What can be lost sight of is what's going to drive sales in three to five years? We came up with the concept called the Science & Technology (S&T) exploratory group, an effort to mirror the environment of our customers. The S&T group is an effort to understand the milieu that the researchers—our customers—work in, so we talk the same language. We set up S&T with the responsibility to look at opportunities as opposed to product development or continued development of products we already had on the market (Figure 1).

S&T is focused on looking at the next quantum leap, as opposed to the next incremental improvement. It is able to frame, monitor, and quickly coordinate possible business opportunities, but also has the responsibility of selling those to the business units to develop. That is, we have to frame those opportunities in such a way that they represent a significant business opportunity. So we wear two hats.

	Technical		Business	
Engineering	Optics	Chem/Bio	Strategic Alliances	Business Development
Research/ evaluate technologies	Laser specifications	Synthesize novel chemistries	3M oversight	Coordinate planning
Design specifications	Design detection systems	Design assays	Aclara oversight	Monitor/seek opportunities
Build prototypes	Valid sensitivities	New material characterization	Cross business unit coordination	Information management

Figure 1   Applied Biosystems' S&T programs.

S&T gets a set slice of the research budget for Applied Biosystems every year. If it isn't looking at what's going to be prime time in three to five years, then it's not doing its job. It develops at the prototype stage, providing a source of funding for researchers, who are able to look at what the next new idea is.

S&T became viewed as an idea incubator by third parties. Many big companies come to smaller companies and say, "I'm focused on today and I don't have the time; can you finish that idea off yourself?" Often, researchers just don't have the funds to do that kind of activity. By creating S&T, we've provided them with support, and therefore had easier access to intellectual property (IP), which is the lifeblood of our industry.

What we basically had done was create a small company within a big company (see Table 1). S&T was designed as an exploratory group that acts as a portal for nascent technologies. It has independent funding, so when times got rough and budgets got cut, it operated as a stand-alone unit and could continue because its focus was into the future. Smaller companies in the Bay Area and around the world are able to approach S&T directly and avoid a lot of the red tape you get when you approach the front door of a large corporation. And academics can approach us much more easily.

S&T also has the ability to apply for government grants. Millions of dollars go into public research labs and funding at universities, and the government wants tangible proof of results. S&T can demonstrate that investments in basic research can be commercialized rapidly.

One of the key strengths of having a small company in a big company is: You can generate ideas, which are never very far away from reality. S&T combines technology and business capability.

S&T is set up with various areas that are complementary—and, more importantly, ones that can come up with answers—so that by the time we go to the operating units and say, "We've got an idea we want you to turn into

Table 1   The Need for a Small Company within a Big Company

Creating an exploratory group as a portal for nascent technologies.
- Independent internal funding encouraging risk taking.
- Early start-ups can partner with less red tape.
- Ability to apply for government grants to leverage spending.
- Internal researchers drive "insider access" to academic labs.
- Academics can approach easily.

a product," we already have a prototype to show the idea can work. We already know that the materials in that product can meet the specifications required, and we already know that all aspects of the optics, which are really the critical aspects of these systems, will work and deliver the results wanted.

PARTNERSHIPS AND EXTERNAL STRATEGIC ALLIANCES

DNA is not always available in large quantities, and researchers needed a way to amplify small DNA samples. We looked outside and found that a small company called Cetus had come up with a solution called polymerase chain reaction, or PCR. Hoffmann-LaRoche had licensed the rights to sell diagnostic products based on this technology, but Perkin-Elmer had the rights to research applications, which was our business. We approached Perkin-Elmer, studied each other, and found we'd be a complementary fit—Perkin-Elmer sold analytical and measurement equipment, while we were focused on life sciences. In 1993, Applied Biosystems merged with Perkin-Elmer and became PE Biosystems (although, in July 2000, our name reverted to Applied Biosystems). We not only gained rights to PCR research applications, but also capital for expansion, synergistic sales and support operations, and complementary geographic strengths, while Perkin-Elmer obtained a way to capitalize on IP that they had licensed.*

We saw from the microchip revolution that through miniaturization you can take a process and apply it to many new applications. We decided to parallel this development and to reduce the size of the technologies we had developed, in order to carry out experiments on a smaller scale while maintaining reproducibility of results, with the eventual goal of miniaturizing to "labs onto a chip."

We looked outside again. A company called Aclara BioSciences had some unique intellectual property in terms of systems to overcome barriers to miniaturization. S&T sent a delegation of scientists and engineers to Aclara to discuss whether its IP was practical to develop commercially. As soon as we ascertained it was, the businesspeople were already involved because they were part of the S&T group, and we could rapidly establish a

---

* In March 1999, slow-growth businesses (including analytical instruments) and the Perkin-Elmer name were sold. PE Corporation is today comprised of Applied Biosystems and Celera, a separate genomic-content company established in 1998.

relationship. This provided a benefit to our customer and made us more attractive to the partner, because they were looking for funding and for commercialization capability. By working with the S&T group at a much larger corporation, they were quickly able to gain access.

A decision many companies face is: Do we continue to invest in new hard assets? Do we build new manufacturing plants? Or is there someone we should partner with? We were faced with this decision. Looking out at the marketplace, we found that indeed there was in 3M, a company that had a very comprehensive material-science capability. By forming an alliance, we were able to utilize 3M's high-volume manufacturing capabilities, as well as other benefits we needed to capitalize on miniaturization (Table 2).

Importantly, 3M wanted to move into the life-sciences business. They saw the margins and the growth opportunities there. They were as hungry as we were to put together a collaboration. By investing in the relationship versus more hard assets, we were able to build miniaturization capability profitably.

OTHER EXTERNAL COLLABORATIONS

The projected growth curve for Applied Biosystems means bringing new partnering strategies to a company that has built itself from its roots in university laboratories and came to be a leading player in the race to unravel the mysteries of the human genome.

We have set up many external collaborations. That's simply because we can't afford the NIH (not invented here) syndrome. When you've gotten some successes under your belt, you begin to think that you're the only ones who can do it. Our key way of making sure that doesn't happen is setting up a broad range of collaborations in various areas, where we're constantly exposed to new ideas and we're constantly humbled by what other

Table 2   Scale Up and Manufacturing: The 3M Alliance

- Comprehensive materials-science capability.
- High-volume manufacturing methods.
- State-of-the-art metrology capability.
- Laminated interconnect technology.
- Microreplication technology.
- Mandate to develop life-science business.

people can do (the results of some of these external partnerships/strategic alliances are summarized in Table 3).

Responding at "Warp Speed"

In 1997, work was progressing on a next-generation DNA sequencing system. Field personnel were reporting strong interest in a "Big Biology" sequencer program and a possible competitive product launch. The race to sequence the human genome was exponentially accelerating sequencing needs. Clearly, there was a need to protect our market position as this new segment grew in importance.

With updated competitor surveillance from the field, the in-house program raced ahead. In September 1998, a prototype factory-scale instrument was demonstrated. Orders were placed even without a production model. By January 1999, Celera (a separate company within PE Corporation that delivers genomic content) had ordered 240 units, and other customers ordered 170 units (at approximately $300K per unit plus reagents). In April 1999, our 3700 Analyzer System shipped. Its automation capability targets the large genomic companies and government labs,

Table 3 Proactively Attract Ideas

External Strategic Alliances

- 3M (materials and manufacturing)
- Aclara BioSciences (microfluidics)
- AMC (prototyping and manufacturing)
- Cornell Med. (ZipCode™)
- HySeq (microarray methodology development)
- Hitachi (technology development)
- Phase-1 (molecular toxicology)
- Third Wave (NDA/RNA detection methods)
- Illumina (microarray SNP profiling)
- BMI/Becton Dickinson (cell surface analysis)
- Genomical (bioinformatics)
- Symyx (polymer technology)
- Standord (Y2 hybrid)
- University of Colorado (DNA synthesis)
- Caltech (protein/DNA sequencing)

and the competition can't match its automation or throughput. By December 1999, the 1,000th unit had shipped!

AN INWARD FOCUS, TOO

Shifting gears, much as it's important for us to look outward, we also can't lose sight of the fact that many ideas come from inside. So we also foster internal collaborations (Table 4). If you have a good idea and want to develop it, you have the opportunity to take a sabbatical in S&T. We have postdoctoral students coming into S&T, bringing fresh ideas. A secondary benefit is that the labs they come from now know more about us, and we have better access to the intellectual property coming out of those labs.

By providing seed funding for our own people to develop ideas, we lose fewer employees to the outside world (or to their own start-up companies). By setting up "New Idea" days, we allow people an opportunity to submit ideas for review by their peers. And by having personnel rotations back in and out of S&T, we avoid the syndrome of getting stale after a number of years because we're just continuing to do what we've already done.

What we don't do is divorce people off in a separate section. By having constant interaction with the project teams, by constantly sitting down for lunch because we're all sitting in the same site, S&T is not divorced from the operating units. They work together, they play together, and they talk together. We rotate people out of the operating units when they have a good idea and want to tackle something new. When those people leave the S&T group, they're back out in the operating units, and bonds have been formed. This rotation is critical to keeping ideas flowing, and keeping us focused on what is going to be real, not what's going to be "nice to have."

It's not just the scientists or the people in the labs who come up with good ideas; a manager in our customer-service department identified that one of the needs of the customers was to keep their machines and systems up and running—that avoiding research downtime was critical for them.

Table 4   Internal Collaborations

- Sabbaticals, postdoctorals
- Seed funding for early opportunities
- New Idea Day
- Personnel rotations

He had an idea for a system that would remotely monitor the installations we had in our customers' labs, so we could pull that information back and provide service earlier. This idea is now being implemented.

COORDINATION AND COMMUNICATION

As well as alliances to oversee, we have a need to coordinate planning across the company, because when you get larger, there's so much more information that needs to be processed if you're going to stay in touch with what's going on.

We recognized that with 23 buildings in Foster City, several sites out west, manufacturing in Singapore and elsewhere, we had to create systems so that one hand knew what the other hand was doing.

We created a database system in Lotus Notes for everyone in the company (Figure 2). It tracks what we're doing, who we're looking at, what aspects of that relationship are important. If in one area of our Foster City offices we're working with a company, there's a description of what's going on there. Someone in our operations back East may look at that and say, "You know, that may be applicable here. Why don't I get in touch with the person who's doing this?"

One of the worst things you can do when you create a database is make it basically an electronic filing cabinet. An important element of this database is its discussion boards, so that if something happens between the researchers or the engineers involved in a project, their actual discussion is captured. A year down the road, when someone else is facing that same problem, they'll know how it was solved. Creating dynamism within the information tracking tools is critical to the success of actually leveraging opportunities across a large company.

Someone in Singapore can know what someone in Foster City is doing, and what someone out in Framingham thinks of it. That's the only way that you instill an ability to keep looking for new ideas on the outside.

THE FUTURE

Going forward, how will the future be different? We'll need to continually develop new products and technologies that exploit advances that we can't even perceive today. Ideas are going to come from different places

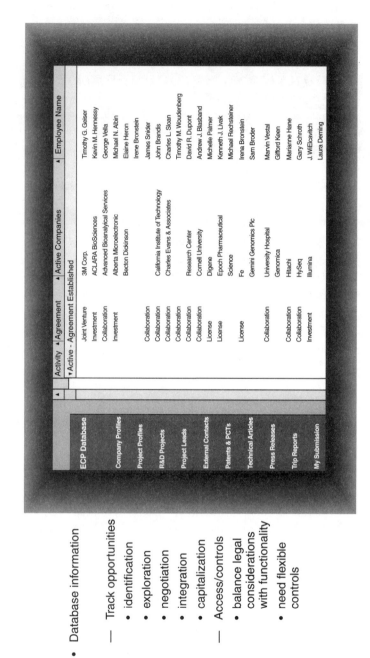

Figure 2 Leverage ideas and relationships.

284

than they have in the past. There will be new markets to focus us, more products and technologies to exploit advances in genomics, and more global manufacturing and R&D.

Preventive medicine—pharmaceutical genomics—will be customized to you personally—an enormous opportunity. No one knows what it's going to look like yet, but we do know that new instrumentation and new diagnostic capabilities will be right in the doctor's office.

Success will continue to come from attracting the right partners to move the company into new areas. But critically, the Science & Technology group within Applied Biosystems will manage the risk, ensure that we're not just doing development for development's sake, and keep an eye on the commercial opportunities.

Applied Biosystems will continue to look to the outside for new ideas and new partners, and combine that with innovative structures internally so that we can maintain our focus on the customer and keep moving quickly enough to stay ahead of the competition.

RELATED READING

SCIP's CTI Symposium: Shedding Light on Science & Technology, *Competitive Intelligence Magazine,* 3(4), October–December 2000, pp. 12–14. Online at www.scip.org/news/cimagazine.html.

ABOUT THE AUTHOR

Tim Budd is director of business development at Applied Biosystems, one of the leaders and innovators in the area of biotechnology and advanced applications, and the second largest employer of high-tech people in the Bay Area. After graduating from the University of Toronto with a master's degree in neurophysiology, he entered the pharmaceutical industry in sales, marketing, and business development. Prior to joining Applied Biosystems, he served as director of marketing with Syntex Pharmaceuticals. He can be contacted at Applied Biosystems, 850 Lincoln Centre Drive, Foster City, CA 94404; Web site: www.appliedbiosystems.com.

Benchmarking the "External Technology Watching" Process: Chevron's Experience

Derek L. Ransley
CHEVRON RESEARCH AND TECHNOLOGY COMPANY

EXECUTIVE SUMMARY

"External Technology Watch," or ETW, is Chevron's term for monitoring how emerging technologies can impact the company. Traditionally, as with other companies, Chevron's long-range research efforts were focused on serving the research needs of existing business units. The additional efforts of its technology awareness committee are geared toward monitoring technologies not now within any business unit's planning horizons. A benchmarking study comparing technology monitoring at several companies showed the importance of paying attention to the context within which ETW is carried out. Chief technology officers, or senior technology committees, can help position efforts to better meet the CEO's initiatives. Identifying enabling technologies that support core competencies was a key issue, as was having formalized ETW processes linked to mainstream R&D activities, including joint activities with universities, government labs, and other companies.

L ooking outside one's own company for technology developments has become an increasingly important process. There are several reasons for this:

- Few companies can rely on their own developed R&D to meet their technology needs because of both cost and time constraints.

Competitive Intelligence Review, Vol. 7(3), 28–33 (1996). © 1996 John Wiley & Sons, Inc.

- Relying on self-developed R&D leaves your company open to being blind-sided.

- It's good practice to leverage the R&D dollar by taking advantage of other's progress.

In a recent paper, Herb Fusfeld (1995: 52–56) states that "Technology managers have had to develop access to external sources of technology, not simply to have more information but to identify partners for future research programs." It's Fusfeld's contention that sometime between the mid-1970s and the late 1980s, "industrial research came up against a limiting characteristic of technical progress," creating "a steady rise in the cost and complexity of generating technical advances." Thus the technical self-sufficiency of corporations began to decline.

"External Technology Watching" (ETW) is Chevron's term for monitoring changes in the technology arena that can impact our company, both positively and negatively. As with other companies, we have become aware of technology changes through our long-range research program, which we leverage through joint programs with universities, government labs, and other companies. However, our long-range research effort is governed by the needs of the existing businesses and, while the company sponsors research both inside and outside of Chevron, the program is not charged with monitoring technologies that are not now within any business unit's planning horizon.

In contrast, Chevron's Technology Awareness Committee was formed in 1988 to "watch" for technologies that might impact our company in the future, even though they are not now an issue for any of our business units. The committee is a corporately funded group of middle managers from both our technology and our operating units. The committee identifies areas of technology to watch and supports networks of interested Chevron employees who agree to attend external conferences, follow the literature, interact with academia, and so on. However, neither the committee nor the networks sponsor or conduct research.

> The committee identifies areas of technology to watch and supports networks of interested Chevron employees who agree to attend conferences, follow the literature, interact with academia, etc.

Typical of this effort are a network focused on global climate change and another on electric vehicles. The former subject is not one that a Chevron business unit would want to spend its R&D dollars on, although we would certainly benefit from being aware of any possible impact on the industry. As to the Electric Vehicles network, since electric vehicles have now advanced into Chevron's planning time frame, this network has turned over to the business its knowledge, accumulated over several years (e.g., how batteries became more efficient over time).

The networks focus on technology rather than the social/political issues (e.g., when cold fusion had its day, the committee was able to respond to senior management's concerns by assembling the facts that assured them it was not a threat to our business).

Overall, the Technology Awareness Committee was satisfied with the ETW process but wanted to see if it could be improved. For that reason, a benchmarking study was commissioned.

THE BENCHMARKING STUDY

Once we decided to undertake a benchmarking study, we sought an external consultant to assist in the process. We had learned about Verna Allee and the Integral Performance Group (Allee, 1995: 50–57) at a meeting of the Strategic Planning Institute's Council on Benchmarking. We hired IPG to help us do the secondary research, identify best practice partners and to develop the questionnaire that we used in the data gathering phase of our study. A joint presentation was made by the author and Ms. Allee at SCIP's 10th Annual International Conference in 1995. The methodology used is described more fully in her paper (Allee, 1995: 50–57).

The final participants—our partners in the Chevron-sponsored study—were:

- Amoco Corporation
- British Petroleum
- Elf Aquitaine
- Electric Power Research Institute (EPRI)
- DuPont
- Eastman Chemical Company

- 3M
- Monsanto Company

The questionnaire, developed in conjunction with IPG, was sent to the participants (see Allee, 1995: 55–56, for a sample questionnaire). Subsequently, data was then gathered by face-to-face interviews, telephone interviews and video conferences.

THE FINDINGS

We had fully expected to learn about different approaches other companies used to learn about external technology threats and opportunities. This was the case. However, we quickly realized that we also had to pay attention to the context within which ETW was occurring. By context we mean the organization, systems, and processes used by our benchmarking partners that made them successful in this area.

The Context

Figure 1 summarizes the context findings. It shows that all participants had a Senior Technology Committee. In many cases the committee was chaired by a chief technology officer. Several companies had formal external technology watching groups or individuals who had taken on this task. About half of the participants had spent considerable efforts to understand their core competencies. All these factors were perceived as being strong positive influences on the external technology watching process.

		Companies							
Contextual Areas	*Chevron*	*A*	*B*	*C*	*D*	*E*	*F*	*G*	*H*
Senior Technology Committee		X	X	X	X	X	X	X	X
Chief Technology Officer		X	X	X	X		X	X	X
Formal ETW Process	X			X	X	X		X	
Core Competency Focus				X	X	X	X		
Baldridge Criteria Used	X			X	X	X	X		

Figure 1 Summary of context findings.

> Several companies in the benchmarking study had formal ETW groups or individuals who had taken on this task. About half of the participants had spent considerable efforts to understand their core competencies.

We also learned that many companies with technology watching efforts use the criteria of the Malcolm Baldrige National Quality Award to focus their improvement efforts. We were not clear whether this affected their ETW process. However, it does indicate a process-driven company.

SENIOR TECHNOLOGY COMMITTEES AND THE CHIEF TECHNOLOGY OFFICER

The role of the committee is to make high-level R&D decisions, to effectively integrate the total corporate technical resources, to resolve cross-operating company issues, and to identify areas to be studied that are not now part of the immediate technical program. It has the ability to bring resources to external technology watching efforts and can identify the needs and interests of senior corporate officers. Chief technology officers, depending how close they are to their CEOs, can bring key technology issues to their attention as well as help to better position technology efforts to meet the CEO's initiatives. Subsequent to our study, a paper by Ed Roberts (1995: 44–56) of MIT decried the fact that so few U.S. companies had chief technology officers. Our partners were strongly supportive of the CTO position.

FORMAL ETW GROUPS/PEOPLE

Four of our participants had formal ETW processes with staff in place to do the work. These groups were an integral part of the mainstream technology activity. They were well known throughout their companies, occupied positions of prestige, and were recognized as valuable contributors. Usually, the process was tied to a technology needs assessment with a focus on the long term.

CORE COMPETENCIES

The tests for core competencies, as defined by Prahalad and Hamel (1990: 79–91) questions whether the competency:

- Provides "potential access to a wide variety of markets."
- Makes a significant contribution to the perceived customer benefits of the end product.
- Is difficult for a competitor to imitate.

Understanding their core competencies and identifying enabling technologies that support core competencies, was a key issue for our partners in focusing the ETW process. Understanding the key capabilities needed to support the core competencies, in turn, helped with workforce planning.

Most of the companies in our study had offices in Washington, DC that were responsible for keeping the company aware of social and political changes. Although most of these companies did not consider this as part of their ETW process, there was substantial variation in the degree to which this high-level information was shared around the company. Often the ETW group or person was aware of these factors but only included them informally in the ETW process.

ETW Approaches

Figure 2 summarizes the findings related to approaches used by different companies to learn about technology changes external to their companies. These include the "tried and true" approaches as well as some unique methods. Even with the more common approaches there were lessons to be learned.

University Programs

Joint programs with universities used to be thought of as an aid to recruiting and something of a charitable donation. This is far from true today. Companies enter into joint programs with the full expectation of a return. It is now thought of as a mutual benefit. Although an immediate project may be the focus, the interaction provides the industry an opportunity to become aware of new developments and to begin planning for their application.

ETW Activities	Chevron	A	B	C	D	E	F	G	H
Government/Public Affairs					X	X	X	X	X
University Programs	X	X	X	X	X	X	X	X	X
Government Programs	X	X		X	X	X	X	X	X
Alliances w/Other Companies	X		X	X	X	X		X	X
Offices in Other Countries				X	X	X		X	X
Professional Societies	X	X	X	X	X	X	X	X	X
Internal Networks	X	X	X		X			X	X
Scientist Forums		X			X		X	X	X
Key Expert Panels					X				
Sabbaticals (In/Out)				I/O	I/O	O			
Ext. Advisory Committee					X	X	X		
Consultants	X		X	X	X	X	X		X
Customer Partnerships					X	X			X
Future Needs Terms					X				

(Column group header: *Companies* spanning Chevron through H)

Figure 2   Summary of ETW approaches.

Government Lab Associations

Government laboratories are aggressively seeking opportunities to work with industry. The message is (with only a bit of exaggeration), "we have great people, wonderful equipment, and we will do anything you want." Despite this effort, our findings indicated that government labs are difficult to work with. The problem appears to be rooted in a cultural difference between government and industry people. Often, those on the government side still have less interest in applying their work and would prefer to operate in a more academic environment. Industry people feel strongly that "it doesn't count if it's not applied."

We were offered some tips by our participants for working with government labs. They suggested that companies considering such a partnership:

- Make sure that they have an effective infrastructure in place, especially regarding finances.
- Avoid product research where intellectual property concerns are highest.
- Focus on work that takes advantage of the government's excellent equipment.

- Use government labs to improve the cycle-time of well-defined projects.
- Be prepared to take the business to a different lab if difficulties develop.
- Realize that the position of Program Manager in government labs is a high-level position. The person elected by the company to lead the project is equivalent to a Program Manager and should act accordingly.

GLOBAL EFFORTS

Almost half of our U.S. participants maintained offices outside the United States strictly for ETW purposes. Some of these were in Eastern Europe, where difficulties with unstable political environments were encountered.

Internal networks and scientist forums were used by two thirds of the participants. They were afforded low-level funding and made use of the interest of middle-level technical managers, as at Chevron. These networks tended to be more aligned with existing company activities or were focused on specific technologies used across a variety of projects.

> Key expert panels and external advisory committees were not widely used but, when they were, added value.

Key expert panels and external advisory committees were not widely used but, when they were, were said to add value. The latter involves a rotating committee of highly acclaimed scientists. The former are brought together as a need is identified. Experts are willing to donate their time for the opportunity to learn and discuss with other experts.

Consultants play an important but ill-defined role. Technology vendors, on the other hand, were not perceived as adding much value. "There is so much stuff out there that I don't have the time to sort through it all" was a common lament. Vendors were encouraged to learn about a company's needs and offer only selected opportunities that meet those needs.

An ETW Model

The diagram shown in Figure 3 is an attempt to map the findings of this study into a model for ETW. Input on social and regulatory changes (Box 1), which act as an "environmental umbrella" around the technology screening process, influences the senior technology committee (Box 2). The committee and the corporate and business unit plans (Box 3), in turn, screen for appropriate topics for the ETW process (Box 4). The screening process can be enhanced by consultants (Box 5), internal scientist forums or networks (Box 6), and/or key expert panels (Box 7).

Further inputs come from the operating company or business unit needs (Box 8). The screening stage is akin to "doing the right things." This is followed by "doing the right things right," that is, performing the ETW process effectively. There is an individual or a small group that has responsibility for performing the ETW function (Box 9). This involves interaction with a group described here as "technology providers" (Box 11) or possibly through internal networks (Box 10).

The screening stage, in particular, is enhanced by determining core competencies. An overlapping, more detailed but consistent model is shown

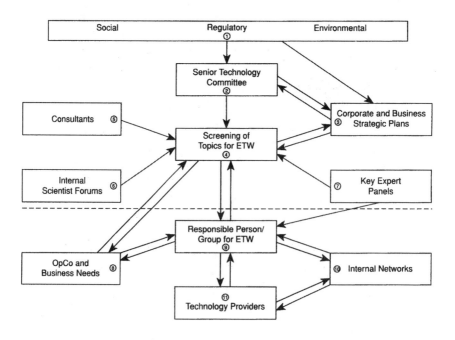

Figure 3   A model for ETW.

in a recent paper (Ashton et al., 1994: 5–16). The Science and Technology scanning process proposed in that paper has six steps. These are:

• Define user needs.
• Prepare a monitoring plan.
• Acquire source materials.
• Analyze results.
• Disseminate monitoring products.
• Review monitoring performance.

These describe in more detail the activities in Boxes 4 and 9 in the model proposed in this article.

We believe that the model shown in Figure 3 is a sound one for ETW. Several of our partners had excellent processes in place. Perhaps the weakness was that the "environmental umbrella" was not in place in many instances. It may be that these issues were addressed in their scenario planning, which was not a focus of our interviews. We did not uncover any "silver bullets" in terms of processes for performing ETW. There were those processes that were well established, such as alliances with universities, government labs, and other companies. These were supported by a variety of alternative processes—expert panels, one- or two-day off-site meetings of a company's senior scientists, informal internal networks that focus on specific competencies—which might flourish in different organizations.

It was clear, however, from the level of activity that our initial premise— that the ETW process is growing in importance—was well founded.

ADDENDUM

In August 1996 Chevron announced the creation of a Chief Technology Officer position reporting to the CEO. This benchmarking study may have had some small influence on this decision.

SUMMARY

Our findings from the benchmarking study of the ETW process fell into two categories: the expected lessons related to the approaches used by others to monitor technology opportunities and threats and those related to the context in which the process was conducted. The latter involved the use of senior technology committees and chief technology officers, formalized ETW processes linked to mainstream R&D activities and understanding core competencies. The former involved mainly joint activities with universities, government labs, and other companies plus a variety of less frequently used approaches.

ABOUT THE AUTHOR

Derek L. Ransley served as a senior planning consultant at Chevron Research and Technology Company, where he worked since 1962. His first 27 years with Chevron were spent in petrochemicals R&D and R&D management. His portfolio includes benchmarking, competitor assessment, cycle-time reduction, and best practices. He received a B.S. degree from the University of Wales (Cardiff) and an M.S. and Ph.D. in Organic Chemistry from Yale University.

REFERENCES

Allee, V. (Winter, 1995). Breakthrough Benchmarking: An Organizational Learning Approach for Comparative Analysis, *Competitive Intelligence Review,* 4: 50–57.

Ashton, W., Johnson, A., and Stacey, G. (Spring, 1994). Monitoring Science and Technology for Competitive Advantage, *Competitive Intelligence Review,* 1: 5–16.

Fusfeld, H. (July–August, 1995). Industrial Research—Where Its Been, Where Its Going, *Research-Technology Management,* 4: 52–56.

Prahalad, C.K. and Hamel, Gary. (May–June, 1990). The Core Competence of the Corporation, *Harvard Business Review,* 79–91.

Roberts, E. (January–February, 1995). Benchmarking the Strategic Management of Technology—Part I, *Research-Technology Management* 1: 44–56.

Past, Present, and Future Directions for Technical Intelligence

Wayne A. Rosenkrans, Jr.
ZENECA PHARMACEUTICALS

EXECUTIVE SUMMARY

The following is an excerpt from remarks delivered by past SCIP President Dr. Wayne A. Rosenkrans, Jr., at SCIP's symposium on "The Value of Technical Intelligence," held November 1997 in Arlington, Virginia. Dr. Rosenkrans discusses how competitive technical intelligence (CTI) has proved its value as a means of enhancing executive decision making and looks at past, present, and potential future valuation models. Using case studies from the pharmaceutical industry, he examines how the traditional CTI process (needs assessment, planning, collection, analysis, and presentation) has evolved by being grounded within a company's overall "knowledge culture." The new CTI model adds a number of key elements, along with more sophisticated ways of measuring CTI's contribution to strategic decision making. The future evolution of CTI will make it part of the core business process—creating corporate knowledge across the entire spectrum of product or service development, and measuring the degree and direction in which knowledge is developing internally and externally.

What is the value of competitive intelligence to a highly technical service or industry? It must be to enhance the effectiveness of executive decision making. If you, as a competitive technical intelligence (CTI) professional, aren't conducting CTI to enhance the decision-making capacity of your executives, why are you doing the activity? Why are you spending the money for these marvelous systems? Why

Competitive Intelligence Review, Vol. 9(2) 34–39 (1998). © 1998 John Wiley & Sons, Inc.

bother about knowledge management and ways to pull information together to create a final product? If you're not supporting decision making within your corporation, it's an academic exercise. Why bother? This is the linchpin of CTI's value, tying it to successful decision making within your corporation.

To examine the evolution of valuing CTI, and suggest some directions for how to value the activity in the future, we will look at some past, present, and potential future valuation schemes. The method will focus on first examining the process, the measures used, an illustrative case study, and finally the value assessment. Our focus will also be high-level, looking mostly at concepts and paradigms.

TECHNICAL INTELLIGENCE—VALUES PAST

The Process

The traditional CTI process has become known as the "Herring Model" of competitive intelligence after its most elegant articulator, Jan Herring (Figure 1). This is by now, quite familiar and consists of a five-step process:

1. *Needs Assessment*—What is it the decision makers need to know? What problem do they need to identify? What decisions do they need support for?

2. *Planning*—How are we going to go about finding the answers that will support these decisions? What sources are we going to use? Who can I talk to? Where do I go to find my basic secondary

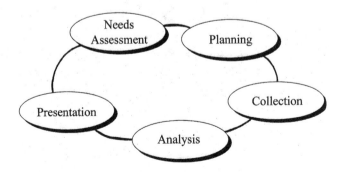

Figure 1   Process: Herring Model.

information that will give me leads of additional people to talk to so I can start my primary collection activity? How will the data I end up with be analyzed, and what is the time frame?

3. *Collection*—Getting the information in; database searches, phone interviews, working the network and the net.

4. *Analysis*—Organizing the data into something that's meaningful, and that will support the decision you've been asked to support. Looking at it forwards and backwards, and creating new insights and conclusions.

5. *Presentation*—Communicating what you've found to the decision maker who's going to use that intelligence to make a decision, providing suggestions for action.

The Measures

How do we measure this kind of activity or how did we measure this kind of an activity (Figure 2)? Inevitably you get the question from higher up, how do we value what you're doing? Justify your budget to me.

> Inevitably you get the question from higher up, how do we value what you're doing? Justify your budget to me.

Usually the more easily tracked statistics, that is, those with a numerical determinant, have been the ones used: number of alerts, number of reports, number of users, and so on. But eventually somebody says, "But that doesn't really tell me anything." How many decisions did you support?

- Quantitative
  - # of Alerts
  - # of Reports
  - # of Users (Associated Databases)
- Qualitative
  - Quality of Intelligence Product
  - Overall Approval Rating

Figure 2   Measures.

What was the quality of the intelligence product? Who assesses that quality? Then there's those infamous words that often spell disaster down the road, the overall approval rating: "You guys are doing a great job. Not sure what you're doing exactly, but keep it up." There's this funny little thing that happens in this industry, something called NDA, "Now Do it Again." Your own success becomes the problem because the overall approval rating becomes, "You did a good job this year. What are you going to do for me now?" Its very difficult to make a successful value case under these conditions.

Case Study 1

Here's a case study of how this model works. SmithKline was developing an anti-cancer compound. A key competitor in the expected market was a Bristol-Myers-Squibb (BMS) compound. The launch window for the SmithKline product relative to the BMS compound launch was critical to the marketing strategy.

Evidence began to accumulate that Bristol-Myers Squibb was moving with their compound: evidence of increased compound production (derived from seemingly unrelated congressional testimony); increased monetary resources; increased human resources; and early indicators of a publication strategy beginning (stoppage in related scientific publications).

Overall conclusion: Bristol-Myers had moved up its New Drug Application filing date for licensing the compound, possibly significantly, which would have a massive impact on the launch window for SmithKline's product.

> Bristol-Myers had moved up its New Drug Application filing date, which would have a massive impact on the launch window for SmithKline's product.

The Action: Based on an alert to senior executives at SmithKline citing the evidence, analysis, and conclusions, Project Management was directed to develop a rapid response contingency plan. And, as a bellwether, Regulatory visited the FDA to ask about the use of NIH-derived clinical data (formerly denied to both companies).

The eventual outcome: Bristol-Myers-Squibb issued a press release the following quarter, stating that their compound's regulatory filing has been moved forward 18 months—a year and a half ahead of schedule—due to rapid patient recruitment into pivotal trials.

Value Assessment

A success story. But what was the value here? It was:

1. Tactical.
2. One time.
3. Tightly focused.

"Well, that's very nice but," says management, "What are you going to do for me next year? Now do it again." The value didn't embed the CTI activity into the core framework of the organization where it would survive changes in direction, orientation, and decision maker. In some ways, however, this case study also suggests evolution in the models and values used to assess CTI. Case study 1 is an exercise in stringing nuggets together which presages several aspects of a more evolved model and value system—namely the concept of an integrator and a knowledge culture.

TECHNICAL INTELLIGENCE—VALUES PRESENT

The Process

The Herring Model is good; it works, and there are numerous applications. But, we're working now in a "knowledge" culture (Figure 3). How do we embed that process into something that takes advantage of a knowledge culture? A new process has emerged, with the Herring cycle in the middle. The newer model represents years of experience and a lot of synthesis done by the SCIP board. It is the best reflection we have at this time of what we see going on in industry.

The new model adds a number of key elements to the Herring model:

1. The concept of an intelligence integrator.
2. The concept of an intelligence protector.
3. The concept of a knowledge background to the activity.

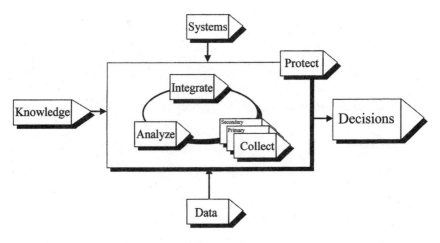

Figure 3   Process: New thoughts.

The intelligence integrators can be an individual or group that not only is developing the intelligence, but also using the intelligence and communicating it to the senior decision makers. It wasn't really clear before who these people were, but now they are beginning to emerge as a key element in the intelligence process: the ones who are going to string the nuggets together created by the core Herring process in the context of the corporate strategy to create a higher value intelligence product.

The intelligence protectors again can be an individual or group that is developing intelligence, but recognize that others are trying to extract your knowledge from you, and to use it to develop their own knowledge. A whole new discipline is appearing growing out of both intelligence and security, the protection of not just internal intellectual capital, but internal knowledge capital as well.

This new model also recognizes that the intelligence process sits within the knowledge context of the company, both internal (i.e., cultural) and external (i.e., intertribal). There is knowledge within your organization which you access through your network (the intelligence professionals most valuable asset), and knowledge outside your company which you access through your network also, but incorporates additional elements. These include knowledge creators—academics and other theoretical thinkers, who are creating the new paradigms you and your competitors will be following in 5–10 years; systems creators creating elegant systems, both electronic and conceptual, which can augment the core process; data creators creating new data models, again both electronic and conceptual, which can streamline the process.

It's important to be mindful that even the most sophisticated systems, data, and frameworks are not the knowledge itself, or by inference, the intelligence. Knowledge is cultural, hence a knowledge, or intelligence, database can really never exist—much as many might like one to.

> The new model recognizes that the intelligence process sits within the knowledge context of the company, both internal (i.e., cultural) and external (i.e., intertribal).

Lastly, and most significantly for assessing value, this new model focuses the output stage on the decisions. That becomes the linchpin—not how many decisions you supported, but what was your contribution to the strategy that that decision supported?

The Measures

Now you're talking about value. You're not talking about numbers of reports or number of users—it's what was your contribution to the strategy and to the decision that was being made (Figure 4). We now have a new set of measures:

1. *Quantitative*—What was the opportunity, value, or cost that was realized through the activity? If you're looking at a strategic acquisition, what was the opportunity cost or the opportunity profit that was supported by this activity? What was the market entry value or cost that was supported by the activity?

- Qantitative
  - Opportunity Value/Cost
  - Market Entry Value/Cost
- Qualitative
  - Innovation
  - Linkage to Strategy

Figure 4 Measures.

2. *Innovation*—How is your activity supporting the innovative process within your corporation? To keep it ahead of the curve constantly? And the other side of that coin is how innovative are you being to support your process within the company?

3. *Linkage to Strategy*—What is the link to the corporate strategy? Not just the problem I have right now, but where is the decision supporting the strategy and how do I contribute to that? That becomes the primary value driver for the organization today.

Case Study 2

Here's a case study under this new model, about a company I'll call "Big-Pharm." The company was considering a major new technology agreement with a genomics company which could substantially remake the way Big-Pharm did R&D. BigPharm believed that the genomics company conferred a strategic advantage, placing it ahead of the industry in adopting this technology. The key strategic question was the nature of BigPharm's actual competitive position, and how it could cement a leadership position.

A threefold approach was utilized to examine this question:

1. *Scientometric analysis of the genomics area*—developing an objective measurement of the knowledge structure underpinning the new technology.

2. *Network analysis of the area*—Where were existing relationships between technology users and downstream technologies? Where were new ventures appearing superimposed on the knowledge structure derived from the scientometrics?

3. *Directed primary research*—Where were specific problem areas moving based on expert opinion from, for example, venture capitalists, academic leaders at centers of excellence, and CEO's at new start-ups?

Based on this strategically focused analysis, the conclusion was that BigPharm did indeed have the leadership position at that time. However, that position was eroding rapidly, as companies nibbling around the edges began to make their moves. Likely challengers included "USPharm," and "FrPharm." USPharm was aligning with major academic centers. FrPharm was developing a network of affiliated technologies that was downstream to BigPharms'. Several boutique companies were emerging or likely to emerge from the key academic clusters commercializing various aspects of the overall technology.

A strategic alliance with FrPharms for access to complementary technology should be considered in addition to an agreement, or agreements, with one or more of the boutiques. It was also clear to expect rapid entry of competitors once success of the venture was recognized.

Value Assessment

Another success story. But this time the value equation was based on a different set of criteria:

1. Strategic.
2. Ongoing.
3. Broadly focused.

The value embedded the CTI activity into the core framework of an evolving portion of the organization, which was considered pivotal for the future. A location where it could now survive changes in direction, orientation, and decision maker. Management now says, "This mission is critical to the ongoing success of this division. We must maintain this level of strategic support for decision making." As before, case study 2 also suggests evolution in that one of the central aspects of the analysis was use of a "knowledge map." This could be considered a pointer toward the future in that use of "knowledge maps" may herald an era in which value is assessed through measurement of contributions to corporate knowledge.

TECHNICAL INTELLIGENCE—VALUES FUTURE

The Process

What does the future hold for evolution of the CTI process (Figure 5)? As any good futurist would do, we need to broaden out our perspective here to make a viable, educated guess. There is a strong academic underpinning for many of the currently popular concepts of "knowledge management." This would imply that while many other so-called management paradigms (which have been "flavor of the year") have had their day and passed on, knowledge management in some form may become a more central aspect

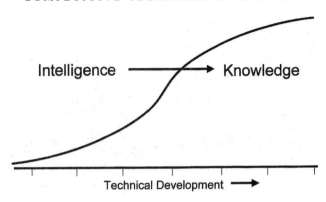

Figure 5   Process: Future.

of continuing business. If that is the case, then a successfully evolved CTI process will not only take advantage of the knowledge architecture, but will become part of the core business process creating corporate knowledge across the entire spectrum of product, or service, development. It will also be involved in measuring the degree and direction in which that knowledge is developing not only internally, but externally as well.

Measures

This evolution in process suggests a similar evolution in measures (Figure 6). As the CTI process evolves into the core process supporting knowledge management, parameters more indicative of this progression will emerge:

1. Degree of corporate knowledge progression.
2. Direction of corporate knowledge progression.

- Quantitative
  — Company/Division Value
  — Corporate Knowledge Progression
- Qualitative
  — Change Agency
  — Impact on Direction

Figure 6   Measures.

3. Influence on corporate change agency.
4. Impact on corporate/divisional strategic value.

These are a far cry from the original, and in some areas still current, measures of value focused on numeric determinants, i.e., number of reports. They also will require much innovative thinking from the "knowledge creators" on how to assess these measures. Such are the challenges facing the evolution of CTI today.

Case Study 3

Watch this space. Elements of this case study are doubtlessly being conducted out there by innovative and creative practitioners of CTI now.

Value Assessment

Showing that all progress stands on the shoulders of those who have gone before us, and a nod to those who believe that all history is circular, I believe the best assessment of future value of CTI still resides within a classic quote delivered by the keynote speaker at a SCIP annual conference some years ago:

> The winners of this game will be those who *know* the most, *know* it first, and are the quickest to turn *knowledge* into action.
> —*Robert E. Flynn, chairman and CEO*
> *NutraSweet Co.*

ABOUT THE AUTHOR

Dr. Wayne A. Rosenkrans, Jr., a former president of the Society of Competitive Intelligence Professionals, spent eight years at SmithKline Beecham in licensing and as head of the firm's strategic intelligence unit in R&D. He is currently with AstraZeneca Pharmaceuticals in Wilmington, Delaware.

Starting a Competitive Technical Intelligence Function: A Roundtable Discussion

EXECUTIVE SUMMARY

What is competitive technical intelligence (CTI)? What benefits can businesses derive from developing a CTI operation, and how would they go about doing so? To answer these and related questions, the Society of Competitive Intelligence Professionals held a roundtable discussion on the topic in Boston, as part of SCIP's 1997 Competitive Technical Intelligence Symposium. The following is an excerpt from that conversation.

Moderator:

Patrick J. Bryant, PharmD, director of the Drug Information Center, University of Missouri–Kansas City School of Pharmacy.

Panelists:

John Chu, technical director of Information Management, Baxter Healthcare Corp.

Jan P. Herring, president, Herring & Associates.

Jay Young, director of International Operations and Strategy, Battelle Memorial Institute.

Dr. Bryant: What exactly is competitive technical intelligence? Essentially, competitive intelligence involves two parallel information tracks. That is, competitive information is derived from either business or technical data, which is gathered, organized, and analyzed into intelligence.

Competitive Intelligence Review, Vol. 9(2) 26–33 (1998). ©1998 John Wiley & Sons, Inc.

Our working definition of competitive intelligence has always been "information that has been analyzed to the extent that an action can be taken or a decision made." Very simply, your choice of technical data or business data, and the background of the analyst, will define whether the result is competitive technical intelligence or competitive business intelligence. Often, you will combine these two sets of information to make your final business decision.

WHAT ARE THE BEST FIRST STEPS IN ESTABLISHING A CTI OR CI PROGRAM?

Mr. Herring: The first step is making sure that management understands its value. If they don't value it, it is not going to be developed properly. They are not going to provide the resources to get started. So, you have got to work at educating the management about its value, winning their hearts and minds, and then go from there. There is no better way, quite frankly, than by having people who others see and admire come and talk to your management.

If the first step is getting management's attention, the second step is understanding management's needs and showing how your program could meet those needs. The third step is beginning to build networks of the people who will be doing the work and

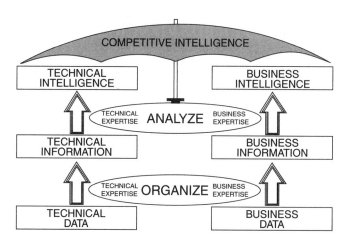

Figure 1   Technical and business intelligence.

developing the skills that they need to produce understandable intelligence and communicate it effectively.

Mr. Young: One effective way of getting people's attention about the importance of setting up a CTI system is to say, "Hey, look. Our competitors are doing it." And if, in fact, you have indications that CTI is being done in an effective and organized way by competitors, that often is a way to get people to pay attention to the need for setting up an organized function.

> One effective way of getting people's attention about the importance of setting up a CTI system up is to say, "Hey, look. Our competitors are doing it."

You have to, as Jan mentioned, present to people a compelling case for why such an organization should exist. That must be linked in a compelling way to the business rationale. You can't just say that we want to set something up to go out and look for neat technology. You have to show management that this is something that will enable them to carry out strategic decision making with technology aspects to it far more effectively than is now being done.

One of the ways that we do this is by helping companies identify what their strategic technologies are. From that, we begin to build a series of what we call lines of inquiry, as a way of making it clear to management what is important and why it helps to get people focused on the need and the importance of this.

Mr. Chu: I would add the need to tie in key technology. Our current effort is to maximize the use of Internet/intranet at Baxter. So, we picked the right information technology and we were also the first beta test site for cutting-edge software. We were able to get a senior management champion for CTI functions because he was already familiar with the technology.

Dr. Bryant: I can't emphasize the importance of a champion. And, even more importantly, try to diversify just as you do your own stock portfolio, because you never know when one of your champions is going to depart the company. All of a sudden you are "out of business." So, if you can diversify across divisional lines, that will help you in those situations.

WHAT RESOURCES ARE NEEDED TO START THE "BAREBONES" PROCESS OR A PILOT STUDY?

Mr. Chu: One manager, perhaps two specialists—one in technical, one in business, plus clerical support. In terms of compensation, maybe a quarter of a million dollars a year; eventually, information systems add another $50,000; information access, subscriptions to various services, add another $100,000; internal technical support for computer $50,000. If you add all of those up, about $400,000 or $450,000 to start with.

Dr. Bryant: Now, that's for a formal group?

Mr. Chu: Yes.

Dr. Bryant: How about where you don't have the opportunity to start a formal group because you can't find $500,000, and you're just trying to do a pilot type of a study to determine if there is really a need out there. What do you think you would need, "barebones"?

Mr. Chu: Hopefully, you have the right technology. Pick a single system that will fulfill people's needs, and then do an internal PR campaign.

Mr. Young: You don't need to make a heavy financial investment initially to demonstrate the efficacy of having a CTI system. What is essential to launching such a pilot function is the selection of a critical technology issue that you believe can be addressed by a much more organized and effective process of technology acquisition and analysis. That has been the case to date. Select a critical technology issue that has been identified as being of concern to senior management. Once that has been identified, come up with a structured plan, which would probably involve the use of very few people—perhaps one person who is in charge initially, who is pushing the idea of a competitive intelligent system to coordinate the acquisition, analysis, and dissemination of intelligence on that particular issue.

Ideally, this person should have a clear understanding of the resources around the company, or know where to go to get information on this particular issue, and then work through a virtual network of people to pull together a solution to this particular question.

You can start a pilot program with a very small commitment of resources, maximizing the use of information technology to connect people in a virtual way around the organization. And also, of course, if you have an established library function, these are people who will be very useful in helping you do that.

As I say, one person, maybe two, working diligently can show a skeptical senior management how this can be beneficial to them on a regular basis.

Mr. Herring: I certainly agree with that and go along with what both of you have said, particularly, what Jay has pointed out. In my earlier life, I was in the Marine Corps. You start with the basic building block and it is a rifleman. Give me eight riflemen, and I will give you a squad. Give me 32, and I will give you a platoon.

In intelligence, the basic building blocks are two minds—the mind of an analyst is different from the mind of a person who gathers human intelligence.

Give me these two different minds, a library, and a well-defined set of management needs, and I will give you an intelligence system.

You are building a pilot program. Tell management, "I can't handle too many projects, but I can handle a few. If you want more, you will have to add analysts."

The analytical function is much more time and resource-intensive. In my experience at Motorola, the ratio of collectors to analysts was about five-to-one. One good human collection manager could tap the brains of about 100,000 people, if he was doing it well, but I needed five analysts to address all of management's analytical issues to their full extent.

Dr. Bryant: Those are good points and I would agree with all of them. In fact, when Tom Krol and I started a concerted effort in competitive technical intelligence for a pharmaceutical company about seven years ago, we found that we spent our first year trying to "drum up" business. We did a needs analysis, and then worked to generate business from the various divisions within the company.

After about six months, we had more business than we knew what to do with. After that, it was a pretty easy sell to go to our manager and get additional resources. So, I've actually seen that work.

How Do You Motivate the Organization to Form a CTI Function?

Dr. Bryant: R&D, in general, is a risky business and technical intelligence is one probable way to try to either decrease or manage that risk. Every head of R&D lays awake at night worried about that risk. So, if you have some way that you can at least try to minimize the risk, or decrease it, or manage it, you are in a situation of being able to sell your service.

Mr. Young: One of the things that we found when we have gone in and talked to companies, in terms of advising them on how to set up a system is that when you come in with an idea and a plan for a more systematic way of collecting information and analyzing it, you begin to get people interested. In many cases, there is a lot of enthusiasm for wanting to see information that people have in their heads or have in their drawers used in a more effective way than it has been used in the past.

At first, we didn't know anybody was interested in this. We have watched this kind of thing for years and were surprised that somebody is actually showing an interest in it now. One of the ways you motivate people to do this is to show that there is interest in it from a senior level, that, in fact, people are now focusing on these issues.

We have identified, at Battelle and at other companies I'm familiar with, key cross-cutting technologies that are going to be priorities for the collection and analysis of information on. This gets people engaged.

Build on that enthusiasm, build on that knowledge, build on those people that you know are there and can be motivated to work with you. You will find there is a lot of willingness to help you.

Dr. Bryant: Let me give you just a quick technique. Every two to four weeks, I would try to get to our head of R&D. My question to him was pretty simple: "What are the things that keep you awake at night?" And then I would discuss with him how I might be able to provide some competitive technical intelligence that would help alleviate one of those things. As soon as he realizes that you are concerned with his or her "health," it makes a big difference in the bonding you can make with that person.

SWITCHING GEARS FROM STARTING TO MAINTAINING THE CTI FUNCTION, HOW DO YOU DEVELOP AN EVALUATION SYSTEM FOR THE CTI FUNCTION; WHAT ARE THE MAIN INDICATORS TO EVALUATE OR ASSESS THE CTI ACTIVITIES AND SERVICE WITHIN AN R&D ORGANIZATION?

Mr. Herring: There are several basic measures that can be applied, but they all go back to the user, the person who, in fact, says, "I need this intelligence for this R&D decision. I need this intelligence to acquire this company."

In almost all cases, you have got to understand what that user's expectations are and how to translate those into measures of effectiveness. If you do that upfront, as you go through the project you will preserve the data to measure the effectiveness at the end of the process. That is very straightforward. I would recommend you buy one of the SCIP reports on this subject. I wrote it. It's a little too theoretical. It needs some practical application, but the way to do it is there.

The first thing is identifying management's expectations upfront. In other words, they have a meeting. It may be an acquisition. It may be to make a decision. At the same time, they are talking about the intelligence needs. They should define what they expect to achieve in the end. You will find, in most cases, it is qualitative, not quantitative.

The next step is to decide if this is a project which lends itself to quantitative measures. Are we going to have more clients, or is it something more qualitative? Is our product going to be seen as the better product in the market?

The intelligence operations that take place after that are intended to not only deliver management the answer it needs, but to gather data that can be used in the evaluation process at the end.

A critical point: The final evaluation of whether or not you have met management's needs with intelligence has to be done jointly with them. You sit down together and you jointly ask, "Did we do it? Did you get the expected number of new clients? Did you get the market share?" Management has to make this evaluation.

The evaluation process starts by asking what management's intelligence needs are, setting up the appropriate CI operations, selecting the right measures of effectiveness. Then, as the intelligence comes in—whether it is applied to the business decision or sales—you can actually measure the results, or at least get management to tell you, "Yeah, you did good. We have 240 more new accounts." Or, "We really did good. Our product was the first to market." If you wait until the end of the CI operation to measure your effectiveness, you may not have the data to do it.

> The evaluation process starts by asking what management's intelligence needs are, setting up the appropriate CI operations, and selecting the right measures of effectiveness. Then, as intelligence comes in, you can actually measure the results.

How Do You Measure Benefits and Translate That into Dollars Attributed to the CTI Function?

Mr. Herring: You can use four basic quantitative measures: Time saving—how much time did we save? Cost savings—how much costs did we save? Cost avoidance—what didn't we spend because we knew this? The fourth measure is revenue enhancement—how much additional revenue did we achieve?

Those four can be combined in different ways. If you understand what the measures of effectiveness are as you go through a complex, intelligence operation, you can be gathering the measurement data during the process. At the end of the CI operation, you can actually do the effectiveness calculations.

Mr. Chu: Within the pharmaceutical industry, it is fairly common to make measurements by using a shortened drug-development cycle—if your key information resulted in a one-month reduction in this cycle, based on potential sales.

SHOULD CTI FUNDING BE BUSINESS UNIT OR PROJECT BASED, OR A CENTRALIZED CORPORATE FUNCTION? HOW DO YOU FUND A CTI EFFORT IN AN ORGANIZATIONAL STRUCTURE WHERE YOU HAVE INDIVIDUAL BUSINESS UNITS WITH SEPARATE FUNDING?

Mr. Herring: There are some intelligence activities that benefit the whole organization, such as setting up the information system for gathering data. That needs to be funded centrally because during tough times businesses start cutting those things pretty rapidly.

In terms of the actual application of intelligence, this needs to be funded at the business unit level. So general funding of intelligence should include maintaining the structure, providing access to information, even funding some conferences like this ought to be a central function, so you can keep the life blood of the intelligence function alive.

When it comes time to go out and hire consultants to help you do the right kinds of things, or maybe to set up programs to gather intelligence in Europe, I think the application unit, which may be the business unit, is the best place to go for funding.

Mr. Young: I would agree with that. Because more and more corporate organizations are becoming highly decentralized with a business-unit focus, much of the funding should come from that particular area. There is, however, and remains a critical role for a central coordinating function, especially in a highly decentralized organization. Now, that function may do several different things, such as helping fund some of the larger infrastructures such as libraries that benefit the entire CTI organization, or information technology.

Another central area involves horizon scanning. Looking out longer term and trying to find the types of challenges that may be over the horizon, that the business units don't have the time and necessarily the need to look for on a regular basis.

The central function can do something else—act as a clearinghouse, a facilitator for disseminating to the business units tools and techniques for doing CTI more effectively.

So, again, the emphasis should be, in many cases, on the business-unit level, but there remains an essential function for some sort of central coordinating point.

As more corporations decentralize, much of the funding for CTI should come from the particular business units. There is, however, and remains a critical role for a central coordinating function, especially in a highly decentralized organization.

APPENDIX
CI-Focused Organizations Referred to in This Book

Acadia University
Aclara BioSciences
Advanced Information
  Technologies (AIT)
Alcoa
Allied Signal Aerospace
Allina Health Systems
American Express
American Productivity Quality
  Center
AmeriGas Propane
Amoco
Applied Biosystems
Arthur Andersen
Asahi Beer
Astra Merck
AT&T
Avnet
Battelle Memorial Institute
Baxter Healthcare
Bell Atlantic
Boehringer Ingelheim
Bristol-Myers-Squibb
British Petroleum
Business Week
Caterpillar
Celera
Central Intelligence Agency
Chevron Research and Technology
Compaq

Corning
CPC International
Daimler-Benz Aerospace AG
Deloitte Consulting
Digital Equipment Corporation
DOP Corporation
Dow Chemical
Dow Jones & Co.
Dupont
Duquesne University
Duracell International
Eastman Chemical
Educational Test Service
Electric Power Research Institute
  (EPRI)
Elf Aquitaine
Embraco
Enron Energy Services
Fairleigh Dickinson University
Fidelity
Ford Motor
The Futures Group
GlaxoWellcome
Health Net
Herring & Associates
Hoffmann-LaRoche
IBM
Integral Performance Group
Intel
Japanese National Railways

Johnson & Johnson Medical Inc.
Joint Military Intelligence College
Kaiser Permanente
Kirin Beer Company
Kirk Tyson International
Knowledge Link
Kodak
Lanier Worldwide
Larscom
Lexis-Nexis Group
MAPCO
Marist College
Mercator Consultants
Merck
Microsoft
Mohegan Technologies
Monsanto
Motorola
National Research Council
    (Canada)
Nationwide Insurance
Northern Telecom
Novartis
NutraSweet
Oakland University
Open Source Solution
Oracle
Paap Associates
Pacific Bell
Pacific Enterprises
PE Corporation
Pfizer

Phoenix Consult
PPG
Procter & Gamble
Public Service Electric & Gas
Rockwell International
Rutgers University
SBC
Scenario Management
    International AG
SCIP
Sequent Computer
Shell
Shell Services International
Stentor Canadian
Telcordia
Texas Instruments
3M
University of Missouri-Kansas
University of Ottawa
University of Pittsburgh
UPS
US West
USAA
Wake Forest University
Warner-Lambert
WarRoom Research
Washington Information Group
Wisconsin Electric
Wisconsin Public Service & Gas
Xerox
Zeneca Pharmaceuticals

INDEX

321

About the Editors

John E. Prescott, executive editor of *Competitive Intelligence Review,* is professor of business administration at the Katz Graduate School of Business, University of Pittsburgh. His research focuses on the network of relationships among a firm's industry, strategy, organizational processes, and performance, as well as the design and implementation of CI systems. Currently, he is the content expert for CI benchmarking studies conducted by the American Productivity and Quality Center, dean of the business analyst program at Texas Instruments, and international consultant. Dr. Prescott was a founder of the Society of Competitive Intelligence Professionals and the 1991–1992 president of the Society's board of directors. In 1994, he received SCIP's meritorious award for outstanding contributions to the field of CI. Dr. Prescott earned his Ph.D. in business administration at the Pennsylvania State University.

Stephen H. Miller, managing editor of *Competitive Intelligence Review,* is editor-in-chief of *Competitive Intelligence Magazine,* published by the Society of Competitive Intelligence Professionals. Previously, he was news editor for the American Institute of CPAs' *Journal of Accountancy.* He has also been part of the communications teams at KPMG Peat Marwick and at the Depository Trust Company. Mr. Miller has a bachelor's degree from Wesleyan University and a master's degree in journalism and mass communications from New York University.